COMPETENCE-
BASED
COMPETITION

THE STRATEGIC MANAGEMENT SERIES

Series Editor
HOWARD THOMAS

STRATEGIC THINKING
Leadership and the Management of Change
Edited by
JOHN HENDRY AND GERRY JOHNSON
WITH JULIA NEWTON

COMPETENCE-BASED COMPETITION
Edited by
GARY HAMEL AND AIMÉ HEENE

Further titles in preparation

THE STRATEGIC MANAGEMENT SERIES

COMPETENCE-BASED COMPETITION

Edited by
GARY HAMEL AND AIMÉ HEENE

WITHDRAWN

JOHN WILEY & SONS
Chichester · New York · Brisbane · Toronto · Singapore

Published 1994 by John Wiley & Sons Ltd,
Baffins Lane, Chichester,
West Sussex PO19 1UD, England

National (01243) 779777
International (+44) 1243 779777

Reprinted December 1994

Other Wiley Editorial Offices

John Wiley & Sons, Inc., 605 Third Avenue,
New York, NY 10158–0012, USA

Jacaranda Wiley Ltd, 33 Park Road, Milton,
Queensland 4064, Australia

John Wiley & Sons (Canada) Ltd, 22 Worcester Road,
Rexdale, Ontario M9W 1L1, Canada

John Wiley & Sons (SEA) Pte Ltd, 37 Jalan Pemimpin #05-04,
Block B, Union Industrial Building, Singapore 2057

Library of Congress Cataloging-in-Publication Data

Competence-based competition / edited by Gary Hamel and Aimé Heene.
    p.   cm. — (Strategic management series)
  Includes bibliographical references and index.
  ISBN 0-471-94397-5 (cased)
  1. Competition.   2. Strategic planning.   I. Hamel, Gary.
  II. Heene, Aimé.   III. Series.
  HD41.C638   1994
  658.4'012 — dc20   93–47494
                                                                CIP

British Library Cataloguing in Publication Data

A catalogue record for this book is available from the British Library

ISBN 0-471-94397-5

Typeset in 10.5/12pt Palatino by
Dobbie Typesetting Ltd, Tavistock, Devon
Printed and bound in Great Britain by
Biddles Ltd, Guildford and King's Lynn

Contents

Contributors

MAURIZIO BARBESCHI
Consorzio Universitario in Ingegneria per la Gestione d'Impresa, Politecnico di Milano, Via Rombon 11, 20134 Milan, Italy.
Maurizio Barbeschi obtained a Masters degree in Theoretical Chemistry at the University of Rome, with a thesis on FTIR spectroscopy and carried out at the Academy of Science's Isotope Institute of Budapest, Hungary. He has been Visiting Researcher at the University of California at Berkeley. He spent several years in the Royal Dutch-Shell group developing an international network aimed at linking R&D and marketing and is currently Researcher at MIP-Politecnico di Milano in the Strategy and Strategic Management Centre. His research interests are in the areas of R&D management and corporate strategy. He is author of several papers published in international journals.

ILSE BOGAERT
UFSIA, Antwerp University, Prinsstraat 13, 2000 Antwerp, Belgium.
Ilse Bogaert has an MBA from UFSIA, Antwerp, Belgium/ Georgetown, USA. She is currently involved in an empirical research project on strategic investment decision processes in Belgian companies.

WILLIAM C. BOGNER
Department of Management, College of Business Administration, Georgia State University, PO Box 4014, Atlanta, GA 30302-4014, USA
William C. Bogner is an Assistant Professor of Management at Georgia State University in Atlanta. He received his PhD in Strategic Management from the University of Illinois in 1991. He also holds a JD from the University of Illinois and a BS from Indiana University. His research interests include patterns of intra-industry competition,

core competencies of competition and the effect of strategic alliances on both of these. He also conducts research which seeks to mix cognitive processes of management with competitive strategy. His work in these areas has primarily focused on the global pharmaceutical industry.

VITTORIO CHIESA
Consorzio Universitario in Ingegneria per la Gestione d'Impresa, Politecnico di Milano, Via Rombon 11, 20134 Milan, Italy.
Vittorio Chiesa obtained a Masters degree in electronic engineering at the Politecnico di Milano. He was previously with Ciba-Geigy and Pirelli in the Organization Division. Currently he is Visiting Researcher in the Operations Management Department at the London Business School. He is Senior Researcher on the National Research Council in Milan and Lecturer in the Management of Innovation and Strategic Management at the MIP-Politecnico di Milano. His research interests are technology management and business strategy. He is the author of several papers published in international journals.

MICHAEL CRAWFORD
Australian Graduate School of Management, The University of New South Wales, PO Box 1, Kensington, New South Wales, Australia 2033.
Michael Crawford has a PhD in organization theory and management from the University of New South Wales and a science degree and a Masters in management from the Australian National University. Dr Crawford worked in computing and systems analysis and in public administration before starting his own consulting organization (Corex Pty Ltd), which advises and implements in areas of corporate strategy, organization design and corporate change. He holds an adjunct appointment as Senior Research Fellow at the Centre for Corporate Change in the Australian Graduate School of Management.

FRANCESCO DE LEO
SDA Bocconi Milan, Via Bocconi 8, 20136 Milan, Italy.
Francesco de Leo (PhD Advanced to Candidacy in Policy and Organization at the Anderson Graduate School of Management, at UCLA) is Professor of International Marketing Research and Analysis at SDA Bocconi, the Graduate School of Management of University Bocconi, Milan, where he also serves on the Board of the International Development Division. He is the Head of the

Corporate Strategy Research Program at SDA Bocconi and a member of the Scientific Committee of the New Winners Project. His interests are the relationship between corporate strategy and competitive advantage and the role of internal markets for mobilizing knowledge within organizations.

RICHARD HALL
Durham University Business School, Mill Hill Lane, Durham DH1 3LB, UK.
Richard Hall has an MA (Cantab.) in physics and a PhD in business policy. His early industrial career was in operations management both as a line manager and as a consultant. Thereafter he was, for 14 years, the chief executive of a company manufacturing consumer products. He is currently a senior lecturer at the Durham University Business School. His research interests are the role of intangible resources in business success, and the role of judgement in strategic management. His publications are largely in the area of intangible resources.

GARY HAMEL
London Business School, Sussex Place, Regent's Park, London NW1 4SA, UK.
Dr Gary Hamel is Professor of Strategic and International Management at the London Business School. He came to the LBS from the Graduate School of Business Administration, University of Michigan, where he taught international management. Gary has worked extensively at board level in many of the world's most successful multinationals. His current research interests centre on the challenge of competing in global industries, on the problems of managing international strategic alliances and on the value-added of top management. Gary has written for the *Harvard Business Review*, the *Strategic Management Journal* and numerous other journals. His articles on 'Strategic intent' and 'Core competence' won McKinsey awards. His most recent article is 'Strategy as Stretch and Leverage' in the March-April 1993 issue of the *Harvard Business Review*. Gary's path-breaking concepts have been put to work in hundreds of companies, including Kodak, AT&T, EDS, Dow Chemical and many others. With his co-author, C. K. Prahalad, Gary is preparing a book, *Competing For The Future* to be published by the Harvard Business School Press in the autumn of 1994. He is also a member of the editorial board of the *Strategic Management Journal*. Gary has recently completed a *Fortune Magazine* video

seminar, 'Competitiveness'. Dr Hamel's ideas are also the subject of a one-week executive course, 'Building Global Leadership', offered at the London Business School each spring.

AIMÉ HEENE
De Vlerick School voor Management, Bellevue 6, 9050 Ledeberg, Belgium.
Aimé Heene has a PhD in educational sciences and an MBA from the De Vlerick School voor Management (University of Ghent, Belgium). After a ten-year career in consulting he joined the De Vlerick School voor Management in 1989. He is head of the Department of Strategic Management and a partner at the De Vlerick School voor Management and Assistant Professor at the University of Ghent. He chaired the International Workshop 'Competence Based Competition'. His main areas of interest are competitive strategy, human resource management and organization. He has published a number of articles on competitive strategy and the relationships between human resource management and competitive strategy.

DUANE A. HELLELOID
School of Business, DJ10, University of Washington, Seattle, WA 98195, USA.
Duane Helleloid is a doctoral candidate in business policy and international business at the University of Washington. He holds previous degrees in mechanical engineering, economics, and industrial engineering from the University of Minnesota and Stanford University. Before beginning his doctoral studies, Duane worked for IBM, McKinsey and Company, and Hewlett-Packard. Earlier articles have appeared in the *IEEE Transactions on Engineering Management* and several conference proceedings. His case studies have been published by Harvard and Stanford Universities. His research interests focus on issues relating to the strategic actions firms can take to adapt to the globalization of business, and how multinationals can best utilize the individual core competencies of various national entities.

PETER HISCOCKS
Scientific Generics, King's Court, Kirkwood Road, Cambridge CB4 2PF, UK.
Peter Hiscocks has a degree in materials science and an MSc in management from Imperial College, London. He has worked for a number of engineering companies in both scientific and

commercial roles. He is a senior consultant within Scientific
Generics, where he has specialized in business development issues
in the chemicals and engineering sectors.

RICHARD KLAVANS
146 Cheswold Valley Road, Haverford, PA 19041, USA.
Richard Klavans has a PhD in strategic management from Wharton,
an MS in management from MIT and a BSME from Tufts University.
His main research and consulting interest is on the formation of
strategies in science- and technology-intensive environments. He
has published a number of articles on related topics (technology-
based diversification; competitive interaction in technology-based
industries; and the measurement of scientific/technical capabilities).
He serves on the editorial board of *Interfaces* and *The Competitive
Intelligence Review*.

JEREMY KLEIN
Scientific Generics, King's Court, Kirkwood Road, Cambridge CB4 2PF, UK.
Jeremy Klein has a PhD in medical physics and an MBA from the
London Business School. He started his career in computer software
but moved towards business consultancy, where he has specialized
in developing strategies for technological companies. He is a Senior
Consultant with Scientific Generics, where his main interest is the
development of tools and frameworks, particularly those which can
be modelled by computer. He has published articles on the relation
between strategy and technology, and on skills and meta-skills.

RUDY MARTENS
UFSIA, Antwerp University, Prinsstraat 13, 2000 Antwerp, Belgium.
Rudy Martens has a PhD in applied economics (strategic
management) from UFSIA, Antwerp, Belgium. He teaches courses
on strategy and organization theory and has several publications
on business strategy and general management. His main domain
of interest lies in the process of strategy formation in large
companies.

RICHARD P. RUMELT
INSEAD, Boulevard de Constance, 77305 Fontainebleau Cedex, France.
Richard Rumelt has been Professor of Business Policy at INSEAD
since 1993. He is also on long-term leave from the UCLA Anderson
Graduate School of Management where he holds the Elsa and Harry
Kunin Chair in Business and Society. Professor Rumelt received

his BS and MS degrees in electrical engineering from the University of California, Berkeley, in 1963 and 1965. He studied management at the Harvard Business School, receiving his PhD in 1972. He joined the faculty of the Harvard Business School in 1972, and UCLA in 1976. He is the author of *Strategy, Structure, and Economic Performance*, a book that won the Irwin prize, and numerous scholarly articles and papers on strategy and the economics of competition. His current research projects include the quality of coordination within organizations, the sources of organizational inertia, and changing patterns of diversification among large firms. Professor Rumelt serves on the Board of Financial Institutions Advisory Group and Management Education Associates. He is President Elect of the Strategic Management Society and is on the editorial boards of the *Strategic Management Journal*, *Industrial and Corporate Change*, and the *California Management Review*.

BERNARD L. SIMONIN
University of Washington, School of Business, DJ10 Seattle WA98195, USA.
Bernard L. Simonin received a PhD in international business from the University of Michigan, an MBA from Kent State University, and a graduate degree in computer sciences from l'Ecole Supérieure d'Informatique in France, where he worked in the field of information systems for three years. He is currently an Assistant Professor of Marketing and International Business at the University of Washington, where he teaches courses in international strategy, management and marketing. His research interest focuses on international strategic alliances, symbiotic marketing, as well as on issues of knowledge transfer and organizational learning in multinational organizations. He has published in the *Journal of International Marketing* and various conference proceedings.

HOWARD THOMAS
College of Commerce and Business Administration, University of Illinois at Urbana-Champaign, 260, Commerce West-Box 110, 1206 South Sixth Street, Champaign, IL 61820, USA.
Professor Thomas holds degrees from Edinburgh University (PhD), University of Chicago (MBA) and London University (MSc and BSc). He is the James F. Towey Professor of Strategic Management, Professor of Business Administration, Director of the Office of International Strategic Management and Dean of the College of Commerce and Business Administration at the University of Illinois at Urbana-Champaign. In addition, he is a permanent visiting professor at Imperial College (London), holds a visiting chair at

Manchester Business School, is an honorary professor at St Andrews University (Scotland) and is a visiting fellow at Templeton College (Oxford). He received several awards for excellence in teaching and serves on the editorial boards of world-class journals in (strategic) management. He is Vice-President for Publications for the Strategic Management Society and author of books on strategic management, which include the *Anatomy of Decisions, Risk Analysis, Strategic Management Research* and *Managing Ambiguity and Change.*

DENNIS TURNER
Australian Graduate School of Management, The University of New South Wales, PO Box 1, Kensington, New South Wales, Australia 2033
Dennis Turner completed a BSc (Econ) at the London School of Economics in 1948 and has spent 30 years in senior management posts in both private and public sectors in the United Kingdom and Australia. He joined the Australian Graduate School of Management in the University of New South Wales in 1981 and became responsible for the schools executive programs. In 1985 he co-authored a book on industrial relations reform. In 1991 Dennis moved to the school's Centre for Corporate Change where his main focus, in teaching, research and consulting, is on the general management of organizational change.

ANDRÉ VAN CAUWENBERGH
UFSIA, Antwerp University, Prinsstraat 13, 2000 Antwerp, Belgium.
André Van Cauwenbergh studied law and economics at the University of Leuven, Belgium, and at the London School of Economics. He teaches general and strategic management at UFSIA, Antwerp, Belgium. He has a large consultancy experience with business and public organizations, and serves on a number of boards of directors. His publications include several articles in international journals (e.g. *Strategic Management Journal, Journal of General Management*) and a book on *Strategic Behavior. Structures and ideas in movements* (1978, 1986; Dutch language).

PAUL VERDIN
INSEAD, Boulevard de Constance, 77305 Fontainebleau Cedex, France
Paul Verdin is Assistant Professor of Strategy and Management at INSEAD (France). He has been a visiting professor at IESE (Spain) and holds degrees in law and economics from the University of Leuven (Belgium) and a PhD in economics from Harvard University. His current research focuses on the empirical relevance of '(core)

competence', 'competence-based competition' and the 'resource-based view' of strategy and their practical relevance for actual strategy formulation, especially in contrast to more 'traditional' concepts of strategy based on industry analysis and positioning. Additional interests regard the formulation and implementation of 'European' strategies across a variety of industries in the evolving European context.

PETER WILLIAMSON
London Business School, Sussex Place, Regent's Park, London NW1 4SA, UK
Peter Williamson has a PhD in business economics from Harvard University. After a number of years with the Boston Consulting Group, he joined the London Business School in 1987 where he is currently Dean of MBA Programmes and Associate Professor of Strategic and International Management. Dr Williamson has acted as consultant to multinational companies in the Far East, Europe and the USA, as well as the World Bank and the Commission of the European Communities. His publications and research interests have focused on export strategy and international expansion, strategies of Japanese firms, and building corporate capabilities.

BEVERLY C. WINTERSCHEID
European Institute for Advanced Studies on Management, Rue d'Egmont 13, 1050 Brussels, Belgium and Baldwin–Wallace College, 274 Eastland Road, Berea, Ohio 44017, USA.
Beverly C. Winterscheid is a professor at the European Institute for Advanced Studies in Management and Assistant Professor of Management at international Baldwin–Wallace College (Ohio). After an eight-year career in industry, she obtained a PhD in management policy from Case Western Reserve University, USA. Her research and consulting interests concentrate on new forms of strategy implementation for established firms, with a particular emphasis on how insiders interpret and act upon changes in strategy. She has conducted research and consulting in the following areas: the identification and development of strategic capability, the transfer of knowledge across intrafirm boundaries, and the management of technology and innovation in established firms.

Foreword

RICHARD P. RUMELT

The idea of 'core competencies', as introduced by Prahalad and Hamel (1990), has generated enormous interest. When it appeared, both academics and corporate managers sensed that this idea was important—there was an immediate and unusually broad resonance within these communities. This resonance owed much to Prahalad and Hamel's craft and persuasiveness, but it also drew on the audiences' readiness for this message. After decades of seeing corporate strategy treated as a portfolio problem, academics and practitioners were ripe for a view of corporate strategy that placed technology, skill and synergy ahead of cash flow and control. In this short foreword I want to explore this notion of resonance in more detail. In particular, I want to describe how Prahalad and Hamel's contribution differs from other work on competence and how that difference fits with weaknesses in mainstream strategic management's treatment of corporate strategy.

CORE COMPETENCE IN STRATEGIC THINKING

The concept of corporate core competence developed by Prahalad and Hamel has four key components:

1. *Corporate span.* Core competencies span business and products within a corporation. Put differently, powerful core competencies support several products or businesses.
2. *Temporal dominance.* Products are but the momentary expression of a corporation's core competencies. Competencies are more stable and evolve more slowly than do products.

3. *Learning-by-doing*. Competencies are gained and enhanced by work. Prahalad and Hamel (1990, p. 82) say that 'core competencies are the collective learning in the organization, especially how to coordinate diverse production skills and integrate multiple streams of technologies. . . . Core competence does not diminish with use . . . competencies are enhanced as they are applied and shared'.
4. *Competitive locus*. Product-market competition is merely the superficial expression of a deeper competition over competencies. Hamel (1991, p. 83) says 'conceiving of the firm as a portfolio of core competencies and disciplines suggests that inter-firm competition, as opposed to inter-product competition, is essentially concerned with the acquisition of skills'.

The idea that competence is an important element of successful strategy is not novel. However, the traditional role ascribed to competence is less central, less integrative and less dynamic than that proposed by Prahalad and Hamel. For example, in the classical Harvard approach to strategy, competence was a key determinant but it was treated as a given rather than as an objective. Drawing on Selznick's (1957) concept of *distinctive competence*, Andrews wrote:

> The strengths of a company which constitute a resource for growth and diversification accrue primarily through experience in making and marketing a product line. . . . The 'distinctive competence' of an organization is more than what it can do; it is what it can do particularly well. . . . In each company, the way in which distinctive competence, organizational resources, and organizational values are combined is unique (Learned *et al.*, 1969, pp. 179, 180, 182).

In this framework, competence poses a constraint on opportunity. Although Andrews (p. 79) noted that firms may 'unexpectedly' develop new capabilities, the perspective is essentially static. Competencies are given, opportunities are given, and the strategist's job is to engineer a creative fit.

The experience curve, popularized by the Boston Consulting Group, brought some dynamics into strategy. According to this doctrine, costs respond dynamically to learning-by-doing. Current costs, therefore, are not simply outlays but are also (partially) an investment in lower future costs. This viewpoint has great power, explaining how one firm might have more competence (lower cost) than another in equilibrium and how the development of competence (lower cost) entails much more than research or development. However, as purveyed, the experience curve was almost wholly restricted to production cost—nothing was said about more general sets of competencies.

Another way of looking at the roots of core competence is to see it as an expression of the new resource-based view of the firm (see Wernerfelt, 1984; Rumelt, 1984; Barney, 1986). This view has emerged in recent years as a counterpoint to market structure analyses of competitive strategy. The resource-based view asserts that competitive advantage does not rest in industry structure or the firm's membership in a collective (e.g. strategic groups), but rather in its possession of unique difficult-to-imitate skills, knowledge, resources or competencies. Recent contributions to this stream have focused on the processes of asset or competence accumulation. Dierickx and Cool (1989) have stressed the limits on speeding up the accumulation of strategic assets and Teece, Pisano and Shuen (1990) argue that strategic *capabilities* are both tacit (difficult to transmit and imitate) and subject to learning. These perspectives finally unite the classical *distinctive competence* view with the learning-by-doing dynamism of the experience curve. These arguments contain the kernel of the core competence concept, but Prahalad and Hamel have taken the resource-based point of view even further and have been even bolder: their concept of core competence admits a proactive construction of competence, sees competence as spanning multiple businesses, and, most importantly, sees competition as being over the acquisition and development of competence.

The issue of competence as a corporate characteristic, spanning a number of business units, also has roots in the literature on diversification strategy. In my own work I defined seven categories of diversification strategy, identifying the *related constrained* strategy as one in which each of the firm's businesses 'draw on the *same* common core skill, strength, or resource' (Rumelt, 1972, p. 360). Interestingly, the related constrained firms tended to have the highest absolute level of performance and to participate in the highest performing industries. Yet this concept, like the idea of distinctive competence, was essentially static—there is scant (if any) attention in the literature on diversification to the development of core skills or to competition over the acquisition of core skills.

RESONANCE

It could be argued that business strategy, as a professional activity, owes its existence to the rise of the diversified firm. As Chandler

(1962) has documented, the strategy of product diversification placed great strains on traditional functional structures and the innovative response was the creation of the multidivisional (M-form) structure. This new form 'removed the executives responsible for the destiny of the entire enterprise from the more routine operational activities and so gave them the time, information, and even psychological commitment for long-term planning and appraisal' (p. 309). It is these general managers, freed from operating responsibilities, who have generated most of the demand for methods of formulating and evaluating business strategies and for concepts of corporate strategy that can lend coherence and meaning to their jobs.

Moreover, neither the corporate structures nor the intellectual paradigms adopted by senior managers have remained static. From the end of the Second World War through the mid-1980s, there was a clear trend towards pushing responsibility for strategy to lower levels and for elaborating the hierarchy of general managers involved in the strategic process. The result has been a proliferation of general management levels and roles. At General Electric, for example, the 1980 organization had three and sometimes four levels of general management: the CEO, Sector management, SBU management and, sometimes, business segment management within SBUs (Aguilar and Hammermesh, 1981, p. 9).

This trend was driven, in part, by increasing diversity and size, but it was also driven by the intellectual toolkit of the times—strategic business units, management by objectives, portfolio planning, etc. These tools and management techniques achieved great clarity by isolating each business from others. With minimal interconnections among businesses and few shared resources, planning was simplified and the responsibility for results unambiguously pinpointed. Attention was focused on products, profits were measured and tracked with precision, and the whole structure served as a school for the development of general management talent.

But this clarity of view was purchased at a cost. Perhaps most costly were the lost opportunities for co-ordination and resource sharing. For co-ordination—across functions, across regions, across products and across time periods—is at the heart of strategic advantage. The clarity of measurement achieved by extreme profit-center decentralization also reduced the gains from scale and scope in particular functions and technologies, reduced the coherence of the corporation as a whole and enmeshed senior management in a world of administrative processes with little or no business context.

It is to this sense of lost coherence that Prahalad and Hamel's work on core competence has been responsive. Their framework has produced a resonance with all who recognize that corporate management must be more than an exercise in control, more than the construction of portfolios. The challenge to academics is to recognize the validity of this resonance and to attempt to test, refine, extend and improve on the concepts offered. There is grist here for the research mill[1] but there is also the call for an evolving theory of strategic management that steps beyond portfolio concepts and agency theory and sees the diversified firm as a bundle of unique resources to be shaped through investment and use.

REFERENCES

Aguilar, F. J. and Richard Hammermesh, R. (1981). General Electric: strategic position—1981. Harvard Business School Case No. 381–174.

Barney, J. B. (1986). Strategic factor markets: expectations, luck, and business strategy. *Management Science*, **32**, 1231–41.

Chandler, A. D. (1972). *Strategy and Structure*. Cambridge, Mass.: The MIT Press.

Dierickx, I. and Cool, K. (1989). Asset stock accumulation and sustainability of competitive advantage. *Management Science*, **35**, 1504–11.

Learned, E. P., Christensen, C. R., Andrews, K. R. and Guth, W. D. (1969). *Business Policy: Text and Cases*. Homewood, Ill: Richard D. Irwin. The text was written by Andrews.

Prahalad, C. K. and Hamel, G. (1990). The core competence of the corporation. *Harvard Business Review*, May–June, 82.

Hamel, G. (1991). Competition for competence and inter-partner learning within international strategic alliances. *Strategic Management Journal*, **12**, 83.

Selznick, P. (1957). *Leadership in Administration*. Evanston, Ill.: Row, Petersen.

Rumelt, R. P. (1972). *Strategy, Structure, and Economic Performance*. Boston: Harvard University Press.

Rumelt, R. P. (1984). Towards a strategic theory of the firm. In R. B. Lamb (Ed.) *Competitive Strategic Management* pp. 566–70. Englewood Cliffs, NJ: Prentice-Hall.

Teece, D. J., Pisano, G., and Shuen, A. (1990). Firm Capabilities, Resources, and the Concept of Strategy. CCC Working Paper No. 90–8, University of California at Berkeley.

Wernerfelt, B. (1982). A resource-based view of the firm. *Strategic Management Journal*, **5**, 171–180.

---

[1] For example, the proposition that competition over competence is more fundamental than competition over product-market positions can be refined and tested. It seems likely that in some contexts (i.e. ready-to-eat cereals) market position may have more to do with performance than corporate core competences.

Series Preface

The purpose of the Strategic Management Society is to bring together, on a world-wide basis, academics, business practitioners and consultants for the development and dissemination of information.

Recognizing that the membership of the society is a relatively small, albeit important and representative, sample of the total population of academics, business people and consultants, The Strategic Management Series of publications is intended to play a key role in bringing information and ideas on strategic issues that are being discussed in the society to the attention of the broader interested audience. To that end, the purpose of the series is to illustrate 'The Best of Strategic Management' by publishing three types of books:

1. An annual volume based on a selection of papers from the annual Strategic Management Society conference. Selection may be based either on a particular theme or on a collection of 'best' papers from the conference, whichever seems to the editors to best exemplify that particular conference.
2. Volumes based on selected papers. Each volume is selected from mini-conferences on topical issues in strategy.
3. Short monographs on current research or novel conceptual frameworks identified, chosen and periodically reviewed by an editorial committee.

This volume is the second in the series representing Strategic Management Society mini-conferences. The society's aim in holding such conferences is to select interesting, cutting-edge topics and to encourage analysis of their content in small, discussion-type conferences of around 100 interested people. This allows examination of issues, in detail, by academics, business practitioners and consultants, and encourages presenters to develop their ideas in a manner that will appeal to a broad range of participants.

The ultimate vision is to stimulate ideas, concepts, and research about new issues and areas in the field of strategic management. Although not every Society member can attend, selected writings can illustrate the flavor of the conference, from the multiple perspectives of academics, practitioners and consultants.

This volume is based on the Proceedings of the Strategic Management Society's International Workshop 'Competence-Based Competition: Towards the Roots of Sustainable Competitive Advantage', held in Genk (Belgium), and co-sponsored by the Strategic Management Society, De Vlerick School voor Management, the Vlaamse Strategievereniging and Coopers & Lybrand.

As the field of strategic management develops, it is clear that the integration of organizational cognizance with the more economic perspectives advanced by such authorities as Michael Porter becomes an increasingly important theme. In the next ten years strategy will take an increasingly general management focus as we grapple with firm-level issues such as: how to manage change; how to design organizations; how to empower individuals while utilizing culture as a source of competitive advantage; how to manage strategic alliances; and how to effectively pair team-based management with more traditional methods.

If you conceptualize firms as bundles of resources, it is folly to think they can be effectively managed without the recognition that both organizations and people are critical resources and elements in the management of strategic change.

This second volume is, I feel, an interesting and effective integration of strategic perspectives that exemplify many of the most important issues facing strategic management, both now and in the immediate future.

An eclectic ensemble of contributors, including academics, business executives, consultants, and administrators, addresses one of the Society's primary concerns—building and maintaining bridges between management theory and business practice.

Editorial commentary provides integration among the papers included, and references some of the more appropriate previous research in each subject area, for the reader's convenience, in supplementary reading. The result is not just a volume of currently relevant papers, to be read once and set aside, but a reference manual that explores currently relevant issues and links them with previous research streams.

HOWARD THOMAS
Series Editor

Preface

At the annual meeting of the Strategic Management Society held in Stockholm (1990), G. Hamel and C. K. Prahalad summarized the key concepts underlying their particular view of corporate strategy management and the role of senior management. These concepts were first laid out in a series of *Harvard Business Review* articles. Prior to the Stockholm conference, four *HBR* articles by Hamel and Prahalad had been published ('Do you have a global strategy?' September–October 1985; 'Collaborate with competitors and win', January–February 1989; 'Strategic intent', May–June 1989; and 'The core competence of the corporation', May–June 1990), and two additional *HBR* articles published since the conference ('Corporate imagination and expeditionary marketing', July–August 1991; and 'Strategy as stretch and leverage', March–April 1993).

While the strategy perspective of Hamel and Prahalad is certainly not unique in each of its particulars, their body of work does seem to add up a view of strategy quite distinct from, though not at odds with, the industrial-organization paradigm developed so thoroughly by Professor Michael Porter of the Harvard Business School. Hamel and Prahalad have sought to complement rather than to replace the traditional conceptual base of strategy along the following dimensions:

Core concept	*Complement*
Strategy as fit	Strategy as stretch
Resource allocation	Resource leverage
Portfolio of businesses	Portfolio of competencies
Competition as confrontation	Competition as encirclement
Markets as product and customers	Markets as needs and functionalities
Competition for market share	Competition for opportunity share

The Hamel and Prahalad perspective received substantial endorsement: 'Strategic intent' and 'The core competence of the corporation' each won a McKinsey Prize for excellence, and by 1993 'The core competence of the corporation' had become *HBR*'s most reprinted article ever, with 'Strategic intent' also in the top five *HBR* reprints. More importantly, their writings prompted many companies to enquire, 'What are our core competencies and how do we better manage them?' Though the question was provocative, companies typically found that the answers were not easy to come by and models of best-practice competence management were few and far between.

As a result of the Stockholm meeting I decided to undertake to develop the 'core competence' perspective further. Organizing a Strategic Management Society 'workshop' was one important way of achieving this objective. The workshop formula allows the organization of intensive discussion and debate among a limited number of academics, business people and consultants, all of whom share a common interest in a given topic and are keen to see advances in theory and practice. Many months of hard work in close co-operation with the 'organizing committee' gave rise to a workshop proposal that the board of the Strategic Management Society was able to support. As a result of this support (and that provided by the De Vlerick School voor Management, the Vlaamse Strategievereniging and Coopers & Lybrand), an international workshop on core competence entitled 'Competence-Based Competition: Towards the Roots of Sustainable Competitive Advantage' was held in Genk (Belgium) in November 1992. Almost 100 participants from all over the world registered for this workshop and 90% of these actively participated in the event, as an author, discussant, session-chair or a member of the opening or closing panel.

Thirty-six papers were submitted for the workshop. The organizing committee accepted 24 of these for presentation and discussion. (Papers written by academics were discussed by business people or consultants and vice versa.) The debates and discussions among academics, business people and consultants were animated, constructive and amicable. In the course of the workshop, the Strategic Management Society proposed that the 'most attractive papers' presented during the workshop be published in a single volume. Nineteen of the 24 authors revised their contribution to the workshop and submitted their papers to the review committee who screened and evaluated them. In the end, 12 papers were accepted for inclusion in the volume, most having been revised three times. Review criteria included coherence, 'clusterability', academic soundness, pragmatism and managerial relevance. All authors were requested to 'line up' with the definitions and typologies outlined in the contribution by Bogaert, Martens and Van Cauwenbergh (Chapter 3). This helped to ensure at least a modicum of conceptual coherence among the papers.

I truly hope that this whole process has been worth enduring for all contributors and, above all, that this book, in its way, will further contribute to the development of an exciting and useful new approach to the practice of strategic management.

AIMÉ HEENE

Acknowledgements

As a sign of true gratitude, the editors wish to thank the many people whose efforts were indispensable in bringing this book to fruition. We first want to thank all those who contributed to the considerable success of the International Workshop 'Competence Based Competition', on which proceedings this book is based. We thank the sponsors of the workshop: the Strategic Management Society, the De Vlerick School voor Management, the Vlaamse Strategievereniging, and last but not least, Coopers & Lybrand, the main financial sponsor.

We thank the organizing committee of the workshop: L. Bartholomeeusen (Coopers & Lybrand, Brussels), I. Greaves (Lancashire Polytechnic, Preston, UK), J. Klein (Scientific Generics, London), N. Konno (Engine Corporation, Tokyo), R. Martens (UFSIA, Antwerp), B. Van Lierde (Boston Consulting Group, Paris) and N. Venkatraman (MIT Sloan School of Management, Boston), who all did a splendid job of laying the groundwork for the conference.

We also wish to thank all the active participants of the workshop: authors, discussants, session-chairs, members of the opening panel and members of the closing panel.

We thank Ann Coopman, the workshop's secretary who managed the workshop perfectly from an administrative point of view, and who took care of the wellbeing of all participants before and during the workshop.

We thank all the authors that were willing to revise (several times) the papers they presented at the workshop for inclusion in this book. We thank the members of the review committee and the editorial board: M. Barbeschi (MIP—Polytecnico, Milan), V. Chiesa (MIP—Polytecnico, Milan), F. De Leo (SDA Bocconi, Milan), N. Konno (Engine Corporation, Tokyo), E. Rühli (Institüt für betriebswirtschaftlichen Forschung, Zürich), E. Scheerlinck, (Gemeentekrediet, Brussels), H. Thomas (College of Commerce and Business Administration, Champaign-Illinois) and B. Winterscheid (EIASM, Brussels). They thoroughly screened all the papers submitted for this publication and provided substantial guidance to the authors during the review process. The quality of this book owes much to their contribution. The editors would like to thank Mark Bleackley of London Business School for his editorial support on an early draft of the manuscript.

Finally, we wish to thank Inge Degraeve for smoothly and perfectly running the administrative organization of this publication.

The editors believe that the effort of all these people has brought about a publication that can be highly recommended to academics, business consultants and managers around the world.

Introduction: Competing Paradigms in Strategic Management

After almost 40 years of development and theory building, the field of strategic management is, today more than ever, characterized by contrasting and sometimes competing paradigms. While each new theoretical construct (experience curves, growth-share matrices, the PIMS research, industry structure analysis, game theory, transaction cost theory, agency theory, etc.) has attracted both acolytes and critics, the strategy field seems to be as far away as ever from a 'grand unified theory' of competitiveness. Indeed, there is still much divergence of opinion within the strategy field on questions as basic as 'what is a theory of strategic management about?' and, more importantly, 'what should a theory of strategic management be about?'

Strategy scholars and practitioners differ widely in their views on whether strategic management is about 'reacting', or about 'anticipating', on whether strategy is created or emerges. We find little consensus when we ask questions such as: Is the process of strategy formulation top-down, bottom-up or middle-out? Is strategy more about doing or more about thinking? Is it 'content' that matters in strategy making, or should the emphasis be put on the 'process' by which strategies are created? Is strategy prospective or retrospective? Is strategy about 'positioning' within an extant industry

Competence-Based Competition.
Edited by G. Hamel and A. Heene.
Copyright © 1994 The Strategic Management Society. Published 1994 by John Wiley & Sons Ltd.

structure or about redrawing industry boundaries for one's own advantage? Is the essence of strategic management the creation of sustainable advantage or the continuous discovery of new sources of advantages as old advantages lose their potency? Does the dynamic of strategy derive from the search for 'fit' between the firm and its environment or from a 'deliberately created misfit' between resources and aspirations? Does industry 'attractiveness' set the boundary conditions for firm profitability or is managerial capability the critical determinant? Is devolvement and decentralization the key to strategic vitality or does vitality stem from the clarity of strategic direction emanating from the top of the company? Are corporate winners the product of Darwinian selection or purposeful action?

A lack of agreement on these points and many others is, for some, a sign of the continuing immaturity of the strategy field. (The implicit comparison, on this point, is often with the finance field. What often seems to be missed is that the certainty and clarity so early reached in the finance discipline, on issues like efficiency of capital markets, the rationality of investors and the application of the capital asset pricing model, is now acting as a substantial brake on the field's ability to come to terms with a wealth of new data and research which challenges the pillars of the faith.)

The task of coming to an agreement on what strategy is, or should be, is complicated by the fact that the phenomena under study are changing faster than they can be described. Where is a robust theory of coalition management that can help the strategy student make sense of General Magic, the US firm developing software protocols for personal digital assistants in conjunction with several investor companies, or America's HDTV consortia? Where is the theory that can help companies make wise strategic choices in perpetually underdefined industries like financial services and telecommunications? Where is the theory that can account for differences among companies in their capacity for dynamic advantage creation? Strategy academics should make no apologies for devoting as much time to the development of new paradigms as to the testing of existing ones. If there is a shortage of anything in the strategy field, it is not of well-tested theory but of administratively sophisticated, contingency-sensitive and operationally subtle theory.

If we have learnt anything about strategic management it is that strategy is about contingencies, trade-offs, paradoxes and uncertainty. Why should we expect to find a grand unified theory of competitiveness? Diversity and variety in paradigms is less a sign of confusion than of the multifaceted phenomena of corporate success and failures and the limited usefulness of any single strategy dictum. The problem comes when strategy choices and perspectives are posed as dichotomies: centralization versus decentralization; competition versus collaboration; emergent strategy versus designed strategy, and so on. What is needed is subtlety, balance and perspective. Rather than seeing the notion of competition for competence as somehow in competition with the idea of competition for market share and position, it should be regarded as complementary. Broadly, the notion of core competence is a much-needed *yang*, to the current and dominant *yin* of strategy theory, which has emphasized more the firm's competitive environment than its internal capacity to create and exploit unique capabilities or competencies. The core competence perspective is simply an additional lens through which to view issues of competitiveness and firm performance.

THE MISSION OF THIS BOOK

Among competing paradigms (some of which give rise to dilemmas) the concept of 'core competence' deserves further research and management attention for several reasons. The issue of the sustainability of competitive advantage from the perspective of grounding competitive advantage on a bundle of (invisible) resources, (intangible) assets, skills or 'stocks' of the company has been part of the theory of strategic management for around 10 years. Though the term 'core competence' is a novel one, a number of ideas that it encapsulates refer to frameworks that have previously been explored by more than one author. The fact that the ideas 'behind' core competence are regularly put forward in the literature proves, at least, that scholars should care about the concept of 'core competence' and the underlying ideas and 'mindsets'. In particular, the 'core competence' concept and approach are of much significance for those academics exploring the roots of sustainable competitive advantage.

The core competence idea is 'attractive' for the business community as well. This can be seen in three instances.

First, the *Harvard Business Review* article 'The core competence of the corporation' by C. K. Prahalad and G. Hamel was a great success in the business community, clearly demonstrated by the number of reprints sold. Second, the Call for Papers of the

International Workshop on which proceedings this book is based was answered by almost 30 business people (out of about 500 to whom the Call for Papers was sent). Finally, one can observe that a considerable number of companies have been keen to co-operate with management schools in order to develop and implement their strategy from a core competence point of view. At the De Vlerick School voor Management (Belgium), for instance, eight medium-sized companies have engaged in a one-year research project concerning the process of strategy making based on the fundamentals of the core competence approach. Similar initiatives (with comparable success) exist at the London Business School, SDA Bocconi (Milan) and several other management schools.

Consultants also seem to be interested in the competence-based approach. The International Workshop 'Competence Based Competition' attracted about 30 consultants and a considerable number of papers presented during the workshop were contributions prepared by leading, internationally recognized consulting companies. In addition, we observe that many consulting companies have added 'core competence' to their own list of skills, competencies and techniques. The justification for this book, however, resides not only in the 'attractiveness' of the concept and the approach but also in the 'steering' or at least 'guiding' effect that this book could have within the strategic management field.

Given the attention that is actually paid to the core competence approach, a number of phenomena need to be watched and 'managed' in order to prevent the 'core competence' approach being rejected justly, but at the same time prematurely. Academics working with the 'core competence' approach (and theoretically related approaches) should avoid developing theories of strategic management just for the sake of theory development without considering (too greatly) the pragmatic relevance of their work. We (academics, business people and consultants) do need a sound theory of strategic management. Above all, we need a theory with obvious pragmatic relevance, with validity for the business community and close links to the daily practice of strategic management.

Academics solely interested in fundamental research (and looking, for example, for the 'fine-tuned' differences between 'invisible assets' and 'intangibles') will therefore be disappointed in the content of this book. It is much more intended to be a contribution to a theory of strategic management with very close and direct links to the daily reality of strategy making.

Business people should avoid 'jumping on' concepts and approaches where they do not fully understand the starting points or consequences in terms of the underlying 'mindsets' and paradigms. This should prevent them from 'playing with words' and abusing the concepts, thereby losing sight of the many advantages offered by the chosen approach. Business people should also keep in mind the limits, constraints and boundaries of the concepts and approaches they apply in strategy making. Losing sight of those limits can indeed lead to 'quick fix' strategies, potentially resulting in decreased profitability.

Consultants do not have any (unless a very short-term) interest in turning 'core competence' into the latest 'buzzword', though they may easily be seduced into doing so. One could imagine certain business people being willing to pay a premium price for apparently 'innovative' consulting approaches. Turning core competence into 'fashion' is the main phenomenon this book tries to avoid. In developing techniques, toolkits and methodologies in what is meant to be an operationalization of the core competence approach, consultants (just like business people) therefore need to understand the underlying theories. This alone will allow them to assist business people (looking for above-average profitability) to implement theoretically sound paradigms.

THE STRUCTURE OF THE BOOK

The chapters in this book are organized into three sections. The first defines the concept of 'core competence' and the related concepts within the field of 'competence-based competition'. This section clarifies the assumptions, models and basic ideas underlying strategy making from a core competence point of view, and determines the 'conceptual environment' within which this approach finds its place.

The second section looks at traditional concepts, approaches and techniques in strategic management (such as industry structure, the value chain and competitive advantage) from a competence-based perspective. Linking new concepts and approaches to the old ones can have great advantage in speeding up the process of theory development (the potential disadvantage being that the process could end up as 'old wine in new bottles') and in promoting the acknowledgement of the new approaches by practitioners (business people and consultants) used to the more traditional concepts.

Though the first two sections primarily address the academic reader, we strongly recommend all to read the chapters very carefully. Given the objectives of this book, we invite all business people and consultants to think through the managerial consequences of these chapters.

The chapters in the third section of the book explore 'The practice of strategic management from the core competence point of view'. Conceptual frameworks and 'taxonomies of core competence' are presented in this section in order to assist business people in identifying the core competencies of their company or of their competitors, as well as methods and techniques for discovering and assessing core competence at an industry level. The process of acquisition and development of core competence is also treated in this third section from a (theoretically sound but at the same time) pragmatic point of view. Particular attention is paid to the process of innovation from a core competence perspective and to the building of 'strategic architectures' to assist in the acquisition and development of core competence as part of the innovation process.

The majority of the chapters in this book concern 'business unit strategy'. This should not lead to the conclusion that a core competence point of view should be limited to address strategic issues solely at the business unit level. In order to prevent this false conclusion the editors invited Professor Rumelt, President-Elect of the Strategic Management Society, to explore the relationships between core competence and corporate strategy. In his Foreword Professor Rumelt highlights four key components of the concept of corporate core competence in order to see how the Prahalad and Hamel approach differs from other work on competence and how that difference fits with weaknesses in mainstream strategic management's treatment of corporate strategy.

THE PURPOSE OF THIS BOOK

This book is meant to be an invitation to academics, to business people and to consultants. To academics, it represents an invitation to engage in the debate on competing paradigms in today's theory of strategic management. The authors hope that this debate can contribute significantly to the development of the theory of strategic management, as companies strive to survive and remain profitable into the next century. To business people, the book is an invitation to think over their actual approaches to strategy making. It is an invitation to apply new mindsets and new 'mental models' and to test thoroughly the assumptions, concepts and approaches that could be(come) the building blocks of a forthcoming theory of strategic management in daily practice. To consultants, this book is an invitation to develop toolkits, techniques and methodologies that have the power to motivate business people to include the core competence approach in their strategic management practice. Through their effort, consultants can contribute to taking sound theory (developed by academics) closer to the daily struggle for competitiveness.

Given these objectives, in publishing this book the editors hope to contribute to the development of a theory of strategic management and to the process of strategy making. They therefore invite all readers to reflect on the chapters and to react to them. We hope that the book will contribute to the founding of a 'world-class research community' that takes the concepts of 'core competence' and 'competence-based competition' as its main field of interest.

GARY HAMEL
AIMÉ HEENE

Section I

Towards a Theory of Strategic Management from a Core Competence Point of View

In order to make a theory of strategic management 'acceptable from a theoretical point of view' and 'workable in practice', the constituent concepts and constructs must be defined and linked into coherent conceptual frameworks. In addition, the assumptions, limits and boundaries of the theory need to be made explicit. But the theory of strategic management does not only have to be clear and consistent. It should also guide day-to-day management decisions and actions that contribute to the long-term survival and to the creation of a desirable future for the company. It is important therefore that a credible theory of strategic management enables managers to ask themselves the relevant questions as they develop their strategy, and to question their own assumptions about the nature of long-term profitability, survival and competition. The chapters in this first section should primarily be looked at from this perspective as they sketch the 'building blocks' of a theory of strategic management from a core competence point of view.

In Chapter 1 Hamel and Prahalad define the concept of core competence, describe different types of core competence and outline four respects in which the concept of core competence complements other strategic perspectives. Furthermore, they go into details on how to manage core competence. The core competence concept is an attractive lens through which to view competitive advantage. Founding a competitive advantage on core competence satisfies a number of requirements regarding sustainability, in particular, that the advantage is both hard to copy and to alienate. However, one might question whether core competence reaches a level of analysis which provides a sufficient degree of detail to explain, 'in a sustainable way', long-term survival and profitability of the company.

In Chapter 2 De Leo discusses the 'ultimate sources' of sustainable competitive advantage. He argues that strategy making based on core competence is only one possible layer of analysis of the long-term success of the company. Thinking about the company as being a bundle of resources, hard to imitate and alienate must be complemented by additional levels of analysis. In his view, strategy should be considered a multi-layered 'game'. De Leo provides a conceptual framework for (thinking about) strategy making within which the core competence approach is coupled to complementary techniques and approaches.

Whereas both Hamel and Prahalad and De Leo stress 'misfit' as one of the crucial fields of attention in strategic management, Chapter 3 by Bogaert, Martens and Van Cauwenbergh treats strategic management as a process of external and internal 'fit'. In the opinion of these authors, strategic management processes can be looked at as very complex 'puzzle games' through which management creates 'organized' core competence out of a collection of skills and competencies and through which 'fit' is pursued between the core competence of the company and the external requirements.

'Fit' and 'misfit' are thus treated in this first section as being 'poles' of one of the important dilemmas in strategic management. Their reconciliation is symptomatic of the very nature of strategic management and its ultimate objective: the long-term survival of the company.

1

The Concept of Core Competence

Gary Hamel

What is a 'Core Competence?'

The purpose of offering a definition here is not to preclude any other (the competence perspective on the firm is still too underdeveloped to permit a single, tight definition), nor is it to develop a subtle typology of different forms of 'resources', 'knowledge' or 'intangible assets'. The goal is simply to provide a working definition that is sufficiently tight to be of some use to practitioners and researchers (in that the term can be distinguished from 'competitive advantage' or 'capability'), but broad enough to encompass the conceptual elaboration that will inevitably issue from further research.

An Integration of Skills

The working definition we employ has several elements. First, a competence is a bundle of constituent skills and technologies, rather than a single, discrete skill or technology. For example, the competence Federal Express possesses in package transport and delivery includes barcoding technologies, linear programming skills and much more besides. A core competence represents the integration of a variety of individual skills. It is this integration that

Competence-Based Competition.
Edited by G. Hamel and A. Heene.
Copyright © 1994 The Strategic Management Society. Published 1994 by John Wiley & Sons Ltd.

is the distinguishing hallmark of a core competence. Thus a core competence is very unlikely to reside, in its entirety, in a single individual or small team.

The dividing line between a particular skill and the core competence to which it contributes may be difficult to define. As a practical matter, if in defining the developed and/or nascent core competencies of a particular business a team of managers comes up with 40, 50 or more 'competencies' they are probably describing constituent skills rather than core competencies. On the other hand, if they list only one or two competencies they are probably describing broad 'meta-competencies' rather than what we would call core competencies. The most useful level of aggregation is typically one that yields somewhere between five and fifteen core competencies for any individual business. If, however, the team has a good understanding of the entire hierarchy of competencies—from meta-competencies ('logistics' in the case of FedEx), to core competencies (package tracking), to constituent skills (barcoding)—then the question of just where to draw the line between contributing skills and competencies is primarily a question of convenience.

Not an Asset

Second, a core competence is not an 'asset' in the accounting sense of the word. A factory, distribution channel or brand cannot be a core competence, but an aptitude to manage that factory (e.g. Toyota's lean manufacturing) or channel (Wal-Mart's logistics) or brand (Coca-Cola's advertising) may constitute a core competence. A core competence is not an inanimate thing, it is an activity, a messy accumulation of learning. A core competence will undoubtedly comprise both tacit and explicit knowledge.

Core Versus Non-Core

We use the terms 'competence' and 'capability' interchangeably. Our starting proposition is that competition between firms is as much a race for competence mastery as it is for market position and market power. Of course, there is nothing very novel about the proposition that firms 'compete on capabilities'. The subtlety comes when one attempts to distinguish between those capabilities which are 'core' and those which are 'non-core'. If one produced an inventory of all the 'capabilities' that are potentially important to success in a particular business, it would be a long list indeed—too long to be of any great managerial usefulness. Senior management cannot pay attention to everything; there must be some sense of what activities *really* contribute to long-term corporate prosperity. The goal, therefore, is to focus senior management's attention on those competencies that lie at the center, rather than the periphery, of competitive success. To be considered a 'core' competence a skill cluster must meet three additional tests, beyond the two tests (an integration of skills, and more than an asset) already identified.

Customer Value

A core competence must make a disproportionate contribution to customer-perceived value. Core competencies are the skills which enable a firm to deliver a fundamental customer benefit. Examples of such benefits might be reliability (in the case of a fault-tolerant computer), image recording (in the case of a videotape competence), user friendliness (the benefit that Apple delivered via the Macintosh), management of complexity (a benefit that EDS brings to its customers in large systems integration projects), and so on. The distinction between core and non-core competencies thus rests, in part, on a distinction between core and non-core customer benefits.

It is this distinction that leads us to describe Honda's knowhow in engines as a core competence, and its management of dealer relationships as a secondary capability. While the experience a potential buyer has in a Honda dealership is not unimportant in the sales process, it does not constitute a core customer benefit. Nor would Honda argue that its dealer network provides customers with a substantially better experience than that of Toyota, Mazda or Ford. On the other hand, Honda's ability to produce some of the world's best engines and powertrains does provide customers with highly valued benefits: i.e. superior fuel economy, zippy acceleration, easy revving, and less noise and vibration. It is interesting to note that in the advertising supporting the recent relaunch of Honda's Accord in America, the car's engine receives several column inches, while the dealer network has scarcely a mention. This is not to say that the sales mechanism can never be a core competence. For years, IBM's extraordinarily well-trained salesforce was a significant factor in its ability to intermediate between customer needs and the company's technological prowess.

That a core competence must make an important contribution to customer-perceived value does not imply that the core competence will be visible to, or easily understood by, the customer. Few customers could express in words exactly why the Honda driving experience may be better than that experience in, for example, a Chevrolet Lumina, but many would attest that the Honda just 'feels' and 'performs' better. Likewise, few computer users could tell you much about the competencies that support the user-friendly interface of Macintosh, but they do know that the computer is easy to use. What is visible to customers is the benefit, not the technical nuances of the competence that underlies that benefit.

There is an important exception to the rule that a core competence must make a substantial contribution to customer value. Process- and manufacturing-related competencies that yield substantial cost benefits to the producer may also be considered core competencies, even though little or none of the cost benefits are passed on to the customer. A chemical company, for example, may have a process competence that enables it to produce a certain kind of plastic 20% cheaper than any other firm in the world. The plastic may very well be a commodity, with a world price level which reflects the cost structure of the least efficient or 'marginal' producers. The more efficient producer, with its process competence, may well choose to 'bank' its cost advantage, rather than pass it on to customers. Thus any bundle of skills which yields a significant cost advantage in delivering a particular customer benefit may also be termed a core competence.

Competitor Differentiation

To qualify as a 'core' competence a capability must also be competitively unique. This does not mean that to qualify as 'core' a competence must be uniquely held by a single firm but rather that any capability that is ubiquitous across the industry should not be defined as 'core' unless, of course, the company's level of competence is substantially superior to all others. Thus you could argue that while powertrains have truly been a core competence at Honda, they have not, over the past decade or two, been a core competence of Ford, even though Ford is certainly capable of producing engines—as uninspiring as they may be. In some cases, managers may believe that a particular competence, while ubiquitous within an industry, has remained substantially under-developed. Such a competence might be targeted as a potential 'core' competence if managers believe there is scope for great improvement. In short, it makes little sense to define a competence as 'core' if it is ubiquitous or easily imitated by competitors.

Gateway to New Markets

To be considered 'core' at least from the corporate as opposed to the business unit perspective, a core competence should provide an entrée into new markets. Honda's engine competence has propelled the firm into a variety of product-markets, as have 3M's competencies in adhesives and abrasives, and AMR's information competencies. Core competencies are the gateways to new markets. Sharp's competencies in flat-screen displays give it access to product markets as diverse as laptop computers, video projection screens, pocket televisions, and camcorders employing flat-screen viewfinders.

So while a particular competence may be 'core' in the eyes of a particular business, in that it meets the tests of customer value and competitive differentiation, it may not be a core competence from the point of view of the corporation if there is no way of imagining an array of new product-markets issuing from the competence. As a practical matter, this means that in defining core competencies, managers must work very hard to abstract away from the particular product configuration in which the competence is embedded and attempt to imagine how the competence might be applied in new product arenas.

For example, while SKF, the world's leading manufacturer of roller bearings, might be tempted to define its core competence as bearings, such a definition would be unnecessarily limiting in terms of access to new markets. No doubt, SKF engineers and marketers have considered all the potential uses of roller bearings. Fortunately, the company's growth is not totally dependent on finding new uses for roller bearings, because when SKF moves away from a product-based view of its competencies, to a skill-based view, new opportunities quickly emerge. SKF has competencies in anti-friction (understanding how different materials work together to either generate or reduce friction); in precision engineering (it is one of a very few European companies that can machine hard metals to incredibly tight tolerances); and in making perfectly spherical devices. One can speculate on whether SKF might be capable of manufacturing the round, high-precision recording heads that go inside a VCR, most of which are now manufactured by Japanese firms. Perhaps SKF could make the tiny 'balls' that go into rollerball pens—another component usually made by Japanese firms. Again, the point is simple: to increase its potential 'opportunity horizon' a firm must be able to move beyond an orthodox, product-centric view of its competencies.

TYPES OF CORE COMPETENCIES

There are probably hundreds of different ways to categorize core competencies. We have found it useful to distinguish among three broad types: *market-access competencies* (management of brand development, sales and marketing, distribution and logistics, technical support, etc.—all those skills which help to put a firm in close proximity to its customers); *integrity-related competencies* (competencies like quality, cycle time management, just-in-time inventory management and so on which allow a company to do things more quickly, flexibly or with a higher degree of reliability than competitors); and *functionality-related competencies* (skills which enable the company to invest its services or products with unique functionality, which invest the product with distinctive customer benefits, rather than merely making it incrementally better).

It is our contention that functionality-related competencies are becoming more important as a source of competitive differentiation, relative to the other two competence types. This is happening because companies are converging around universally high standards for product and service integrity, and are moving through alliances, acquisitions and industry consolidation to build broadly matching global brand and distribution capabilities. Interestingly, the Japanese concept of quality has shifted from an idea centered on integrity ('zero defects') to one focused on functionality ('quality that surprises' in that the product yields a unique functionality benefit to the customer).

For example, Ford has long had a strong dealer presence in most major countries and a world-wide manufacturing base (albeit the company was and is under-represented in some parts of Asia). The ability to manage this world-wide market access infrastructure was a core competence for Ford in the days when it alone had such a global position. While Ford was enjoying the fruits of its global reach, Japanese car makers were working hard to increase vehicle integrity. By the end of the 1970s defects per hundred vehicles among Japanese-made cars were often a mere 25% of the defects per hundred cars to be found in US-made cars. Not surprisingly, quality and reliability became key differentiators in the minds of customers, and integrity-related disciplines constituted a genuine 'core' competence for Japanese producers. In the 1970s and 1980s Japanese producers began to put their own worldwide market access capabilities in place, including local manufacturing where required, strong dealer networks, and logistic networks for spare parts. Ford's core competencies in these arenas stopped being so unique, and thus ceased to be 'core'. (Though if Ford could again make them unique in some way, they might regain their status as 'core'.) In the early 1980s Ford began working to close the product integrity gap with its Japanese competitors. As it did so, quality also ceased to be a differentiator for Japanese car companies and thus became somewhat less 'core', though, and this is an important point, product integrity continued to be essential if one was going to hold one's own in the intensely competitive global car business.

While Ford was succeeding in improving its integrity-related competencies it was paying too little attention to building functionality-enhancing competencies. For most of the 1980s Ford, by its own admission, seriously under-invested in powertrains, suspension and engine competencies. The result was that Ford became a global manufacturer and distributor of well-made but often deadly boring automobiles. This deficit was partially offset by Ford's apparent efforts to build a core competence in vehicle design (i.e. the Sierra model in Europe and Taurus/Sable models in the USA). However, when later designs did not reflect the same daring and panache, some observers wondered whether Ford really did possess an unequivocal commitment to building a core competence in design leadership. As quality came to be taken for granted, the new 'core' competencies were skills that could help a company win the excitement sweepstakes. Such skills included 'agile' manufacturing techniques which allowed companies like Mazda to produce 'lifestyle niche' cars in volumes too small to be economical for Ford and GM. To meet their higher minimum efficient model runs, American car companies had to design cars for a wider spectrum of buyers, and thus often ended up with cars that were plain vanilla ice cream rather than double-chocolate, macadamia nut.

The point here is that what is 'core' changes over time, and top management must ensure that it is working today to build the competencies that will be 'core' in the future. What is core and non-core may also differ between firms competing in the same industry. Dell Computers built a core competence in mail-order selling. Dell would not claim that it has a core competence in software or microprocessors, but its core competence—the ability to manage a 'remote' telesales and teleservice function in support of a reasonably sophisticated product—does create customer benefits for those consumers eager to buy a PC with minimum hassle. Although Apple and IBM may develop mail-order sales channels, these companies would be unlikely to see mail-order sales management as a core competence. On the other hand, if all PC vendors begin to explore this sales channel, it may well cease to be a core competence for Dell, though it may continue to be a very important capability within the industry.

CORE COMPETENCE AS A COMPLEMENTARY PERSPECTIVE

There are at least four respects in which the concept of core competence complements other strategy perspectives.

CORE COMPETENCIES VERSUS COMPETITIVE ADVANTAGES

A core competence is, most decidedly, a source of competitive advantage, in that it is competitively unique and makes a contribution to value and or cost. But whereas all core competencies are sources of competitive advantage, not all competitive advantages are core competencies. A firm might have a licensing agreement which allows it unique access to a particular technology; a company might be granted an exclusive import license for a particular product; a business's factories might be preferentially positioned close to raw material supplies; a firm's plants might be located in a low wage cost location; customers may prefer to buy from the company because its products are locally produced, as in 'Buy American', or because they are produced abroad, as in 'real' (i.e. French) champagne. All these are examples of competitive advantage, none of them are core competencies.

A competence is just what the name implies, an aptitude, a capability, a skill. A business may possess many advantages, *vis-à-vis* competitors, that do not rest on skills and aptitudes. This does not make these advantages any less valuable or critical to success, but it does mean they will be 'managed' in quite different ways from core competencies.

CORE COMPETENCIES VERSUS PRODUCTS

The dominance of the product perspective in strategy can be traced back to the field's roots in marketing strategy. Concepts like experience curves, product portfolios, rivalry, signaling, order of entry effects, and profit–market share relationships all had their genesis in marketing. Indeed, if in the early 1980s one compared a Michael Porter strategy text and a typical strategic marketing text one would have seen a substantial amount of overlap. The competence perspective goes a long way in helping strategists differentiate their contribution from that of marketers, whose focus tends to be the end product or service, rather than the underlying competencies.

The Longevity of Competencies

Product and service leadership is the outgrowth of core competence leadership. Core competencies are more lasting, typically, than any individual product. While the constituent technologies and skills that go into Sony's miniaturization competence have changed markedly since the company first licensed the transistor from Bell Labs, and while the range of products where Sony exploits that competence has grown and changed, miniaturization has been at the heart of Sony's competitiveness for three decades. The same could be said for Apple's competence in user-friendly digital products. Apple has recently expanded its conception of itself to include not only computers but also any product where digital technology can be applied to humanize the human–machine interface. Again the particular skills that underlie this competence will change over time. Individual products and technologies tend to be more transitory than competencies.

The Transcendence of Core Competencies

Core competencies are not, for the most part, product-specific. They contribute to the competitiveness of a range of products or services. In this sense, core competencies transcend any particular product or service, and indeed may transcend any single business unit within the corporation.

INTER-FIRM COMPETITION VERSUS PRODUCT-TO-PRODUCT COMPETITION

For the most part, the unit of analysis for competitive strategy has been a particular product or service. Issues of positioning, pricing, cost and differentiation, competitive signaling, and barriers to entry are typically discussed in the context of a single product or a closely related line of products. Likewise, competitive battles are described in product terms: Diet Coke versus Diet Pepsi, Apple's Powerbook versus IBM's ThinkPad, or the first-class service of British Airways versus that of American Airlines. But companies compete in a more fundamental and deeper way, as well. American Airlines competes with British Airways to develop competencies in fleet management, cabin service and reservation systems. Sharp competes with Toshiba to build global leadership in flat-screen displays. Ford competes with Honda, Toyota, GM and others to build world leadership in engines and powertrains.

There are several reasons why it may be appropriate to view competition for competence leadership as inter-corporate competition, as opposed to inter-product or inter-business. First, because a core competence contributes to the competitiveness of a range of products or services, winning or losing the battle for competence leadership can have a profound impact on a company's potential for growth and competitive differentiation; a much greater impact than the success or failure of a single product. If Motorola lost its leadership position in wireless competencies, a broad spectrum of businesses would suffer. Likewise, because the investment, risk taking and time frame required to achieve core competence leadership often exceeds the resources and patience of a single business unit, some competencies will not get built in the absence of direct corporate support. Third, only by building and nurturing core competencies can top management ensure the continuance of the enterprise. As we argued earlier, core competencies are the gateway to the future; they are the well-spring of future product development; the 'roots', if you like, that nourish the product 'fruit'. If top management fails to take responsibility for nurturing core competencies it may, inadvertently, mortgage the company's future.

It is important to note that competition for competence not only transcends inter-product competition it also antedates product competition. While the lifecycle for a particular product or service offering might be measured in months, the time to build world-class leadership in a core competence area is likely to take years, and perhaps decades. AT&T tested a video telephone in its labs in 1939, demonstrated one at the New York World's Fair in 1964, and finally introduced it as a consumer product in 1992. Even then, one of the contributing core competencies, video compression, was not sufficiently developed to allow transmission of full-motion, television-quality images. It took JVC almost 20 years to perfect the competencies that contributed to its success with VHS; Philips worked just as long to establish its leadership in digital optical storage and playback. Thus product-to-product competition may represent only the last mile of a competence-building marathon. Surprisingly, traditional competitive strategy virtually ignores the first 25 miles of the race.

CORE COMPETENCIES VERSUS STRATEGIC BUSINESS UNITS

Corporate strategy has typically been concerned with the management of a portfolio of businesses. For the reasons just enunciated, it may be equally useful to conceive of a firm as a portfolio of competencies. Business units are typically defined in terms of a specific product domain: soaps versus detergents versus shampoos; pagers versus cellular phones versus two-way radios. Yet if a firm cannot escape the product perspective, it may limit its potential 'opportunity horizon'. If Canon conceived of itself only as cameras and copiers, it might never have entered the market for laser printers, fax machines, and semiconductor production equipment. Likewise, Honda might never have moved beyond motorcycles. A core competence perspective allows a firm to expand its view of potential opportunities.

Of course, it is not enough to discover opportunities to apply existing core competencies in new ways. There must also be a mechanism for reallocating the individuals who comprise core competencies from one business to another, and from one opportunity to another. While most unit managers will admit that they do not own the company's capital resources, and are willing participants in the capital budgeting process, they are generally much more reluctant to admit that the human capital they manage—the individuals who comprise the firm's core competencies—are corporate, rather than unit property. In most companies there are elaborate and well-articulated procedures for allocating capital across business units, but no similarly explicit mechanism for allocating competence carriers to the most promising opportunities, wherever in the organization those may lie. In this sense, core competencies often become imprisoned within a particular business unit. We believe that core competencies need to be as explicitly recognized in resource allocation decision processes as capital.

CORE COMPETENCE SHARE VERSUS CORE PRODUCT SHARE VERSUS END PRODUCT SHARE

The term 'market share', as typically used by strategists and researchers, refers almost exclusively to 'brand share' or 'end product share'. Yet competence leadership can exist at least somewhat independently of product leadership. While Canon is a leader in laser printing competencies, manufacturing the great majority of the laser printer 'engines' that go into desktop computer printers, it has a very small 'brand share' of the end product market. Canon is content to exploit the brand and distribution power of its partners, and concentrate its investment in building leadership in laser and bubble-jet printing competencies.

Directly measuring Canon's competence share would be difficult, but by looking at its share of 'core products'—intermediary product or services that lie between the competence skill and the end product—one can gain some appreciation of Canon's competence share. Japanese companies, in particular, have concentrated on building core product share as a way of supporting their core competence building efforts. Almost every Japanese company, and all the major South Korean multinationals, have used OEM relationships to bolster core product share. Making microwaves for GE, videotape recorders for RCA, computers for ICL, engines and powertrains for Ford and airframe components for Boeing, Asian companies have typically had a ratio of core product share to end product share that is substantially greater than 1.

The goal may, in fact, be to build a monopoly, or as close to a monopoly as possible, in some particular core competence area. The ability to build an end product monopoly is limited by legal constraints and the fragmentation of distribution channels, but there are often no such constraints on core product share, and hence core competence share. For years, following its invention of VHS, Matsushita made a substantial majority of the world's VCR components, reinforcing its competence in videotape. Between them, Sharp and Toshiba have something close to a monopoly in flat-screen display competencies. They sell many more screens on an OEM basis than they use internally.

The notion of core product share is applicable in service businesses as well. Marriott sells its core competencies in catering and facilities management to companies seeking to contract out management of conference facilities or company cafeterias, as well as delivering its competencies directly to customers via Marriott-branded hotels. Federal Express has created a business where it sells its core products in the form of systems and consulting to any company that has to manage a complicated logistical problem. In this case FedEx is not selling the end product (package delivery) but an intermediate service.

In recent years IBM has begun to reverse a long-standing company policy, and is now willing to sell core products (components, modules, etc.) to just about anybody—friend or foe. The reasons for such a shift are several. In the years when IBM had absolute distribution dominance (when computers were sold almost exclusively through direct channels, and IBM had the biggest and best direct salesforce) there was little incentive for IBM to sell core products to outsiders. IBM's own channels gave the company enough volume and market share to stay ahead in the race to improve semiconductor, software and computer architecture competencies. With the proliferation of channels and new competitors, IBM executives came to realize that they could not guarantee the company's continued leadership in critical core competence areas unless IMB's direct salesforce represented, each year, a smaller and smaller percentage of the total available market. Likewise, the company came to realize that the IBM brand also represented an unnecessarily restrictive gateway to potential markets. Additionally, some of IBM's core competence competitors (NEC, Sony and Sharp, for example), were substantially more horizontally diversified. These companies had a broader product scope across which to amortize competence-building efforts. To maintain core competence leadership IBM thus needed the volume it could derive by selling core products and platforms through other channels.

What is true in most companies was also true in IBM: the decision to sell core products to outsiders, to be incorporated into products bearing a competitor's brand name, caused a fair amount of consternation to the company's direct salesforce. The question that always comes from the direct channel is 'how can we maintain our competitive differentiation if we sell our core products to rivals?' What the marketing and sales function seldom sees is the alternate questions, 'how can we maintain absolute leadership in our core competence areas if we limit our volumes, and therefore our revenues and market learning opportunities, to our own sales channels?' In our experience, the greater the angst of sales and marketing managers over the decision to sell core products to outsiders, the more likely it is that the firm's in-house channels are less efficient than alternate distribution channels. When, by purchasing a company's core products, competitors can offer products with similar performance characteristics, the internal salesforce will be successful only if they can offer customers some additional value-added over and above that inherent in the product itself. If they cannot, and if they are a more expensive channel than the alternatives, there is no reason they should be given a proprietary right to the firm's core products.

In this sense, selling core products to outsiders is often a very healthy discipline for the sales and marketing function—it puts pressure on managers to ensure that they are not merely living off the competitiveness created 'upstream' in the value chain, but are adding sufficient additional value to justify their overheads. Likewise, selling core products to outsiders is a good barometer of whether or not the company really is a competence leader. If competitors and others do not line up to buy the company's core products, the firm's core competencies are probably not as terrific as insiders might claim.

Interestingly, nowhere in the strategy or marketing literature is the distinction between core competence share, core product share and brand or market share clearly drawn. This is a substantial omission, since competition for competence share and core product share often transcends competition for brand share. In fact, it may be impossible for a company to maintain brand share leadership if it has surrendered core competence leadership and core product leadership to others. Where a company's brand share is substantially higher than its core product share, it runs the risk of being 'hollowed out' by its suppliers. This happened, to one degree or another, within the consumer electronics businesses of General Electric and RCA in the 1970s and 1980s. Yet there are very few companies where core competence and core product shares receives as much top management attention, and are as visible to managers, as brand share.

MANAGING CORE COMPETENCIES

There are four key tasks in the management of core competencies: selecting core competencies, building core competencies, deploying core competencies, and protecting core competencies. Each task will be considered briefly, in turn. Given the paucity of clinical research around the notion of core competence, it is impossible, at this point, to present a model of 'best practice'. The goal here is simply to outline a few of the central managerial tasks. Companies are likely to differ in terms of their abilities to select, build, deploy and protect core competencies. These differences are, in turn, likely to yield differences in corporate performance. The following discussion points to some of the vectors along which a company's capacity to manage core competencies may be assessed.

SELECTING CORE COMPETENCIES

If the strength of a company's core competencies determines, in large part, the competitiveness of its current products or services, and its capacity to generate future new business opportunities, then the identity and health of those competencies should be of concern to senior managers. On the other hand, the almost embarrassingly positive reception given to the concept of core competence by managers suggests that the notion, if not entirely novel, has certainly not occupied much 'share of mind' among corporate executives. This is not surprising, given the strength of the product-market paradigm in management theory, and the dominance of the product-market-constrained strategic business unit as an organizing principle inside large companies.

A firm cannot actively 'manage' core competencies if managers do not share a view of what those core competencies actually are. Thus the clarity of a firm's definition of its core competencies, and the degree of consensus that attaches to that definition, is the most rudimentary test of a company's capacity to manage its core competencies. While most managers will have some sense of 'what we do well around here', they may be quite unable to draw any kind of specific link between particular skill sets and the competitiveness of end products. Thus the first task in managing core competencies is to produce an 'inventory' of core competencies.

When we have observed companies attempting to define their core competencies, the process tends to be haphazard and political. The first attempt typically produces a lengthy 'laundry list' of skills, technologies and capabilities—some core, but most not. A substantial amount of effort is required to fully disentangle competencies from the products and services in which they are embedded, to distinguish core from non-core, to cluster and aggregate the skills and technologies in some meaningful way, and to arrive at 'labels' that are truly descriptive and promote shared understanding. The time it takes to arrive at an insightful, creative and shared definition of core competencies is, in a large company, more likely to be measured in months than weeks. Despite the effort, most companies that have been through the process of identifying core competencies have found it a worthwhile exercise.

One company with which we are acquainted succeeded in developing a hierarchy which ran from competencies to skills and technologies down to individual employees—'competence holders'. This hierarchy could be accessed through a computer database. If someone in the company needed to access a particular competence, he or she could roam through the database until the right person was located. Such visibility to a firm's core competence resources is vital if they are to be fully exploited and easily redeployed.

Of course, more difficult than merely accounting for existing competencies is selecting those that should be built for the future. Given that it may take five, ten or more years to build world leadership in a core competence area, consistency of effort is key. Such consistency is unlikely unless senior managers all agree on what new competencies should be built. Without such a consensus, a company may well fragment its competence building efforts, as various business units pursue their independent competence-building agenda; or the firm may simply fail to build new competencies.

Which competencies to build is, of course, an enormously complex question. Yet it is a question that is, in a sense, antecedent to the question of which markets to enter. AT&T and other American companies, and most of their Japanese competitors, are committed to building competencies in and around high-definition television (HDTV). While it is, at the time of this writing, impossible to predict exactly where and how HDTV will be exploited (engineering workstations, personal computers, cinema photography, graphical arts, military applications, and home television are only a few of the possibilities), and therefore equally impossible to produce a convincing business case for a specific application of HDTV technology, the HDTV bandwagon rolls on. The commitment one sees on the part of AT&T or Sony stems from a deep desire to lead the world in the provision of 'life-like realism', a core customer benefit that transcends any particular product.

In competence building, the commitment is to leadership in the provision of a fundamental customer benefit, rather than to a particular product plan or 'business case'. If commitment to competence building were made dependent on an incontestable business case, the firm would risk almost certain pre-emption. At Sony, the quest for 'pocketability' preceded the invention of the Walkman, the portable CD player or the pocket TV. Similarly, Motorola's commitment to wireless communication technologies reflects its belief in the value 'untethered' communications will have for customers not simply the 'attractiveness' of a particular product category. In like manner, JVC's 20-year commitment to perfecting its videotape competence rested not on an uncontestable business case, which would have been impossible to produce until shortly before VCRs arrived on retailers shelves in the mid-1970s, but on a sense of the rewards that would come to a company that was able to allow television viewers to 'take scheduling control away from the broadcasters'.

In the first instance, then, the question of which core competencies to build for the future is one of which classes of customer benefits the firm would like to 'control'. What is involved here is a calculation first of the importance of a particular benefit to customers and then of technical feasibility.

Sometimes one competence may displace another as the most efficient way of delivering a particular customer benefit. For years electronic imaging has threatened to overtake chemical imaging, just as flat-screen displays seem destined to overtake cathode ray tubes. To defend a brand position, such as Canon's in 35 mm photography or Philips' in televisions, a firm may be forced to build new competencies. Thus Canon is experimenting with electronic photography with its Xap Shot cameras, and Philips is rushing to catch up in flat-screen displays. In selecting competencies to build, a company may want to consider not only the question of whether a competence will enable the delivery of fundamentally new customer benefits, such as 'untethered communications' or 'pocketability', but also whether the competence may allow the displacement of a less efficient or less effective competence in the delivery of an existing customer benefit.

BUILDING CORE COMPETENCIES

Building core competencies requires the accumulation and integration of knowledge, residing both within the firm and without. EDS's core competence in managing billing systems, an insurance company's core competence in claims processing, and Sony's core competence in miniaturization are each a tapestry of many individual technologies and skills. The capacity to integrate the individual strands into a core competence requires a rich pattern of cross-discipline communication and learning. As one Japanese manager put it, '[to build core competencies] you need generalists more than specialists'. For example, a car company could have technological leadership in a range of discrete technologies—combustion engineering, materials science, electronics, fluid mechanics and more—and yet fail to successfully integrate them into a world-beating powertrain. In building core competencies a capacity to integrate may be just as important as a capacity to invent.

The goal, of course, is not only to build core competencies but to build them more economically and more quickly than competitors. One way of reducing the costs of competence building is to borrow skills and technologies from other companies. This can be done through small targeted acquisitions, licensing agreements, joint ventures, alliances or competitive hiring. In all cases the goal is to 'borrow' as many of the constituent skills and technologies from competitors as possible, as cheaply as possible. Japanese companies, in particular, have demonstrated a penchant for piggybacking off the development efforts of others. The transistor, charge-coupled device, and liquid crystal display were all technologies born in the United States. Yet it was Japanese companies who picked up these technology threads and wove them into world-class competencies in miniaturization, electronic imaging and flat panel displays. As one executive at Sony put it, 'You [in the West] cut down the trees, and we build the houses'.

There is, today, a global market for technology and individual human skills. This market can be accessed by taking minority equity stakes in Silicon Valley companies, by hiring away the best talent from a competitor, by sponsoring university research, and by searching the world's patent applications. Sometimes the goal is to get access not to the building blocks of a core competence but to the competence itself. Here the preferred route may be an intimate and long-term strategic alliance. Thomson, the French consumer electronics company, used such an alliance to absorb some of the manufacturing competencies of its partner, JVC. Japanese companies are today using alliances to absorb project management and aeronautic competencies from Boeing. (Though Boeing maintains it is getting more in the relationship than it is giving away.) NEC used alliances with Honeywell, Hughes and Intel to build up its competencies in computers, satellites and microprocessors, respectively. GM has used its joint venture with Toyota, NUMMI as a window on Toyota's comparatively low-tech, high-productivity manufacturing competencies. So just as the capacity to integrate may be as important as the capacity to invent, the capacity to absorb competencies from others may be as important as the capacity to invent competencies oneself. A role model, or exemplar, can reduce both the time and risk involved in building a new competence.

Constancy of effort is another determinant of the cost of building core competencies. While, over two decades, RCA spent more than almost any other company in exploring new video recording and playback technologies, it never brought a successful product to market. The rapid turnover in project leaders and divisional management in RCA and the consequent on-again–off-again support for video research projects undermined the slow, persistent, cumulative learning that is at the heart of competence acquisition.

Throwing money at a project, then scrapping it when it does not yield short-term results, then starting it up again when competitors appear to be moving ahead, then de-emphasizing the project when a new CEO comes on board, is a recipe for inefficient and ineffective competence development.

Another determinant of a company's ability to build core competencies at low cost is its capacity to leverage, or amortize, its competence-building efforts across a broad range of products or geographic markets. The broader the family of products that will benefit from the core competence, and the broader the company's geographic reach, the more economies of scope it can reap in competence development. Companies intent on competence leadership are thus likely to end up more horizontally diversified—around the core competence—than vertically integrated. While Canon exploits its competencies across a broad range of products, and is thus able to amortize the development costs of new core competencies, it buys in up to 85% of the componentry needed to turn its core competencies into world-beating products.

Deploying Core Competencies

To leverage a core competence across multiple businesses, and into new markets, it is often necessary to redeploy that competence internally—from one division or SBU to another. Some companies are better at this redeployment than others, and hence get greater effective use out of their competencies than others. We can define the quantity of a company's core competencies in the same terms as a country's money supply: stock (the number of bills printed, or the number of people who 'carry' a particular skill) multiplied by velocity (how fast the bills change hands, or those competence carriers are capable of being redeployed into new opportunity areas). Many companies have a sizable stock of core competencies—many people with truly world-class skills—but almost zero competence velocity—it is difficult, if not impossible, to redeploy those individuals into new markets.

When a competence becomes imprisoned within a single business the firm suffers in two ways. First, because potential opportunities to exploit the competence in new market arenas go unexploited, growth is slower than it might otherwise be. Second, because the people that comprise the core competence are not as stretched nor as fully utilized as they might be, their skill, and hence the core competence, erodes.

Any manager who has ever gone to a sister division, and asked to 'borrow' that division's top ten or twenty technical employees for a few months, can attest to just how reluctant managers are to share core competence resources. We find it perplexing that while most human resource executives will proudly proclaim that 'people are our most important asset', there is seldom any mechanism for allocating human capital that approaches, in its sophistication and thoroughness, the procedures and processes for capital allocation. In most Western companies the chief financial officer has more organizational status and raw power than does the head of personnel. In many Japanese companies the situation is precisely reversed—as it should be if a company truly believes that competition for competence is the highest order of competitive rivalry, and if it understands that competencies are no more than clusters of highly skilled and inter-dependent individuals.

Sharp uses 'urgent project teams' to allocate scarce competencies to high pay-off projects. When a potential market opportunity is spotted an 'urgent project team' is formed, and the project leader is given the right to raid Sharp worldwide for the best competence resources, i.e. the best people. This raiding is not indiscriminate; the project leader may not get everyone he or she wants, as trade-offs between the priorities of various corporate projects are taken into account. Nonetheless, the principle of the system is that the company should be viewed as a worldwide reservoir of core competence resources. No one manager 'owns' the people who comprise the firm's core competencies. Sharp has had more than 150 urgent project teams, and is a master at redeploying core competencies behind promising new products. Sony uses a similar device, 'gold badge teams'. As a general rule, deploying core competencies requires a company to take a project approach to new business development.

An exercise we sometimes carry out with a company's divisional managers illustrates a critical precondition to the capacity to redeploy competence assets. We provide each divisional or SBU manager with a product/geography matrix, and then ask each executive to rank, 1 through 10, their company's near-term growth opportunities. Not surprisingly, when we compile the completed matrices, there is usually little correspondence between one manager's rankings of growth priorities and any other manager's rankings. Yet in the absence of a corporate-wide consensus on new business opportunities, that is, agreement on what projects truly are 'urgent' or deserve to be labeled 'gold', there can be no logical basis for the internal reallocation of core competence resources.

PROTECTING CORE COMPETENCIES

Protecting core competencies from erosion takes continued vigilance on the part of top management. While most senior managers can easily dredge up competitive measures of sales performance, market share and profitability, few are able to offer a quick and convincing judgment on whether or not their company is staying ahead of competitors in core competence development. There is no way to protect a firm's core competencies from erosion if the health of those competencies is not visible to top management.

Core competence leadership may be lost in many ways. Competencies may wither through lack of funding; competencies may become fragmented through divisionalization, particularly where no single executive feels fully responsibile for competence stewardship; competencies may be inadvertently surrendered to alliance partners; or thrown out with the bath water when an under-performing business is hived off.

For example, in the 1970s, Motorola sold its television plants to Matsushita, and exited the consumer electronics business. While the decision to get out of the virulently competitive consumer electronics business was probably foresightful, Motorola now wishes that it had preserved some of the competencies buried within its former consumer electronics business. Recently, Motorola has recognized that it must rebuild a competence in video displays. To protect core competencies, a company must be able to distinguish between a bad business and the potentially valuable competencies buried within that business. After working on its videotape competence for 20 years, Sony met with disaster when it launched its Betamax VCR. In most companies such a humiliating market defeat would have led to the disbanding of the development team, and abandonment of the competence development effort. While Sony was profoundly embarrassed by the failure of Betamax, it kept the competence team together, and scored a major success when, a few years later, it rebounded with the 8 mm camcorder. Sony recognized that when one loses a core competence, one loses a gateway to a raft of potential new business opportunities.

There are many other issues involved in the management of core competencies than the ones identified here. Nevertheless, it is hoped that this tentative agenda will be a spur to managers, consultants and academics to better understand the challenges and rewards of better managing core competencies.

SUMMARY

There is no argument here with the product-market, SBU and brand share perspectives that predominate in strategy research and writing. The only argument is that these perspectives are incomplete and, if not balanced by a complementary core competence perspective, potentially dangerous. Again, what is important is *yin* and *yang*. Too often, when confronted with the core competence perspective, managers respond by saying, 'what you're asking us to do is to reorganize around core competencies, instead of strategic business units'. Nothing could be further from the truth. For most companies product-market domain is the most sensible organizing principle for corporate structure. What we are asking executives to do is to give substantial visibility and attention to the selecting, building, deploying, and protecting of core competencies; we are not asking for wholesale reorganization. SBUs may be hard-wired into organizational structure, but the core competence perspective must be soft-wired into the minds of every manager. We hope this book is an aid to that wiring process.

2

Understanding the Roots of Your Competitive Advantage. From Product/Market Competition to Competition as a Multiple-Layer Game

FRANCESCO DE LEO

INTRODUCTION

What lies at the roots of your competitive advantage? The common wisdom held within the strategy field was to identify the chain of causality either in terms of cost leadership (Boston Consulting Group, 1968, 1975) or differentiation advantage (Porter, 1980, 1985). It goes without saying that the primary focus of attention was competition in the product/market arena, and that competition was essentially competition for market share (Buzzell, Gale and Sultan, 1975). The inherent assumption was that market share was the

Competence-Based Competition.
Edited by G. Hamel and A. Heene.
Copyright © 1994 The Strategic Management Society. Published 1994 by John Wiley & Sons Ltd.

key-driver to superior profitability (Buzzell and Gale, 1987). This is why it was generally held that the recipe to gain competitiveness was simple: managers had to solve a single equation—how to trade off quality for cost.

But managers and strategy scholars were not alone in making this simple assessment. International economists for more than 20 years went around saying that labor costs were everything in determining foreign investment location decisions (Vernon, 1966), and that the uneven distribution of comparative advantages across and among nations represented an unsurmountable obstacle, beyond the control of the firm (Krugman, 1991). If this is really so, why did BMW decide to build a new plant in South Carolina, where labor costs are higher than in Mexico? The problem is that according to the BMW chief economist 'To sell high-quality auto in the luxury sector, labor costs are not the determining factor' (*Wall Street Journal*, 2 November 1992).

Thus it comes to the following questions: Which are the missing links in explaining competitive advantage?

The trouble is that the focus on both cost leadership and differentiation coupled with the inherent advantages of a 'favorable' national context contributed to consolidate the notion of strategy as a search for 'fit' between the firm's strengths and weaknesses and its environment. Within the traditional strategy framework every industry had an underlying economic logic that determines the degree of competition that the industry faces both internally and externally. Thus, the only game in town was to select a product/market strategy which is consonant with the opportunities and constraints imposed by the environment (Porter, 1985).

With the product/market focus as the only arena of competition it becomes difficult to discern if the success of leading firms is the result of strategic choice, or is due to the invariant nature of competition in the industry. Thus, it becomes increasingly difficult to adequately account for the persisting existence of unfit strategies across firms within the same industry (Rumelt, 1987). If the underlying economic logic of the industry is a given, why are there unfit strategies?

Moreover, equating the locus of strategy with product/market competition contributed to direct managers' attention away from the process of value creation to focus upon maneuvering and positioning, as if they were the only two relevant dimensions of competition. Metaphors like 'guerrilla warfare' and 'high-speed competition' contributed on their own to build the notion of strategy as a game of optimization within constraints.

The way to play the strategy game was to exploit existing asymmetries, build barriers to entry and select industries where the 'five basic competitive forces' were weak enough to provide a greater profit potential (Porter, 1985). To achieve this, managers had to be concerned with administering vertical or complementary activities, with efficient resource allocation and purposeful manipulations of market share to sustain long-term profitability.

While there can be no argument that every firm must, in the end, come to terms with product/market competition, our understanding is that the analysis of the causality chain that explains how firms are able to obtain superior market positions has not yet registered significant progress. Perhaps the product/market arena is just the last stage of a multiple-layered competitive game (Hamel, 1991, p. 83). Perhaps the problem is that competitive advantage is not just a function of how a firm plays the game: it is also a function of what assets the firms has with which to play the game. Perhaps the inherent goal of strategy is not to exploit existing asymmetries but to search for and develop new ones.

If we go beyond the traditional competitive frame, then strategy is not simply maneuvering and positioning. Focusing upon product/market competition as if it were the only relevant competitive arena is of little help in understanding how far back we need to go to explain why some firms are able to attain a consistent superiority in the value-creation process. When British Telecom announced that its profits in 1990–91 were $5.7 billion a quick calculation gave $150 of profits per second. British Telecom is Britain's biggest, most valuable and most profitable firm. Yet its profits are a smaller proportion of sales (at 21.3%), and of capital (at 21.5%) than, say, Glaxo (40% and 35.6%, respectively).

While the product/market arena remains, indeed, a useful yardstick of competitive success, and in many cases, a proxy for the existence intangible-yielding assets it should not be the only focus of concern (Rumelt and Wensley, 1981). In the 1930s Morris was the largest European car manufacturer, but that was largely because it benefited from tariff protection in the largest and wealthiest European market (Britain), not primarily because it was the most efficient manufacturer. Product/market competition is a yardstick of success otherwise created, but it is in the links between core competencies and capabilities that allowed competitive success to be gained that value resides.

Going beyond the traditional strategy frame means discovering the latent linkages which bridge different stages of a multiple-layered

**HOW FAR BACK DO YOU NEED TO GO IN THE
CAUSALITY CHAIN ?**

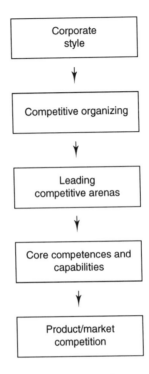

FIGURE 2.1   Understanding the roots of your competitive advantage

competitive game. Instead of focusing exclusively on product/market competition, most of a firm's strategy is concerned with identifying across multiple stages the ones which are the building blocks of competitive success. Under the new rules of competitive engagement, the strategy game becomes not just one of positioning, but one of architecturing, where achieving competitive advantage is the result of a superior capability in bridging different levels of competition.

Under some circumstances, a firm's most critical competence may not be a set of technical skills, however specialized or unique, but its inherent capability to constantly invest in building new bridges across different levels of competition.

STRATEGY AS A MULTIPLE-LAYER GAME

Within the traditional competitive frame, strategy was about selecting those contexts which were in favor of company strengths. The economic logic underlying an industry, as well as its inherent potential for profits, were assumed to be invariant, and beyond the influence and control of a single firm. Competitive success was explained in terms of existing impediments to imitability, or barriers to entry, due to structural or transactional failures, with implications for a firm's competitive positioning (Porter, 1985).

It goes without saying that equating the search for competitive advantage with strategies for diminishing the degree of competition across and within industries in terms of existing barriers to imitability contributed to directing managers' attention away from the process of discovering and creating new asymmetries as a critical source of enhanced competitiveness, towards low cost or differentiation as the only two ways to achieve superior market positions.

Instead of addressing the question: 'What drives our competitive advantage, and where do we need to focus in the chain of causality?' most of the strategy was concerned with 'How do we compete?' Two different questions, two different managerial frames. To attend to the first means focusing on processes, while addressing the latter implies focusing on discrete activities.

If activities are the primary concern, then most managers' work is about gaining competitive advantage by managing the firm as a collection of discrete operations and products. Within this frame the emphasis is placed upon allocative efficiency, generally achieved through cost efficiency, or upon differentiation as a way to command a premium price by performing a given or similar set of activities in a unique way.

The competitive strategy framework holds until it is assumed that cost leadership and differentiation advantage are mutually exclusive objectives. The common wisdom was that low cost was achieved through standardization and economies of scale and differentiation through focusing on meeting the needs of specific customer groups. If strategy is about choice and commitment to hard-to-reverse investments, it follows that competitive advantage could be achieved in terms of either low cost or differentiation.

The trouble is that there is a compelling body of empirical evidence which suggests that this need no longer be the case (Stalk, 1988). Information technology offers the possibility of achieving both, in the sense that it makes it feasible to pursue a market niche strategy in many different niches at once (Glazer, 1989; Braddock, 1989). Even more remarkable is that the impact of information technology is not that it renders you more productive, in the sense of more physical output per hour, but it permits you to have access to a greater variety of information sources, and to process them faster (Milgrom and Roberts, 1990).

Beyond that, the assumption of incompatibility between low cost and differentiation has received a serious challenge by the evolution of modern manufacturing and, more precisely, by the international success of Japanese companies (Womack, Jones and Roos, 1991). When the Japanese challenge became evident in its entirety, the immediate reaction among practitioners and academic circles on both sides of the Atlantic was to ignore the problem, arguing that Japanese firms were different (Dertouzos, Lester and Solow, 1989). Most disconcerting of all, the persistent success of several Japanese companies indicated that it was, indeed, possible to achieve both low cost and differentiation in a way that the traditional competitive frame was not able to accommodate.

To cope with this discontinuity in management practices, the advocates of the traditional strategy frame had to ascribe the cause of superior economic performance to the benign influence of the Japanese institutional context and to the unique characteristics of the Japanese culture. But recent empirical work has contributed to resolving this ambiguity. There is strong evidence with respect to both manufacturing practices (McMillan, 1991) and the crafting of contractual relationships (Kester, 1991) that these characteristics are not unique to Japanese firms neither are they byproducts of the Japanese institutional setting (Henderson 1993).

Looking beyond what was considered to be a deviating case, that is, the possibility to achieve simultaneously both flexibility and specialization, one important lesson was learned: that product/ market competition was about not only managing discrete activities and individual products but also managing processes; and, more important, that the search for competitive advantage was not driven only by administering existing activities but also by persistent commitment to creating new ones.

Besides the traditional focus upon cost leadership and differentiation advantage, research into the evolution of modern manufacturing and the international success of major Japanese companies explored two critical dimensions of product/market strategy: the influence of time-compression economies (Stalk and Hout, 1991) and the role of complementarities (Milgrom and Roberts, 1990).

Time is a dimension of strategy which does not find place in the traditional strategy frame. There is little concern in the competitive frame about the pace of change as a key aspect of competition (Williams, 1991). However, it is clear that time drives strategy and affects the sustainability of competitive advantage. In telecommunications, while cellular phones like Motorola's Micro-Tac has a life of less than 2 years, COS (Central Office Switching) equipment sold by AT&T and the baby Bells lasts more than 10 years. Even more important is to acknowledge that time-compression economies critically affect the trade-off between cost efficiency and variety.

Consider Sony's Walkman. When it was launched, Sony did not rely on standard marketing research but adopted a design-for-response approach to quickly adjust its product/marketing mix to conform to sales patterns. In order to do so, Sony decided to design each Walkman model on a common core platform which allowed a wide range of models to be easily built on (*Wall Street Journal*, 13 February 1993). In a business where competing on short lifecycles is a critical determinant of success, Sony introduced 160 models of the Walkman in just 10 years to stay ahead of the competition. Crucial to this approach, however, was reducing the cost of failure by keeping expenses down, by changing model features while keeping the same platform, thus achieving simultaneously both cost efficiency and customer-driven variety.

However, it would be misleading to advocate that time-compression economies only work in consumer goods industries, where customers value fast delivery and product lifecycles are short. Boeing has recently announced that it aims to cut the production cycle for its 737 from 13 to 6 months, while maintaining the same quality standards (*Business Week*, 1 March 1993). In January, in order to win competition from McDonnell-Douglas and Airbus, it promised to design and build UPS's new aircraft in an astonishing 28 months, well below the 38 it would normally take.

The key to Boeing's fast-flexible response resides in its new factories, where multitask production equipment permits the firm to produce a variety of outputs in very small batches. Although Boeing's largest product has 6 million parts, 8.1% of all batches are of size one and 38% are sixteen or less.

When considering time as a competitive weapon the trouble is that accommodating rapid rates of change should not be considered a goal in itself but a critical dimension of a superior value-creation process. This is why to claim that time is the next source of competitive advantage is misleading if it refers merely to a way of achieving both cost efficiency and variety. The strength of variety can be better explained if we look beyond the narrow boundaries of the traditional strategy frame by considering the role played by complementarities (Milgrom and Roberts, 1990).

Time drives strategy not so much in the sense that it affects the way discrete activities are performed or new products are introduced but because it influences how activities relate to each other. The focus is not upon inputs at different stages of the value chain but upon linkage across groups of activities. These linkages are said to be complementary because they do not stop at the level of technology of manufacturing but also extend to marketing and organization variables. To describe these linkages, economists use the term 'non-convexity', meaning that when the marginal cost associated with the introduction of flexible manufacturing and rapid-response systems falls, the cost of variety also decreases because it becomes increasingly attractive to expand product lines and to update products frequently (Milgrom and Roberts, 1990, p.515). But complementarities also extend to marketing, because designing-for-response permits the reduction of the costs of failures and encourages firms to set lower prices and to respond quickly to customers while maintaining high quality standards. In other words, instead of solving the trade-off between quality and cost, the presence of complementarities among groups of activities allows low cost and variety to be pursued at the same time.

Transferring attention from discrete activities to the nature of complementarities among them requires a shift in perspective from competition viewed as product versus product to competition between alternative organizing logics. Given that cost leadership and differentiation advantage do not exhaust the competitive spectrum of available strategies, it becomes critically important to assess the missing links in the causality chain that explains competitive advantage.

COMPETITION AS A MULTIPLE-LAYER GAME: BEYOND PRODUCT/MARKET COMPETITION

The recent focus on time and how time drives strategy together with the evolution of modern manufacturing suggests that there is much more to firm competitive advantage than a simple listing of cost leadership and differentiation. Increasingly empirical evidence supports the perspective that the quest for competitive advantage is not confined to product/market arena and to the presence of barriers to entry but that it is also a matter of limited asset imitability. Recent developments of the resource-based view of the firm have contributed to consolidating the notion that competitive advantage is about what *assets* the firm has with which to play the game as much as it is about *how* a firm plays it.[1]

The problem with the traditional frame is that no attention is given to the quality of the assets and to the way they are linked together as a source of advantage and little or no attention to the problem of how these assets have been accumulated over time, and how likely this will be so in the future. Yet recent empirical work on the evolution of competition as, for instance, in the pharmaceuticals industry has discovered that competitive success has less to do with size than with the ability to combine capabilities, such as research, clinical testing and marketing.[2]

What this evidence suggests is that the sources of competitive advantage are not so much influenced by the context or industry structure conditions, as they are by asymmetric endowments of unique, and more or less sustainable, resources and capabilities. That is why 'choice sets' are not given or exogenously determined but, rather, much of firm behavior is concerned with discovering and creating new ways to sustain the rent-yielding potential of unique resources and capabilities (Nelson, 1991; p. 62). In contrast to the competitive advantage perspective, instead of merely focusing

---

[1] In recent years, the rediscovery of internal factors as the basis of firms' success can be linked to the revisionist approach (Rumelt, 1987; Teece, Pisano, and Shuen, 1992) to Prahalad and Hamel's contributions about the role of core competencies *vis-à-vis* two other consolidated paradigms in strategic management: that of competitive forces (Porter, 1980, 1985) and the one of entry deterrence (Shapiro, 1989; Fisher, 1989), whose roots lie, respectively, in industrial organization economics and game theory.

[2] In the 1980s according to David Matheson and Craig Wheeler, consultants with the Boston Consulting Group (BSG), there was no clear correlation between the size of drug companies and profitability.

on existing asymmetries, organizational capabilities and core competencies also qualify a firm that has yet to achieve a sustainable competitive position. If this is the case, then strategy is about realizing whether a sustainable competitive position can be reached by investing in developing capabilities in the existing business or if it is more appropriate to move towards a new competitive system to search for new asymmetries.

This implies an analytical reorientation away from the invariant rules of competition within a given industry's economic logic towards the role of firm discretionary choices. Strategy then relates not only to maneuvering and positioning in the context of product market competition but also to ways of mobilizing and bridging competencies among and across different levels of competition.

In our view there is much more to firm competencies than just a simple listing of technical or marketing skills. Under the new rules of competition firms must identify the critical levels of competition and how these can be linked together. This is why under some circumstances a firm's most critical competence may not be a set of technical skills, however specialized or unique, but its inherent capability to constantly invest in building new bridges across different levels of competition. Thus the competitive game becomes not one of maneuvering and positioning but a game of architecturing, where the problem is not simply to decide where or at which level to compete but also how to transfer advantages acquired at one level to the following ones. We believe this is a promising way to further enrich the core competence approach and to add to the traditional enumeration of resources and capabilities a dynamic dimension. Within this perspective, core competencies represent more than just another concept or techniques in strategic management. They are a new way to look at the process and content of business strategy.

To illustrate this, consider the strength of variety as a competitive weapon. The capability of providing low prices while emphasizing high quality supported by frequent product improvement does not translate into competitive success, unless the speed of innovation fits the customer's speed of absorption. There are reasons to believe, for instance, that Japanese car makers have now realized that they went too far in the variety war. One Nissan model offered 86 different types of steering wheel (*The Economist* 27 February to 5 March 1993). Toyota provided 32 types of sound systems in the cars it exported to the United States. However, Toyota's operating profits reported a 63% fall in the year to June, while its operating margins collapsed from 4% to 1.4%. At the same time, Nissan has recently announced the first closure of a Japanese car plant since the Second World War, and it has undertaken a program to reduce the variety of parts in three years by 40% and the number of different variations of models it offers by 50%. Mazda and Toyota have the same drive and plan cuts of 30% in both areas.

What this evidence tells us is that the capability to provide variety to customers does not drive to competitive success by itself but creates the conditions to reach a superior competitive position if the linkages with other levels of competition are explored. This is why managers should be concerned not so much with the question 'What business should we be in?' but with 'Where do we need to focus in the causality chain to identify the roots of our competitive advantage? Which are the critical linkages across different levels of competition and how do we build them?' This also implies a change in logic from retrospective to prospective, from strategy as a game of optimization within constraints to strategy as a search for new ways to challenge a traditional competitive logic. This is why an important question which is often left unattended but which is critical for discovering and creating new ways to sustain a company competitive advantage is 'Where do we want to be in the future?'

To do so, managers need to analyze the causality chain which leads to attaining and defining superior market positions. In our four-year study of a selected group of successful multinational companies equally distributed across United States, Europe and Japan[3] we identified four distinct levels of competition which critically affect the way firms perform in product/market competition, with respect to both existing products and to the industry future: (1) core competencies and capabilities; (2) leading competitive arenas; (3) competitive organizing; and (4) quality of corporate management.

CORE COMPETENCIES AND CAPABILITIES

Focusing upon core competencies means moving back in the chain of causality to explore how competitive advantage is linked to unique resources and firm-specific assets which are the basis of the value-

---

[3]The sample of firms is composed of Benetton, Daimler-Benz, Ciba-Gigy, Alcatel Bell, Matsushita, ABB, Lafarge Coppée, GE.

creation process. This is to say, for instance, that the persistent competitive success of Merck and Glaxo has less to do with their size than with Merck's ability to identify promising categories of drugs early, and Glaxo's rapidly bringing to market a few important drugs in many countries at once[4].

Core competencies and capabilities, however, are not given to the firm, but need to be built from within it (Rumelt, 1984), and their development is subject to the influence of path dependencies. Moreover, some resources are not tradable, and difficult to transfer, like tacit knowhow (Teece, 1980; Shuen, 1993) and reputation (Dierickx, Jemison and Cool, 1989). Thus, resource endowments cannot equilibrate through factor input markets.

Competition, however, is about not discrete core competencies *per se* but how to combine them in ways which are difficult to replicate because of the presence of causal ambiguity (Lippman and Rumelt, 1982). Given that what is crucial is the relationship of complementarity between a set of competencies, it follows that value dependency or asset specificity should be brought into the picture. Managers should be concerned not so much with the existing competence endowment but with the more rent potential increases, the more inputs are specific to the firm's existing asset base.

It is the linkage of an input to the firm's existing asset base and especially the relative strength of that linkage as compared to that which competitors would achieve that determines the rent-yielding potential of a specific combination of resources and capabilities and thus the sustainability of a firm's competitive position (Conner, 1991). Recent research on the nature of competition in the drug industry supports the notion that critical to a firm's success is not a particular set of technical skills as much as a firm's unique ability to combine capabilities such as research, clinical testing and marketing (Henderson, 1993).

However, the 'adhesion' firm and organizational capabilities constrains future business options in at least two ways. On the one hand, the firm must take its existing capabilities into account when projecting its future expansion in related asset bases; on the other, the possibility of obtaining the required capabilities on a timely basis is seriously limited by their weak market mobility.

Thus, firms aiming at this level of competition should be concerned with their 'absorptive capacity', which refers to their ability to

---

[4]Merck and Glaxo, the most successful firms in the drug industry, each holds a mere 5–6% of the market, and there are 14 other firms with at least half of that level of sales.

recognize the value of new, external information and to add it to their own knowledge base (Cohen and Levinthal, 1990). Borrowing from this notion, it can be argued that a firm's ability to expand its capability base is a function of the firm's level of prior related knowledge.

SELECTING LEADING COMPETITIVE ARENAS

A promising way to further enrich the core competence approach is to add a dynamic dimension to the traditional enumeration of resources and capabilities. Thus, managers should focus on how core competencies are developed through the mutual interaction between firm-specific resources and environment-specific resources. The former are owned by the firm, but the latter represent resources that the firm 'has access to', and resources which are shared within the relevant environment (Kogut, 1991b). Thus, it seems interesting to try to understand how a firm can 'appropriate' shared resources (Dornseifer and Kocka, 1991).

This is somewhat different from the traditional resource-based view of competition, which holds that the sources of competitive advantage lie in the fact that different firms have different initial 'traits' or unique 'resource bundles' that constitute 'imprints' on which their distinctive competencies are built, within a context that is favorable or unfavorable to actors having certain 'genetic' properties. The connection between organizational capabilities and country-specific capabilities seems prominent in this respect. By the term 'country-specific capabilities' we refer to the organizing principles which are shared among firms within a specific environment (Kogut, 1991a). One of the most significant conclusions of Chandler's Scale and Scope (1990) is that different economic conditions, institution and cultures in the USA, Britain and Germany played a major role in shaping the organizational capabilities developed by firms within particular regions and industries in which nations developed special strengths (Porter, 1990). At the same time, Chandler tells us that firms have a major influence on the environment in which they are embedded as, for instance, in calling forth significant public investments in education in Germany. In other words, 'choice sets' of core competencies are not given but, rather, firms have discretionary margins to create and discover new possibilities of mobilizing surrounding resources. What we do miss, however, is an understanding of how firms' core competencies can be attributed to specific mechanisms at the firm–environment interface, which allow firms in specific regions in the world economy to build upon each other's strengths (Nelson, 1991, p. 70). If we are to explain what are the ultimate sources of competitive advantage we need to enlarge the core competencies' perspective in order to take into account how specific interaction mechanisms within a given environment contribute to shape the extent to which firms are able to appropriate shared resources.

The only limit of the core competence approach, with its focus on organizational capabilities that are rooted 'inside' the firm as the source of competitive advantage, is that it has left little room for the possibility of incorporating knowledge that may be embodied in firms without being specific to any one of them (Kogut and Zander, 1992). In a purely domestic setting, as the one in which the core competence approach has been articulated, this distinction is frequently lost, because common knowledge shared among firms in the same environment is of no consequence in explaining performance differentials. But this does not need to be so when comparing firms which belong to different region/environments, competing for the appropriation of unique rent-yielding assets. This suggests that a shift in focus towards capturing the role of self-reinforcing mechanisms at the firm–environment interface can help to reorientate the core competencies approach toward the analysis of the sources of international competitive advantage which are related to organizing principles and capabilities that are region-specific.

The central problem which needs to be analyzed concerns the extent to which a portion of the knowledge incorporated into firm routines, skills, organization and capabilities is contingent upon the region or country of origin. The complementarity between organizational capabilities and organizing principles which are shared within the relevant regional environment cannot be considered as given, but is itself subjected to an evolutionary process. But how is this complementarity achieved and sustained? A critical issue is to engage in the relevant, and likely emerging, communities of practice (Rappa, 1990).

It is of interest to concentrate the attention not on all the linkages the firms have within a specific context but on the role played by linkages that can be regarded as strategic. We consider strategic a linkage which provides access to desired strategic capabilities (see Nohria and Garcia-Point, 1991).

Two types of strategic linkages can be identified: those that provide access to complementary capabilities and those through which firms connect their resources with those having similar capabilities (Richardson, 1972; Porter and Fuller, 1986). Thus linkages can be considered as playing two different roles: (1) to create a way for firms to develop or learn new capabilities, or (2) to enhance existing capabilities (Kogut, 1991b).

This finally poses the problem of determining to what extent the capability sets to which the firm has access are given, or instead are 'discovered' and created through the interaction with other parties within the context. The German experience suggests that the second explanation seems more promising (Dornseifer and Kocka, 1991). This also highlights the possibility that different resource environments have different prerogatives with respect to technology diffusion and cumulation and the spread of common organizing principles of work (Kogut, 1991a).

It also seems to be the case that the stock of cumulated shared resources has a rate of decay in value which is less than the decay in the capabilities of single firms. It is in fact often the case that leading-edge companies in a field often change, whereas several measures of a country's technical specialization are stable over several decades (Pavitt, 1987).

This asymmetry can thus be appropriately explained if we consider the different degree of decay between a firm's resources and the environmental resources that the firm is able to access. These resource-environments are subjected to different sources of competition. The first can be identified in the competition between existing firms for appropriating the uses of the commonly shared resources. Another source consists of potential entrants which can be interested in appropriating their uses: the threat of entry can stem from domestic firms in other environments, and from foreign firms within the same competitive arena.

However, because firms are not able to sustain growth for more than few years, while the resource environment can (Pavitt, 1990),[5] it can be argued that competition between different resource-environments is lower. There are, in other words, market imperfections with respect to resources across different environments: these resources, as the system of common organizing principle of work, are less transferable than technology and less subject to the risk of substitution.[6]

---

[5]The question is that while a country's technical specialization remains stable over long periods of time, the leadership at the level of the firm within a country's area of excellence tends to show a rapid rate of change.

[6]Texas Instruments has recently opened a research lab at Tsukuba, following the example of Dow Corning, IBM, Du Pont, DEC and Kodak (*Fortune*, July 1991).

COMPETITIVE ORGANIZING

Firms do not compete in terms of only different combinations of resources and capabilities, nor do they only differ in their capability to select and access specific leading arenas. They also confront each other on the basis of competitive organizing logics.

In the old computer industry vertically integrated companies competed against other vertically integrated companies. IBM and Digital Equipment sold a completely integrated product based on their own proprietary technology. In the new PC age companies like Intel and Microsoft have succeeded in challenging the industry logic by replacing the old vertical model with a new horizontal one.

Different organizing logics are required because different businesses, even in the same industry, are subject to a different rate of change. These discontinuities are a critical factor influencing the sustainability of a firm's competitive advantage. Consider, for instance, that Compaq, once a premium price competitor, has recently announced that it will introduce 39 new notebooks and desktop machines (*Wall Street Journal*, 8 March 1993) while the basic features of LOTUS 1-2-3 have not changed for more than a decade.

Therefore managers need to question where their companies belong with respect to the rate of change in the relevant environment and to consider the extent to which their organizations can cope. The tradition was to think about all the product lines within an industry using one paradigm. Corporations like IBM, NCR and DEC competed against each other as vertically integrated entities, building everything from chips, to computers and software. Of course, each company had its own salespeople, trained on the basis of a single-industry paradigm, to sell those computers to corporate accounts. But, Dell Computers' success against Compaq and the other PC makers has shown that it is not only feasible but also profitable to sell computers by telephone.

What is important to recognize is that there are different organizing logics within the same industry, and that different environments have to be managed and controlled differently. ICI is dividing itself into two companies: industrial chemicals, and specialty chemicals. In the ICI managers' own words, dealing with so many different businesses was undermining their ability to predict where they were going to be in the market in the future (*Wall Street Journal*, 8 March, 1993). Pacific Telesis, in the telecommunications industry, is doing the same, separating highly

TABLE 2.1   Multinational corporations moving global headquarters of major business units abroad

Company	Home country	New location	Operation moved	Year moved
AT&T	USA	France	Corded telephones	1992
Du Pont	USA	Japan	Electronics	1992
Hyundai Electronics	South Korea	USA	Personal computers	1991
IBM	USA	UK	Networking systems	1991
Siemens	Germany	UK	Air traffic management	1991
Siemens	Germany	USA	Ultrasound equipment	1991
Du Pont	USA	Switzerland	Agricultural products	1991
Hewlett-Packard	USA	France	Desktop computers	1990

stable businesses such as local telecommunications exchange, from fast-growing and risky ones such as cellular telephones. Furthermore, there is compelling empirical evidence that multinational corporations have recently started to move the headquarters of important businesses abroad, because they want to operate near key customers and tough competitors in fast-changing markets (Table 2.1). This is why beyond the level of strategy as positioning, strategy as competitive organizing has the merit to shift managers' focus away from a given industry paradigm towards the search for new ways of defining their organizing logic. One of the critical assumptions in Intel's successful effort to challenge the industry's organizing logic is that they think of themselves as a microprocessor company with 100 million customers: not the people who pay their invoices but the PC users, whose minds they have to win in order to succeed. According to Intel's CEO, 'We have to figure out what will be the needs of our 100 million customers years from now, what sort of application software they'll be using' (*Fortune*, 22 February 1993).

Thus, when digging deeper into the causality chain which explains a firm's competitive advantage, it is critically important to assess what discretionary margins managers have to challenge the dominant industry paradigm in order to tailor management objectives and control appropriately.

QUALITY OF CORPORATE MANAGEMENT

One of the building blocks of the competitive strategy frame is that 'diversified companies do not compete; only their business units do' (Porter, 1987). However, an increasingly active market for corporate control and the gap between the stock market value and the equity value reflects, among other things, an underutilization of organizational capabilities by the existing management team (Brennan, 1990). The link between the quality of corporate management and competitive advantage is manifest when considering that competition for the right to control and manage businesses is a function of value-added by corporate parents (Goold and Campbell, 1987).

Think, for example, about the fact that Johnson & Johnson put forward the idea of decentralization as early as the 1930s. Now, after 50 years, J&J has become a model of how to make decentralization work. But having gone far in the decentralization process, J&J's corporate management has now realized that they need to fine-tune their approach to achieve a balance of entrepreneurial spirit and corporate structure, to share more services among units and to cut redundancies (*Business Week*, 4 May 1992). This is why the quality of corporate management becomes critical in identifying a way to maintain the autonomy and identity of units while working hard on integration.

Looking at companies that have been successful over long periods of time suggests that they have been able to nurture a specific ability to anticipate the challenges imposed by a complex and turbulent environment by creating and sustaining a superior management system. The underlying assumption consists of considering that the linkages across different levels of competition are fostered by the ability of the corporate management to ensure that learning in different parts of the organization and at different levels of competition is transferred to superior market positions.

CONCLUSIONS

To move away from strategy as maneuvering and positioning means focusing upon the chain of causality that leads to competitive advantage and adopting a competitive frame where the strategy game is viewed as composed by multiple levels of competition. Instead of assuming that the industry's organizing logic is a given, managers need to be concerned about discovering discontinuities, to expand into related asset bases and to identify the missing links across different levels of competition. Thus there is much more to strategy than just simply maneuvering and positioning. There is also much more to a firm's core competencies than a mere listing of technical and marketing skills.

REFERENCES

Boston Consulting Group (1968). *Perspectives on Experience*.

Boston Consulting Group (1975). *Strategy Alternatives for the British Motorcycle Industry*. London: HMSO.

Braddock, R. S. (1989). Keeping the customer at the fore. 1989 Marketing Conference, Conference Board, October, New York.

Brennan, M. J. (1990). Latent assets. *The Journal of Finance*, 709–30.

Buzzel, R. D. and Gale, B. T. (1987). *The PIMS Principles*. New York: Free Press.

Buzzel, R. D., Gale, B. T. and Sultan, R. (1975). Market share—a key to profitability. *Harvard Business Review*. January–February.

Chandler, A. D. (1990). *Scale and Scope. The Dynamics of Industrial Capitalism*. Cambridge, MA: Harvard University Press.

Cohen, W. M. and Levinthal, D. A. (1990). Absorptive capacity: a new perspective on learning and innovation. *Administrative Science Quarterly*, **35**, 128–51.

Conner, K. R. (1991). An historical comparison of resource-based theory and five schools of thought within industrial organization economics: do we have a new theory of the firm? *Journal of Management*, **17**, 68–72.

Dertouzos, M., Lester, R. and Solow, R. (1989). *Made in America*. Cambridge, MA: MIT Press.

Dierickx, I., Jemison, D. and Cool, K. (1989). Business Strategy, Market Structure and Risk–Return Relationships: A Structural Approach. *Strategic Management Journal*, **6**, 507–522.

Dornseifer, B. and J. Kocka, J. (1991). The impact of the preindustrial heritage. Reconsiderations on the German pattern of corporate development in the late 19th and early 20th centuries. Assi Foundation Conference on 'Organization and Strategy in the Evolution of the Entreprise', Milan, October.

Ghemawat, P. (1991). *Commitment. The Dynamic of Strategy*. New York: Free Press.

Glazer, R. (1989). Marketing and the changing information environment: implications for strategy, structure, and marketing mix. Report No. 89–108, *Marketing Science Institute*, Cambridge, MA, March.

Goold, M. and Campbell, A. (1987). *Strategies and Styles*. Oxford: Basil Blackwell.

Hamel, G. (1991). Competition for competence and inter-partner learning within international strategic alliances. *Strategic Management Journal*, **12**, 83–103.

Henderson, R. (1993). Flexible integration as core competence: architectural innovation in cardiovascular drug development. Working paper, Stanford Graduate School of Business, March.

Kogut, B. (1991a) National organizing principles of work and the erstwhile dominance of the American multinational corporation. *Proceedings*, ASSI Foundation Conference on 'Organization and Strategy in the Evolution of the Entreprise'. Milan, October.

Kogut, B. (1991b). Country capabilities and the permeability of borders. *Strategic Management Journal*, **12**, 33–47.

Kogut, B, and Zander, U. (1992). Knowledge of the firm, combinative capabilities, and the replication of technology. *Organization Science*, Journal of the Institute of Management Sciences.

Kester, W. C. (1991). *Japanese Takeovers. The Global Contest for Corporate Control.* Boston, MA: Harvard Business School Press.

Krugman, P. R. (1991). *Geography and Trade.* Cambridge, MA: MIT Press.

Lippman, S. A. and Rumelt, R. P. (1982). Uncertain imitability: an analysis of interfirm differences in efficiency under competition. *Bell Journal of Economics*, **13**, 418–38.

McMillan, J. (1990). Managing suppliers: incentive systems in Japanese and U.S. industry. *California Management Review*, Summer, 38–55.

Milgrom, P. and Roberts, J. (1990). The economics of modern manufacturing: technology, strategy, and organization. *American Economic Review*, June, 511–28.

Nelson, R. R. (1991). Why do firms differ, and how does it matter? *Strategic Management Journal*, **12**, 61–74.

Nohria, N. and Garcia-Point, C. (1991). Global Strategic Linkages and Industry Structure. *Strategic Management Journal*, **12**, 105–124.

Pavitt, K. (1987). On the nature of technology. Inaugural lecture given at the University of Sussex, 23 June.

Pavitt, K. (1990). The nature and determinants of innovation. Paper prepared for the conference on 'Fundamental Issues in Strategy'.

Porter, M. E. (1980). *Competitive Strategy.* New York: Free Press.

Porter, M. E. (1985). *Competitive Advantage.* New York: Free Press.

Porter, M. E. (1987). From competitive advantage to corporate strategy. *Harvard Business Review*, **65**, No. 3, 43–59.

Porter, M. E. (1990). *The Competitive Advantage of Nations.* New York: Free Press.

Porter, M. E. and Fuller, M. B. (1986) Coalitions and Global Strategy. In M. E. Porter (Ed.), *Competition in Global Industries*. Boston: Harper & Row, pp. 315–344.

Prahalad, C. K. and Hamel, G. (1990). The core competence of the corporation. *Harvard Business Review.* **68**, No. 3, 79–91.

Rappa, M. (1990). The dynamics of R&D communities. Working paper, MIT, Sloan School of Management.

Richardson, G. B. (1972). The organization of industry. *Economic Journal*, **82**, 883–96.

Rumelt, R. P. (1984). Toward a strategic theory of the firm. In R. B. Lamb (Ed.) *Competitive Strategic Management* (pp. 557–70). Englewood Cliffs, NJ: Prentice-Hall.

Rumelt, R. P. (1987) Theory, strategy and entrepreneurship. In D. J. Teece (Ed.) *The Competitive Challenge* (pp. 137–59). Cambridge, MA: Ballinger.

Rumelt, R. P. (1991). How much does industry matter? *Strategic Management Journal*, **12**, 167–185.

Rumelt, R. P. and Wensley, R. (1981). In search of the market share effect. Paper MGL-63, Graduate School of Management, UCLA.

Shuen, A. (1993). Co-developed know-how assets in technology partnerships. Working paper Center for Research on Management, Berkeley, January.

Stalk, G. (1988). Time—the next source of competitive advantage. *Harvard Business Review*, July–August, 41–51.

Stalk, G. and Hout, T. M. (1991). *Competing against Time*. Sperling & Kupfer.

Teece, D. J. (1980). Economies of scope and the scope of an enterprise. *Journal of Economic Behavior and Organization*, September, 223–47.

Teece, D. J., Pisano, G. and Shuen, A. (1990) Firms' capabilities, resources, and the concept of strategy. CCC Working Paper 90-8, Center for Research on Management, University of California, Berkeley.

Vernon, R. (1966). International investment and international trade in the product cycle. *Quarterly Journal of Economics*, **80**, 190–207.

Williams, J. (1993). How sustainable is your competitive advantage? In R. P. Rumelt, D. Schendel and D. J. Teece (Eds) *Fundamental Issues in Strategy*, forthcoming.

Womack, J., Jones, D. and Roose, D. (1991). *The Machine that Changed the World*. Cambridge, MA: MIT Press.

3

Strategy as a Situational Puzzle: The Fit of Components

ILSE BOGAERT, RUDY MARTENS, ANDRÉ VAN CAUWENBERGH

THE SEARCH FOR 'STRATEGIC' COMPONENTS

Over the last decade the mass of publications on the resource-based perspective on strategy has caused some terminological confusion. Competence, core competence, (invisible) assets, strategic assets, strategic stocks, resources, skills, etc. are used to refer to strategic components of one type or another. Table 3.1 gives a chronological review of some of the concepts used in the resource-based perspective. We should like to comment briefly on the particulars of some of the contributions in this matter.

Barney (1991) describes *firm resources* as those that include all assets, capabilities, organizational processes, firm attributes, information, knowledge, etc., controlled by a firm, enabling it to conceive of and implement strategies that improve its efficiency and effectiveness. These firm resources can be classified into three categories: physical capital, human capital and organizational capital. Barney remarks that *not all resources are strategically relevant*.

Competence-Based Competition.
Edited by G. Hamel and A. Heene.
Copyright © 1994 The Strategic Management Society. Published 1994 by John Wiley & Sons Ltd.

TABLE 3.1 A chronological overview of concepts used in the resource-based perspective

Author(s)	Main concept(s)	Description or additional concepts
Wernerfelt (1984)	Resources	Resource position barriers
Itami (1987)	Invisible assets	Information-based resources/dynamic resource fit
Dierickx and Cool (1988)	Strategic assets	Stocks accumulated through investments (flows)
Aaker (1989)	Assets and skills	• Asset: something a firm possesses superior to competition • Skill: something a firm does better than competitors
Akerberg (1989)	Competence	Organizational competence depends on individual competences
Prahalad and Hamel (1990)	Core competence	• Strategic architecture • Collective learning: production skills and technologies • Metaskills: generate core skills
Klein et al. (1991)	Metaskills	
Barney (1991)	Firm resources	All assets, capabilities, processes, attributes, information, knowledge controlled by a firm
Grant (1991)	Resources	• Resources: inputs to the production process • Capability: capacity of resources to perform some task
Hall (1991, 1992)	Intangible resources	• Skills or competences: e.g. the knowhow of people • Assets: things which are owned • Intangible resources may be linked with a functional, cultural, positional or regulatory capability
Stalk et al. (1992)	Capabilities	• Capability: more broadly based than core competence • Key business processes
Amit and Schoemaker (1993)	Resources Capability	• Stocks of available factors owned/controlled by the firm • Capacity of firm to deploy resources using organizational processes, to effect desired end
	Strategic assets	• Set of difficult to trade, imitate, scarce and specialized resources and capabilities

Other authors distinguish *'having'* (what the firm owns) from *'doing'* (what the firm or parts of the firm do). One of them makes a distinction between *assets* ('things which one owns') and *skills or competencies* ('the knowhow of employees and other stakeholders and the collective aptitudes') (Hall, 1992).

Another distinction is made between resources and capabilities. *Resources* are defined as stocks of available factors owned or controlled by the firm (Amit and Schoemaker, 1993). They are the inputs into the production process (such as capital equipment, skills of individual employees, patents). *Capability*, on the other hand, refers to the capacity for a team of resources to perform some task or activity (Grant, 1991) or also the capacity of a firm to deploy resources using organizational processes to affect a desired end. Capabilities are firm-specific, and developed over time, through complex interactions among resources (e.g. manufacturing flexibility, responsiveness to market trends, highly reliable service) (Amit and Schoemaker, 1993).

Dierickx and Cool (1988) distinguish between stocks and flows. *Stocks* (technological expertise, brand loyalty, etc.) are *accumulated* over time through a history of investments or *flows* (R&D spending, advertising spending, etc.). While flows can be adjusted quickly, stocks cannot (Dierickx and Cool, 1988).

Sometimes the *invisible* or *intangible* assets are particularly stressed. A number of authors perceive them to be crucially important to business success.

Invisible assets are described as information-based resources (such as consumer trust, brand image, etc.) (Itami, 1987) or as information-based capabilities (Amit and Schoemaker, 1993). These invisible assets are hard to accumulate, capable of simultaneous multiple uses and are, at the same time, inputs and outputs of business activities. The importance of visible assets is also recognized but the invisible assets are considered by Itami (1987) to be the *most* important resources for long-term success.

Intangible assets range from intellectual property rights (patents, trademarks, copyright and registered design); through contracts; trade secrets; public knowledge such as scientific works; to the people-dependent or subjective resources of knowhow (networks, organizational culture, and the reputation of product and company) (Hall, 1991).

In general, assets are perceived to be(come) *strategic* if they are grounds for establishing a firm's *competitive advantage*. In our literature review, only one author treated 'asset' and 'skill' as *implying* the *strategic* characteristic. An asset is defined as 'something your firm possesses such as a brand name or retail location that is superior to the competition'. A skill is then 'something that your firm does better than competitors such as advertising or efficient manufacturing' (Aaker, 1989).

Strategic assets (Amit and Schoemaker, 1993) or 'firm resources that hold the potential for strategic competitive advantage' (Barney, 1991) have four attributes: (1) they are valuable (exploit opportunities and/or neutralize threats in the firm's environment); (2) they are rare among the firm's current and potential competitors; (3) they are imperfectly imitable; and (4) no strategically equivalent substitutes exist (Barney, 1991). They are, in other words, a set of difficult to trade and imitate, scarce, appropriable, and specialized resources and capabilities. Examples are technological capability, favorable cost structure, a firm's service organization (Amit and Schoemaker, 1993).

Simply put, competitive advantage can evolve from *distinctive competences*, which are the capabilities the organization possesses that set it apart from its competitors (Hall, 1991). The firm should identify its *key business processes*, manage them centrally and *invest* in them heavily, looking for a long-term payback (Stalk, Evans and Shulman, 1992).

In order to *keep* an established competitive position, or 'differential resource position' (Wernerfelt, 1984) or 'sustainable asset stock position' (Dierickx and Cool, 1988), such as technological lead or customer loyalty, a firm should erect *resource position barriers*. Doing so, a firm has to find a balance between the exploitation of existing resources and the development of *new* ones (Wernerfelt, 1984). Strategic management should thus, in essence, be concerned with developing and maintaining meaningful assets and skills, with selecting strategic and competitive arenas to exploit those assets and skills, and with neutralizing competitors' assets and skills (Aaker, 1989). In other words, there should be a *dynamic resource fit*. According to Itami (1987, p. 125), 'effective strategy in the present builds invisible assets, and the expanded stock enables the firm to plan its future strategy to be carried out. And the future strategy must make effective use of the resources that have been amassed'. Prahalad and Hamel (1990, p. 89) state that, therefore, management should develop a corporatewide *strategic architecture*, 'a road map of the future that identifies which core competencies to build and their constituent technologies'.

This development of meaningful assets for future strategy *presupposes the existence of a collective learning* in the organization, especially about the ways in which diverse production skills can be co-ordinated and multiple streams of technologies can be integrated (Prahalad and Hamel, 1990). Learning makes a two-way relationship between people and organization possible (Klein, Edge and Kass, 1991). Along those lines, *organization competence* then embodies (1) the formation of a common conception of key activities and key competences and (2) the creation of procedures and systems which promote the fulfilment of key tasks (Akerberg, 1989). Figure 3.1 presents an attempt to connect the different concepts in one scheme.

In conclusion, this brief review and conceptual scheme lead us to indicate that the most frequent distinctions are these between 'having' and 'doing', i.e. assets are seen versus skills (Aaker, 1989;

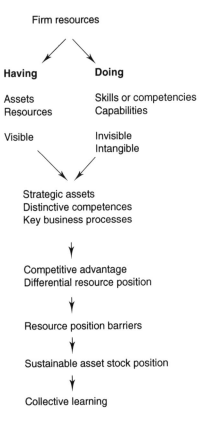

FIGURE 3.1 A review of the search for 'strategic' components

Hall, 1992), resources versus capabilities (Grant, 1991; Amit and Schoemaker, 1993) stocks versus flows (Dierickx and Cool, 1988). Also, some authors (Itami, 1987; Hall, 1991) focus on the invisible, intangible aspects (from brand image to intellectual property rights) as prime sources of competitive advantages. To them, visible assets are of less importance.

Almost all authors agree that strategic assets are accumulated over time and that they are to be considered as the building blocks for a competitively better performance. Many authors (Itami, 1987; Aaker, 1989; Klein and Kass, 1990, among others) associate resources/ assets with long-term success. (None of these authors, however, gives guidance with respect to what 'long-term' success is and, if it can be conceived, how this can be measured.) However, not all authors seem to be convinced that a resource-based view necessitates a dynamic and/or evolutionary perspective.

A very down-to-earth view stated that a dynamic perspective is necessary because it can only be *ex-post* shown which resources and capabilities are key determinants of the firm's profitability. The identification of a set of strategic assets the firm has to concentrate on, at a specific moment and in its near future, is an incessant challenge managers are facing (Amit and Schoemaker, 1993). Some ideas were offered to take up this challenge through *learning*. Prahalad and Hamel (1990) argue that the organization should collectively learn, especially about co-ordination of production skills and integration of technologies. According to Stacey (1991), the nature of organizational learning, also taking place collectively, in groups, stresses the impact of the combination of personalities in the group, the dynamics of the group and the culture the group has developed.

THE ASSEMBLY OF STRATEGIC COMPONENTS

As the above review indicates, many valuable insights have been offered in order to recognize relevant strategic components in business management. Little guidance is given, however, with respect to how critical components, or *strategic assets*, as we will now call them, are or can be used. (An elaboration of the concept 'strategic assets' can be found in Van Cauwenbergh and Martens, 1989.) We believe that some critical reflections on the characteristics of these strategic assets *and on their assembly* may offer a better insight into basic strategy processes.

In our conception an *asset* refers to something available for the firm at some place(s), and may be tangible as well as intangible. An asset may refer both to something you *have* (a brand name, a patent, access to sources of cheap energy or raw materials, etc.) and to a *process* (the way something is done, such as specific technology or team experience) as long as it has a value for some corporate purpose. A *strategic asset* refers then to an asset which is *of high value for a firm (or some part of it)* in *adjusting itself to or preparing itself for a (strategic) opportunity at some point in time.* Although strategic assets are mostly stocks accumulated with time and energy (investments, flows), we admit that strategic assets may also simply emerge in business life (Mintzberg, 1978).

In order to draw up some meaningful messages about strategic assets, one should first get a more thorough insight in the characteristics of these strategic assets. An overview of their main characteristics may then result in a broader view on the *assembly* of these strategic assets.

CATEGORIZATION AND CHARACTERISTICS OF STRATEGIC ASSETS

A categorization of strategic assets is a hazardous and probably infecund task resulting in endless listings (cf. the many SWOT-lists in strategy handbooks). Notably, strategic assets may refer to almost any aspect of organizational functioning: equipment, systems, human resources, knowhow (technological, production, financial), environmental acceptance, etc. Moreover, the categories and variables *useful for a specific business* are *dependent upon the type of industry and context* in which strategy takes place. One important distinction can and should, however, be made between:

1. *All-purpose strategic assets:* corporate-wide assets which *can* be deployed in different situations (e.g. firm reputation, firm culture, brand image, financial resources, etc.) and
2. *Situation-bound strategic assets:* assets which turn out to be of high importance in dealing with some specific strategic situation(s) (e.g. an efficient personal relationship with some government body; a specific technical knowledge which is of crucial importance in responding to a perceived problem).

A promising route to further explore both categories is in trying to identify the general characteristics of these strategic assets, as has, for instance, been proposed by Dierickx and Cool, 1988. It can be argued that strategic assets are:

- Scarce
- Characterized by access barriers
- Generating significant value for the firm (or unit) and
- Mostly *unsteady*.

The last characteristic has been quite often overlooked in many studies. Although *a few* strategic assets may be fairly stable (e.g. a competitive location), most strategic assets are of a dynamic nature and frequently changing with respect to their value and/or utility. Some strategic assets, such as personal networks, may even appear or disappear on the very scene where a strategic action is developing. It can be argued that strategic assets characterized by a high degree of volatility should deserve relatively more attention and nurturing than the more stable ones (because the volatile ones are more difficult to 'catch'). Sometimes the most volatile or dynamic strategic assets may evolve into more stable all-purpose strategic assets.

All-purpose strategic assets such as brand loyalty, firm image, basic technological experience in production processes, etc. have already received extensive attention. These kinds of assets need to be constantly nurtured to maintain or increase the current asset level. Dierickx and Cool (1988) argue that strategic stocks are subject to stock erosion, and therefore need to be constantly monitored. Imitation is often not easy as these assets have mostly been built up very slowly (e.g. Coca-Cola's customers' brand loyalty). Attempts at imitation do, however, occur in business life (e.g. the Pepsi challenge). However, the cost of time compression (Dierickx and Cool, 1989) prevents competitors from rapidly building desired strategic assets.

The Internal Fit of Strategic Assets

One of the major issues in the resource-based perspective refers to the degree of *interdependence* or *mutual convenience*, between strategic assets; this is *the internal fit*. (Strategic assets may also be mutually exclusive. See Stalk, Evans and Shulman, 1992, for an illustration of this.) The synergy between different kinds of assets is rightly considered to be the basis for a superior performance of a firm (or division). One may think of the reciprocal adjustment of the 'hardware' (e.g. machines, logistic processes, etc.) to the 'software' (e.g. the motivation and capability of managers) as the basis of competitive performance. As such it can be argued that, although strategic assets possess a profit potential (the value is greater than the cost of using it), the realization of a profit potential is often dependent upon the availability of and adjustment to other strategic assets and *operating* variables (such as product availability, advertising campaigns, etc.).

Adjusting several strategic assets to each other can multiply the value of each. In fact, the finesse is to reach the best possible impact with the fewest possible resources. Strategic assets do not only have to be attuned to each other, there must also be a close interaction with operating variables. Most people nowadays agree that business strategy does not refer to secluded reflections in the boardroom but deals with (strengthening or adjusting) the *many daily operations* carried out in the firm.

The need to achieve an *internal fit* of strategic assets is a constant concern in strategy formation. The usefulness of some strategic asset may be dependent upon the availability of some other strategic asset(s). Taking into account the volatility of strategic assets, the assembly of components may turn out to be rather complex, constantly changing–and, at times, unpredictable.

THE SITUATIONAL FIT OF STRATEGIC ASSETS

Many publications in the resource-based perspective pay attention to the internal fit or synergy between a firm's strategic assets. As the resource-based perspective originated as a counterforce to a view on competitive advantage that was rather too outwardly oriented, not surprisingly, the *link with external elements* has received relatively little attention. The fit of the assembled strategic assets with the outside situation at hand is, however, of prime importance in a resource-based view. This is what we call the *situational fit* of the strategic assets. It refers to:

1. The fit with the *strategic field* on which the (combination of) strategic assets are being used. Here, some observations with

respect to managers' perceptions and the variety of possible strategic fields result in an evaluation of the usefulness of overarching strategies.
2. The fit with the *time* factor. Here, the time pressure and time horizon will be put forward as essential elements in a resource-based analysis of a business.

THE FIT OF ASSETS WITH A STRATEGIC FIELD

Stalk, Evans and Shulman (1992, p. 65) describe a type of firm they call a '*capabilities predator*': it can come out of nowhere and rapidly move into a position of a major player. Identifying the underlying capabilities and concentrating all actions and processes on these capabilities should result in its growth path. The 'capabilities predator' focuses on its strategic capabilities and can compete in various regions, products and businesses. In short, according to Stalk, Evans and Shulman (1992), once a business has collected its strategic capabilities it is able to cope with a whole range of situations.

Yet we would like to bring to the fore that strategy refers to *(re)actions* of a business in response to some perceived existing, *or* anticipated, strategic field, by which we mean the real or conceptual area in which supporting and counteracting forces are perceived. Viewed as such, the strategy process *does not start* with thinking about strategic assets or capabilities. Strategic reflections are, in the first instance, triggered by the perception of what may or can be done in some perceived strategic field. This field refers mostly to what is being considered, explicitly or implicitly, as belonging to a firm's domains. This perception may *then* result in an attention to and evaluation of available strategic assets to be used in strengthening or adjusting the firm's operations.

The initiation and the subsequent diffusion processes of strategic reflections and actions have already been described in many empirical strategy studies (see e.g. Aharoni, 1966; Bower, 1970; Quinn, 1980; Burgelman, 1983; Mintzberg, 1985, among others). One of the major arguments in this school of thought is that the initiation is situated in perceptions of individual managers. Strategic reflections are *not* found to be the privilege of some few and mighty (usually one thinks of *top managers* or *CEOs* as the sole strategists). Many managers can be taking the initiative and inducing actions in a business at the same time. In large corporations, a high *variation in the kind and number of strategic actions* may be witnessed, depending upon the positions of the initiating managers. *The strategy of a firm should thus be viewed as the sum of several specific strategic actions being undertaken by distinct parts within the firm.* (This has been argued by Van Cauwenbergh and Van Robaeys, 1978, and Mintzberg, 1978. It refers to several emerging strategic actions in which a common pattern may be witnessed.)

This results, of course, in the risk of having a too-wide dispersion of different strategic actions going on. Moreover, most people feel a need for presenting an overarching strategy, in which the diverse specific strategies can be positioned and justified. This induces top management to declare 'the' strategy of the firm or corporation, mostly with some long-term view on internal and external developments. Yet it can be observed in large entities that what is declared 'the' strategy may be remote from actual actions going on. A declared firm or corporate strategy does, however, have a vindication. Mostly, it serves as some *umbrella* to rationalize actions undertaken throughout the corporation. In recent years this 'umbrella' is often presented as a *mission statement*. It refers to some kind of (higher-order) purpose of a corporation and the *domain (the product-market scope)* in which this purpose is then to be realized, together with the underlying corporate values (Campbell and Tawadey, 1990). Some mission statements may be quite specific and, as such, include the drawback of inflexibility (see Langeler, 1992). As most mission statements are, however, intended to serve for a longer period of time, they remain correspondingly vague. This seems logical, as the major aim of these mission statements should *not* be to direct the firm's strategy *but* to have an *impact on the motivation of some participants* whose contribution in the strategic actions is needed. By presenting the different parts as belonging all to one 'large firm', some people may feel more committed to support some strategic initiatives. Furthermore, top managers (in large divisionalized companies) *do* recognize that they do not hold the privilege for the perception of and (re)action to new strategic situations.

The ease with which lower-level managers may perceive potential relevant situations (*opportunities*) is then dependent upon:

- Their competence in a specific field.
- Their willingness to search for new information or opportunities.

The willingness to search for opportunities may be stimulated by a clear articulation of a firm's mission or competence field. Such an articulation may support the organizational culture and give some ideas about which initiatives may have a high chance of being accepted at higher management levels. The same line of reasoning may apply with respect to the search for core competences by top managers. Being too specific may involve the danger of inhibiting the building up of new core competences. Being too general may result in a dilution of the firm's competitive position.

A firm's strategy can thus be viewed as consisting of many uncertain choices, in searching for a fit between assembled strategic assets (puzzle pieces) and perceived strategic situations. For one specific strategy, the strategic field refers in our view to *the specific context in which this strategy is originating and developing*. Strategic assets can only generate value if they are fit to the external situation to which actors are (re)acting. This way, the product/market-perspective and the resource perspective are combined.

THE FIT OF STRATEGIC ASSETS WITH TIME

Strategy takes place in a constantly moving and changing strategic field. Quick actions may be called for. The assembly of strategic assets therefore often occurs without a clear perception of the relevant strategic field. As such, strategy can be analyzed as a sequence of (proximate) tasks deduced from problems emerging at (relatively) unpredictable points in time.

Several empirical studies have shown that strategy processes are typically fragmented, evolutionary and largely intuitive (see e.g. Quinn, 1980; Smith, Child and Rowlinson, 1990). These findings weaken the assumptions (1) that an organization's strategy inherently refers to *long-term objectives* and fits the organization's *mission* and (2) the idea that analysis (resulting in *strategy formulation*) can be completed before the action (or *strategy implementation*). These findings, on the other hand, support the argument that strategic assets are both situation- and time-bound and *fit* with the period in time and with the situation in which they were being activated.

Management's thinking about core competences or strategic assets is normally influenced by the point in time at which they originated. Depending upon the specific opportunities confronted with at a given moment, the result of an exercise on identifying core competences may be quite varying. This may raise questions about the usefulness of such an exercise. But, as is also argued for SWOT-analyses, thinking about it is often considered to be more useful than the eventual outcome of the thinking process.

In our view, then, the formation of *proximate objectives* is a central phenomenon in the strategy process. Some perceived strategic situation (or anticipation of a 'new' situation) evokes the formulation of some 'proximate objectives' for dealing with it. The use of strategic assets to achieve these proximate objectives will be subject to the opinion of managers on the urgency to react to the situation.

In that sense, 'the' overall strategy, referred to above as an 'umbrella' or 'mission statement', can only take the form of fairly vague, long-term objectives, providing some coherence in the large organization. However, these long-term objectives, which may include the articulation of core competences, do not *induce* strategic behavior within a firm. Strategy is to be considered as a dynamic short-term oriented situational assembly. Contrary to a large stream in the strategic management literature, strategy has thus much more to do with the short term. Nevertheless, two important comments must be made here:

1. Short-term objectives do not imply, as such, a short-term effect. Strategic actions mostly have a long-term *effect*. In this sense, strategic actions do concern the long term: although some strategic action associated with some proximate objective may result in a commitment of strategic assets at more or less short notice; such commitment may or will have a long-term impact. The short-term response of a firm to a suddenly perceived external change may limit or promote future strategic actions (e.g. by means of buying, building up or divesting some specific asset). Proximate objectives, arising from suddenly perceived situations, may thus result in long-term commitments of resources. Moreover, while proximate objectives do not necessarily originate from long-term objectives, the support and commitment of some participants may be much more easily obtained if the proximate objectives can be linked in some way or another to the proclaimed long-term objective or mission of the firm.

2. Many managers (especially higher-level managers) are *supposed to have* some long-term views on *external developments* (such as

'the future of our biotechnology firm lies in applied research for the pharmaceutical industry'). Such views may have an impact on resource (re)allocation decisions. The longer the time horizon of such views, the higher the probability of variations in interpretation or perception. Strategies solely based on long-term views carry an increased uncertainty and level of ignorance (Ackoff, 1970) and with this, a greater risk of failing. Many mergers and acquisitions, reflecting long-term views, have been witnessed to end in loss or failure (Porter, 1987). Coca-Cola's diversification experience (into the wine and coffee business) is a good illustration. Assembling strategic assets for some future opportunities, as perceived by some top manager's 'vision', may therefore be an uncertain route to follow. In our view, firm performance benefits more from identifying, supporting, rearranging and using strategic assets in response to opportunities more close at hand.

STRATEGY AS A SITUATIONAL PUZZLE GAME

One more argument still remains to be proposed. The variety of contributions which strategic assets can bring, in also complex and varying situations (all this depending on the perceptions of strategic actors) induces our view that strategy comes close to a game—or gamble—situation. From our 'constructional' view it can be looked at as a *puzzle game*. Strategic assets are then somehow the pieces of a complex puzzle, the strategic fields are then the varying contexts under elusive horizons. *The fit of strategic assets to some situation is thus essentially a function of the perception of committed actors in the organization.* The more experienced the actor, the greater the ease with which perceptions will originate and actions will be played. The situational fit in strategy may therefore have to be considered as a continuous *strive* for fit (Hinings and Greenwood, 1988). The driving force for strategy reflections is the constant feeling of tension or incompatibilities in the adaption of organizations to new perceived (changing) situations. A perfect puzzle will never be achieved. In contrast to some common belief, this view on strategy does *not* imply a *reactive* attitude. A perception of some possible *future* environmental state can also start the strategy process.

It should be mentioned that this avenue of thought was already explored by the work of Penrose (1959), where *resources* render *services*, being functions and activities that are most valuable and specialized to the firm, and combine in a jigsaw puzzle of some sort. In our view, however, strategy is not only to be compared with a jigsaw puzzle, in which the different components have a fixed (predestined) place, but it is rather to be considered as a puzzle *game* bearing *uncertainty* and *ignorance* as inherent characteristics (Ackoff, 1970). The pieces (assets) may fit in different places, depending upon the perception of possible combinations with other pieces, the perceived situation and competitors' (re)actions. Two determining factors for the resulting performance of a firm's puzzle game are: (1) the knowledge of and experience in the strategic field in which the (combination of) strategic assets are used and (2) the perceptions and movements of the counteracting forces (competitors) in this field. This strategic field is, on the one hand, constantly changing; on the other, these changes, inducing puzzle actions, can be perceived in different ways (with respect to the impact on current actions, relatedness with other activities and events, urgency of reaction, etc.). As both observers' *perceptions* of a certain situation and their judgment of strategic assets may differ, the strategic field where strategy takes place can unfold as participants come and go. Using the puzzle-concept, we say that puzzle patterns constantly change with changing situations. This view results in a call for flexibility of the pieces deployed.

CONCLUSIONS

We believe that the framework presented in this chapter delivers a realistic explanation of actual strategic behavior within organizations. Central is the situation-driven and action-impelled inclination in managerial behavior, which is induced by some gamble or play with *proximate objectives*.

The perception of managers of some strategic situation, inducing strategic actions, is frequently the starting point of such puzzle game with strategic assets. Conceiving strategic assets with no link to a specific situation is often a vain exercise. The perception of a situation induces the understanding of strategic assets with the ensuing attempt to link or adjust different strategic assets to each other. This continuous reflection and action results in a learning process out of which new strategic assets may appear. Learning and action go on simultaneously and cannot be seen as separate domains. Strategic assets are retrieved, used and adjusted in a *dynamic* puzzle game.

Finally we would like to point to two research avenues which we believe to be of prime importance in the further development of the resource-based perspective. First, skills are a major component in the strategic assets available to a firm. It should, however, be recognized that organizations *per se* do not have skills. An organization derives its skills from the *people* within it. (A similar line of reasoning has been offered by Akerberg, 1989, and Klein, Edge and Kass, 1991.) Skills are thus kept by individuals. How can the transformation be made from individual skills to what is perceived as organizational skills? Motivation and commitment may turn out to be crucial factors.

This results in a second dilemma, as the former statement assumes that skills need to be managed. Who possesses the skill of *managing the skills*? Perceiving and using skills, and, more broadly, strategic assets, in a relatively successful way is dependent upon the quality of the manager who is confronted with his or her puzzle games. Management talent may, as such, turn out to be among the most scarce and significant components of the puzzles in firm strategy.

REFERENCES

Aaker, D. A. (1989). Managing assets and skills: the key to a sustainable competitive advantage. *California Management Review*, **31** (2), 91–106.

Ackoff, R. (1970). *A Concept of Corporate Planning.* New York: Wiley Interscience.

Aharoni, Y. (1966). *The Foreign Investment Decision Process.* Boston, MA: Division of Research, Graduate School of Business Administration, Harvard University.

Akerberg, A. (1989). *The Process of Transforming Individual Competence into Organizational Competence in Professional Organizations.* Helsinki: Swedish School of Economics and Business Administration.

Amit, R. and Schoemaker, P. J. H. (1993). Strategic assets and organizational rent. *Strategic Management Journal*, **14** (1), 33–46.

Andrews, K. (1971). *The Concept of Corporate Strategy.* Homewood IL: Dow Jones-Irwin.

Ansoff, H. I. (1965). *Corporate Strategy. An Analytical Approach to Business Policy for Growth and Expansion.* New York: McGraw-Hill.

Barney, J. (1986). Strategic factor markets: expectations, luck and business strategy. *Management Science*, **32** (10), 1231–41.

Barney, J. (1991). Special theory forum. The resource-based model of the firm: origins, implications, and prospects; and Firm resources and sustained competitive advantage. *Journal of Management*, **17** (1), 97–98 and 99–120.

Bower, J. (1970). *Managing the resource allocation process. A study of corporate planning and investment.* Boston, MA: Division of Research, Graduate School of Business Administration, Harvard University.

Burgelman, R. (1983). A process model of internal corporate venturing in the diversified major firm. *Administrative Science Quartery,* **28**, 223–44.

Campbell, A. and Tawadey, K. (1990). *Mission and Business Philosophy, Winning Employee Commitment.* Oxford: Heinemann Professional Publishing.

Christensen, C. R. *et al.* (1987). *Business Policy, Text and Cases,* 6th edn. Homewood, IL: Irwin.

Cyert, R. and March, J. (1963). *A Behavioral Theory of the Firm.* Englewood Cliffs, NJ: Prentice-Hall.

Dierickx, I. and Cool, K. (January 1988). Competitive advantage. INSEAD, Working Paper no. 88/07.

Dierickx, I. and K. Cool (1989). Asset stock accumulation and sustainability of competitive advantage. *Management Science,* **35** (12), 1504–14.

Grant, R. M. (1991). The resource-based theory of competitive advantage: implications for strategy formulation. *California Management Review,* **33** (3), 114–135.

Hall, R. (1991). The contribution of intangible resources to business success. *Journal of General Management,* **16** (4), 41–52.

Hall, R. (1992). The strategic analysis of intangible resources. *Strategic Management Journal,* **13**, 135–44.

Hinings, C. and Greenwood, R. (1988). *The Dynamics of Strategic Change.* Oxford: Basil Blackwell.

Itami, H. (1987). *Mobilizing Invisible Assets.* Cambridge, MA: Harvard University Press.

Klein, J. A. and Kass, T. (1990). *The World Beyond Markets and Products: Skills and Metaskills.* Cambridge: Scientific Generics Limited.

Klein, J. A., Edge, G. M. and Kass, T. (1991). Skill-based competiton. *Journal of General Management,* **16** (4), 1–15.

Langeler, G. (March–April 1992). The vision trap. *Harvard Business Review,* 46–56.

Mahoney, J. and Pandian, J. R. (1992). The resource-based view within the conversation of strategic management. *Strategic Management Journal,* **13** (6), 363–80.

Mintzberg, H. (1978). Patterns in strategy formation. *Management Science,* **24**, 934–48.

Mintzberg, H. (1990). The design school. *Strategic Management Journal,* **11** (3), 171–95.

Mintzberg, H. and McHugh, A. (1985). Strategy formation in an adhocracy. *Administrative Science Quarterly,* **30**, 160–197.

Penrose, E. T. (1959). *The Theory of the Growth of the Firm.* Oxford: Basil Blackwell.

Porter, M. (1980). *Competitive Strategy.* New York: Free Press.

Porter, M. (May–June 1987). From competitive advantage to corporate strategy. *Harvard Business Review,* 43–59.

Prahalad, C. K. and Hamel, G. (May–June 1990). The core competence of the corporation. *Harvard Business Review,* 79–91.

Quinn, J. (1980). *Strategies for Change. Logical incrementalism.* Homewood, IL: Irwin.

Smith, C., Child, J. and Rowlinson, M. (1990). *Reshaping work. The Cadbury experience.* Cambridge: Cambridge University Press.

Stacey, R. D. (1991). *The Chaos Frontier. Creative strategic control for business.* Oxford: Butterworth-Heinemann.

Stalk, G., Evans, Ph. and Shulman, L. (March–April 1992). Competing on capabilities: the new rules of corporate strategy. *Harvard Business Review,* 57–69.

Stevenson, H. (1976). Defining corporate strengths and weaknesses. *Sloan Management Review.* 17 (3), 51–68.

Van Cauwenbergh, A. and Martens, R. (October 1989). Corporate strategies and strategic assets. A resource reallocation analysis. Paper presented at the Ninth Annual Strategic Management Society Conference, San Francisco.

Van Cauwenbergh, A. and Van Robaeys, N. (1978). *Strategisch Gedrag.* Deventer: Kluwer.

Wernerfelt, B. (1984). A resource-based view of the firm. *Strategic Management Journal,* 5, 171–80.

Section II

Linking Competitive Advantage and Core Competence

The chapters in this second section link traditional concepts of the theory of strategic management to the concept of core competence. Both contributions build on a number of ideas included in Van Cauwenbergh's 'puzzle game' metaphor and thus can be considered as being complementary to the ideas developed in the first section of the book.

In the first part of Chapter 4 Verdin and Williamson link the concept of 'competitive advantage' (arising from the use of cost drivers or differentiation drivers) to that of core competence. In the second part (based on extensive empirical findings) the authors discuss the role of core competencies as 'catalysts' in the process of advantage building. This allows them to pull together the core competence of the corporation, on the one hand, and structural features of the industry, on the other. The authors show, among other things, that the importance of a given core competence varies systematically with the structural features of the environment. As such, they are reconciling 'internal' and 'external' points of view in strategy making in a remarkable way.

Based on a conceptual description and analysis of the relationships between core competence and competitive advantage, in Chapter 5 Bogner and Thomas formulate three basic research questions in the domain of competence-based competition: 'Is it the environment which determines which competencies are "core"?' 'How is competitive advantage lost over time by firms that succeed in establishing core competence?' 'What is the role of learning processes in maintaining core competence over time?' Addressing these research questions within the pharmaceutical industry brings the authors to the main conclusion that learning processes are the key factor in the successful linking of core competence to competitive advantage and that those learning processes are (partly) the answer to Van Cauwenbergh's 'puzzle game'.

4

Core Competences, Competitive Advantage and Market Analysis: Forging the Links

PAUL J. VERDIN, PETER J. WILLIAMSON

The essential is invisible to the eye
(A. de Saint-Exupéry, *The Little Prince*)

INTRODUCTION

Today's discussions about competitive advantage give conflicting advice to the business world (see e.g. a series of Letters to the Editor, *Harvard Business Review*, May–June 1992, 162–172). One school of thought views competitive advantage primarily as a function of inherent industry attractiveness and the market positioning of individual firms (see e.g. Porter, 1980, 1985). It extols the benefits of looking 'outward'. An alternative, and increasingly vocal, school emphasizes the bundle of resources in the form of tangible and intangible assets on which the firm can draw. It advises business people to focus on expanding their asset stocks and capabilities as

Competence-Based Competition.
Edited by G. Hamel and A. Heene.
Copyright © 1994 The Strategic Management Society. Published 1994 by John Wiley & Sons Ltd.

the basis for sustained competitive advantage.[1] All too often, the debate between these 'schools' has become a 'dialogue of the deaf'.

Some proponents of the latter 'resource-based' view hail it as a new paradigm, sweeping away the old under banners like 'Competing on capabilities: the new rules of corporate strategy' (Stalk, Evans and Shulman, 1992). Others in turn proclaim that 'the resource-based view cannot be an alternative theory of strategy' (Porter, 1992, p. 108). In this chapter we argue that there are important payoffs to be gained by linking and integrating the two views.

More specifically, we develop the following basic propositions concerning the links between core competences and competitive positioning based on market analysis:

- That analyses of markets and competitors have an important role in identifying which competences are key in a particular market environment. The critical competences will be those that can be used to build sources of advantage which are slow and costly for competitors to imitate. Traditional competitive strategy frameworks therefore help practitioners identify which competences to concentrate on.
- That transfer of core competences within a corporate group will provide a powerful basis for entry only in market environments with certain characteristics. In other competitive environments, independent startups will compete on a much more level playing field with corporate affiliates. By linking an understanding of the competitive environment with the concept of core competences, practitioners can determine where to transfer competences within their organizations and identify opportunities for profitable diversification.
- That the scope for leveraging off core competences in order to gain competitive advantage is itself an important element of market structure. Practitioners need to assess barriers to entry relative to the core competences of other potential diversifiers as well as independent startups. Entry barriers to a market will be low if many outsiders have core competences which allow

---

[1]This characterization of the resource-based 'school' is, of course, a simplification. Particular authors have explored different aspects of the relationship between internal capabilities and competitive advantage; see e.g. Wernerfelt (1984), Dierickx and Cool (1989), Prahalad and Hamel (1990), Grant (1991), Barney (1991), Lado *et al.* (1992). Terminology differs between researchers; Bogaert, Martens and Van Cauwenbergh (this volume) set out the various concepts and the relationships between them. For an overview of the resource-based view in contrast to a broader set of theories in a historical perspective, see Conner (1991).

them to quickly and cheaply build the assets and skills required to compete effectively.

In the next section we develop the link between Porter's 'drivers' of cost and differentiation advantage to the underlying resources or asset stocks required to gain and sustain competitive advantage. We then explore the different means of securing these assets: endowment, acquisition, sharing or accumulation and the role of core competences as catalysts in these processes. By linking market analysis to competences in this way, we can use market data to predict the kinds of competences which will be key and how large an advantage they will provide. These predictions are illustrated with case examples and a simple empirical test. In the final section we draw together the implications for business practitioners.

SOURCES OF COMPETITIVE ADVANTAGE

When an infamous bank robber was asked the question 'Why do you rob banks?' he gave a matter of fact, but compelling, reply: 'Because that's where the money is.' Much of the early theory and practice of strategy adopted just this approach, focusing on the problem of how to choose 'attractive' industries in which to compete. Simplistic definitions of 'attractiveness' based on growth or past profitability gave way to richer analyses of 'industry forces' (Porter, 1980) and how these were changing over time.

We have subsequently seen considerable debate over just how important the 'industry factor' is as a determinant of the profitability of an individual firm. Classic cases such as Crown Cork and Seal[2] have alerted countless students to the fact that some firms make high profits in 'unattractive' markets—industry is not destiny. Large-scale statistical studies of the 'industry effect', while they produce different quantitative estimates, generally agree that only between 16% and 19% of the total variations in profit between business units can be directly explained by industry variables (Schmalensee, 1985; Rumelt, 1991).[3] Being in an 'attractive' industry is no guarantee for

---

[2]Crown Cork and Seal Company and the Metal Container industry, HBS Case Nos. 6-373-077 and 9378-024.
[3]These analyses were carried out at the level of the business unit or line of business, *not* at the *firm* level. It may also be noted that Rumelt's study attributes less than 1% of the total business profit variation to corporate effects.

success, while lack of industry attractiveness is not a sentence to poor performance.

Positioning within an industry (or, more correctly, a market) has therefore attracted increasing attention as a key determinant of firm profitability. Investigators like Porter (1980, 1985) have explained differential performance among competitors as a function of each firm's success in harnessing the 'drivers of competitive advantage' in a particular industry so as to place themselves in a more advantageous position relative to 'industry forces' compared with rivals. If scale is an important driver of cost leadership, for example, those firms who operate efficient scale plants will be better positioned to protect their profits against the power of buyers or suppliers and the threat of substitutes or entrants compared with subscale competitors. If reliable, responsive service is a critical driver of differentiation advantage, those forms who can offer such service will be positioned to make higher profits than rivals who offer lower reliability or slower response times. Porter's generic list of drivers is summarized on the right-hand side of Table 4.1.

MARKET POSITIONING—PUTTING IT INTO PRACTICE

To suggest to a manager that his or her company needs to produce in a large-scale plant in order to be profitable in a particular industry is rather like telling a pauper that if he wants to be rich he should operate a gold-mine. Two questions immediately arise:

- How would I go about obtaining access to a gold-mine or even a large-scale plant? (What Bogaert, Martens and Van Cauwenbergh in this volume, Figure 3.1, term 'having' resources.)
- What competences and skills do I need to successfully operate my gold-mine or large-scale plant once I have access to it? (Bogaert, Martens and Van Cauwenbergh term these 'doing' resources.)

It is obvious that for 'drivers of advantage' to become operational we need to consider their link to the assets which underpin them and, in turn, the process by which access to these assets are obtained and developed. Recently Porter (1992, p. 109) has recognized both this need and its relative neglect, noting that 'The existence of such asset is implicit in the concept of drivers but not well-developed . . .'.

TABLE 4.1 Asset stocks and cost/uniqueness drivers

Asset stocks	Cost drivers	Uniqueness drivers
Input assets •R&D capability •Technological know-how •Firm's reputation •Access to inputs •Appropriate production capacity •Relationships with suppliers	Economies of scale Learning and spillovers Pattern of capacity utilization Linkages •Within value chain •Vertical linkages	Discretionary policies •Similar examples to cost drivers, with emphasis on quality, service, etc. Linkages Timing
Process assets •R&D capability •Technological knowhow •Appropriate production capacity •Employee production experience	Interrelationships •With other business units Integration •Level of vertical integration	Location Interrelationships Learning and spillovers Integration
Channel assets •Distribution network •Dealer/distributor/ retailer loyalty •Market share •Customer assets (listed below)	Timing •First mover versus follower advantages •Timing with respect to business cycle/market	Scale Institutional factors
Customer assets •Firm's reputation •Product's reputation/ image •Customer loyalty •Brand awareness •Service network •Installed customer base	Discretionary policies, examples: •Product features, performance •Mix and variety of products offered •Level of service provided •Delivery time	
General assets (support/ infrastructure) •Human capital —managerial skill (strategic and tactical) —firm and industry specific experience —knowledgeable employees/managers •Financial capacity •Information technology systems •Market knowledge •Relationships with government/regulators	•Spending on marketing, R&D, etc. •Wages paid relative to industry norms •Other human resource policies •Procedures for scheduling production, etc. Location Institutional factors •Government regulation, unionization, etc.	

To illustrate these relationships in more detail let us return to the example of scale as one of the most common drivers referred to in industry analysis. As a newly created business unit I might have been endowed with a large-scale plant from my parent. Alternatively, blessed with sufficient financial capacity, I might go to a 'turnkey' engineering company and contract for its construction. Even if I lack the financial capacity, the option of leasing large-scale capacity may be available, as would be the case with a Boeing 747 needed by a startup, long-distance airline.

To reap the benefits of scale, however, I need more than just access to a large-scale plant. I need to be able to operate it. This means access to the relevant process experience. I also need to be able to sell the mass output of such a plant. This may require assets such as access to distribution channels or the consumer brand franchise necessary to overcome customer risk aversion and search costs. Exploiting the benefits of even a relatively straightforward driver like scale is therefore apt to require the services of a complex bundle of tangible and intangible assets as a prerequisite.

The same is true for high and stable capacity utilization, another important cost driver. This can only be achieved to the extent that the firm has the thorough market knowledge, adequate information systems, customer loyalty and consistent quality to keep capacity as high as possible without incurring major bottlenecks.

The need to secure access to the right assets is equally compelling in the case of differentiation drivers. For example, a firm's ability to learn how to perform an activity better may be an important driver of uniqueness. A fast-learning firm could be more responsive to changing consumer needs and preferences. However, several assets are required in order to realize this advantage: good information technology systems to facilitate the collection, processing and dissemination of knowledge and information; motivated employees and a corporate culture geared towards stimulating learning and adapting to change; skilled managers able to facilitate the learning process, etc.

Alternatively, take the example of Rockwell International in water meters: its policy choice to offer meters with superior reliability and durability would only pay off if it could obtain premium prices to more than offset the higher cost involved, e.g. by using more expensive bronze parts (Rockwell Water Meters, HBS Case No. 9-841-060). Higher prices in turn could only be obtained thanks to channel assets (in the forms of its efficient distribution network) and customer assets (its reputation for quality, reliability and service) that Rockwell had been able to build up over many years of successful operations in the industry.

The left-hand side of Table 4.1 provides a more complete listing of the assets on which exploitation of Porter's cost and differentiation drivers depend. We distinguish five main groups:

- *Input assets*—e.g. input access, loyalty of suppliers, financial capacity
- *Process assets*—e.g. proprietary technology, functional experience, organizational systems
- *Channel assets*—e.g. channel access, distributor loyalty, pipeline stock
- *Customer assets*—e.g. customer loyalty, brand recognition, installed base
- *Market knowledge assets*—accumulated information, and the systems and processes to access new information, on the goals and behaviour of competitors, the reactions of customers, suppliers and competitors to different phases of the business cycle, etc.[4]

Explicit recognition of the portfolio of assets which underpins any cost of differentiation driver helps in pinpointing where potential, long-term competitive advantages lie. If all competitors have equal access to the assets necessary to reap the benefits of a driver, then it will cease to be a source of competitive advantage. It is only when it is slow and costly for a rival to gain access to some of the necessary, underlying, assets that a particular driver will offer scope for sustained competitive advantage. The processes by which the services of particular assets are accessed therefore play a critical role.

SECURING THE NECESSARY ASSET SERVICES

The asset services necessary to underpin any market positioning can be accessed in four possible ways:

1. They may be secured from an asset *endowment* which establishes the business. A company established to exploit a proprietary

---

[4]Throughout this paper we use the shorthand term "assets" to mean "strategic assets, distinctive competences and key business processes" as defined more fully in Bogaert, Martens and Van Cauwenbergh (this volume) and illustrated in their Figure 3.1.

technology, for example, often receives a valuable patent asset from its founder.

2. They may be *acquired* by the business either in the form of the asset itself or the right to the services of an asset (as in the case of an equipment lease).

3. Access may be obtained through *sharing* of the asset with a sister business unit or alliance partner. Much of the literature on diversification has discussed the possibilities of sharing as a basis for entry into new, but related, businesses. This route encompasses the sharing of tangible assets like facilities through to intangibles, such as debt capacity.

4. Finally, access may be obtained by *accumulating* the asset inside the company over time.

Asset services which are both tradable and non-specific to a particular industry or product line can, in principle, be accessed via any of these routes. Relative costs will act as the deciding factor. Other assets will be freely tradable, but industry- or product line-specific. In this case, sharing across business units in different industries will not be possible. Instead, the necessary asset services would have to be accessed through acquisition or accumulation, as illustrated in Figure 4.1. Tradable assets of either of these types, however, are unlikely to act as a source of long-term competitive advantage. This is because, to the extent that any such an asset afforded supernormal returns to one or more players, it would be quickly acquired by rivals. As a result, the initial competitive advantage would disappear. Where such assets were in limited supply, asset prices would be bid up, causing the rate of return

Degree of tradability

	Tradable	**Non-tradable**
Specific	Acquisition Accumulation	Accumulation
Non-specific	Endowment Acquisition Sharing Accumulation	Endowment Sharing Accumulation

Industry specificity

FIGURE 4.1   Asset access

to the holder to fall back to competitive levels when properly measured against the asset's new market value.

Consider, then, asset services which are 'non-tradable' because the transactions costs in exchanging them through a market mechanism are prohibitive or the underlying factor market is non-existent or not functioning as an efficient market (Williamson, 1975; Barney, 1986; Dierickx and Cool, 1989). In this case the necessary asset services can only be obtained via endowment, sharing within an organization, or by the business unit accumulating the asset.

Among these assets, those that can be accessed through endowment or sharing will tend to provide only short-lived competitive advantage. This is because most assets will be subject to erosion over time (see e.g. Eaton and Lipsey, 1980). Customer assets such as brands will decay as new customers enter the market or former customers forget past experience or exit the market. The value of a stock of technical knowhow will tend to erode in the face of innovation by competitors. Patents will expire. Thus, assets accessed through initial endowment or an initial asset base shared with another SBU will tend to lose their potency as sources of competitive advantage over time unless they are replenished by internal accumulation processes.

The class of asset most likely to afford a firm long-term competitive advantage comprises those which can *only* be accessed by accumulating the asset inside the business unit. This will be the case where the relevant asset is both non-tradable and industry-specific (the upper right-hand quadrant of Figure 4.1). Once a firm has accumulated more of these assets than its competitors, its rivals will often find it difficult to match this position. This is because to do so, they would need to accelerate their own rate of asset accumulation so as to outpace this leading firm (since the leader is not standing still; unless, of course, the asset were substitutable by another asset which could be accessed through one of the other routes (Grant, 1990; Peteraf, 1991; Barney, 1991).

The implication of this analysis is that the processes by which non-tradable, industry-specific assets are accumulated lie at the heart of the competitive advantage and its creation. To the extent that these accumulation processes present barriers to replication of the relevant assets by rivals or entrants, a business that can increase the speed and reduce the cost of asset accumulation will be in a position to generate competitive advantage over rivals who are less qualified to do so. These processes have been the subject of important theoretical work (Dierickx and Cool, 1989). This literature points to various process characteristics which render rapid replication of these assets costly.

In this context, the notion of 'core competence' may assume an interesting yet largely unexplored role. The deployment of an appropriate set of core competences across business units within a firm may significantly reduce the costs and increase the speed with which new, non-tradable and industry-specific assets can be accumulated. Core competences may, therefore, allow a firm to quickly achieve a desirable positioning within a new market by helping it to rapidly accumulate assets which are necessary, but otherwise difficult to access.

Core competences may also allow a firm to maintain or extend its competitive advantage by enabling it to augment its non-tradable, industry-specific assets more quickly than its competitors. This is especially important in market environments that are undergoing significant change. Even firms with massive asset bases will lose their competitive advantage if they are unable to develop the new assets necessary to serve a changing market, either because they lack the necessary core competences or fail to use the competences they have. It is these relationships between core competences and the assets underpinning competitive advantage to which we now turn.

CORE COMPETENCES AS CATALYSTS TO ASSET ACCUMULATION

According to Dierickx and Cool (1989) there are four main factors which impede cheap and rapid asset accumulation:

1. *Time-compression diseconomies:* the extra cost associated with accumulating the required assets under time pressure (the cost of compressing an activity in time). For example, it may take more than twice the amount of marketing to achieve in one year the same level of brand awareness as an established competitor may have been able to develop over a period of two years (other things being equal). Similar relationships are likely to hold for other types of spending such as R&D costs relative to the rate of product or process improvement.
2. *Asset mass efficiencies:* some types of assets are more costly to accumulate when the firm's existing stock of that asset is small.

It is more difficult, for example, to build the customer base of a credit card when it has few existing users. Prospective customers fear that if they sign up to an unknown card it will not be widely accepted at retail stores. Worse still, the average costs per transaction will be high due to lack of network economies, making it difficult to price the service competitively.

3. *Asset interconnectedness:* the lack of complementary assets can often impede a firm from accumulating an asset which it needs to serve its market successfully. For example, it may be harder for a firm that lacks a service network to improve its product quality. Without the in-house data on actual product performance its own service network would provide, the targeting of improvements becomes more difficult.

4. *Causal ambiguity:* the uncertainty associated with pinpointing which specific factors or processes are required to accumulate a required asset (the precise chain of causality is ambiguous).[5] For example, a long list of key assets may explain the success of Wal-Mart in discount retailing in the USA, but it is unclear which particular assets are really the critical ones. Even if a possible imitator could pinpoint these, it would still need to understand how to go about accumulating them (see Ghemawat, 1986 and 1991, Ch. 1).

When the process necessary to accumulate an asset suffers from one or more of these impediments (or 'asset accumulation barriers'), all firms will face higher costs and possibly time delays in building it.[6] This will restrict their ability to satisfy their market or diversify into a new one by offering the differentiation or cost advantages that the elusive asset would underpin. It may be, however, that deploying existing core competences can help a firm *overcome* some of these asset accumulation barriers. We provide some simple examples in Table 4.2. An important point illustrated in each of the examples in the table is that core competences give the firm an advantage in building the new asset stocks which are required to serve a market. The fact that Honda had a core competence in

---

[5]The term was first introduced by Lippman and Rumelt (1982) to describe the phenomenon surrounding business actions and outcomes that makes it difficult for competitors to emulate strategies; Reed and DeFillippi (1990) identify three characteristics of competency that, individually or in combination, can generate causal ambiguity: tacitness, complexity and specificity.
[6]Barriers to asset accumulation are a prime cause of barriers to survival for young firms (see Verdin and Williamson, 1991).

TABLE 4.2   Core competences as catalysts to asset accumulation

Characteristic	Examples of the impact of core competences
Time-compression diseconomies	In the race to develop a low-cost, high yield production line for small-screen color LCD television sets the makers of large-screen sets found that money was a poor substitute for time. By drawing on its core competences in miniaturization, microprocessor design and material science—all developed in its card calculator and watch businesses—Casio was able to reduce the time-compression diseconomies faced by other players. Its core competences acted as a catalyst to rapidly establishing the assets necessary to manufacture the LCD television product in high volume at low cost.
Asset mass efficiencies	Entrants commonly face a 'catch 22' in establishing a dealer network: they cannot build their skills and systems for providing excellent dealer support without access to a large or dense network of dealers; yet they cannot establish such a network without the necessary skills and systems. Honda, however, was able to break this cycle when it entered the lawnmower business by using its core competences in dealer management originally developed in the motorcycle business to compensate for asset mass inefficiencies in building a new dealer network.
Interconnected asset stocks	Most entrants into the laser printer business lack crucial information on product reliability which is available to competitors with a well-established service network. In seeking to improve their product and design capability they therefore suffer from inter-connectedness of asset stocks. Canon, however, was able to reduce this disadvantage by deploying its core competence in the design of photocopier engines built on the basis of information from a large installed base and worldwide service network.
Causal ambiguities	The process of developing and gaining approval for a new pharmaceutical product has often been likened to a 'jackpot game'—the relationship between R&D spending and successful new products is highly ambiguous. Yet firms with core competences in drug development, such as Glaxo, appear to be able to develop systems and procedures which reduce this causal ambiguity. They must still play the proverbial 'slot machine' in R&D, but compared with other potential entrants into a new market, their core competences allow them to improve their odds of success.

dealer management did not mean it had a ready-made dealer network or support infrastructure which could simply be used in its lawnmower business. Given the differences between the markets for motorcycles and mowers, it still needed to develop distribution and dealer support infrastructure specific to the lawnmower business. Likewise, Casio did not have a production line in another business unit ready and waiting to be switched to cost-competitive manufacture of LCD television sets. Again, a new asset had to be built.

The deployment of core competences across business units therefore differs fundamentally from traditional asset sharing. Competences are not a substitute for asset accumulation, they facilitate it. They improve the efficiency in terms of both cost and time with which a firm can extend its asset stocks to serve new businesses as well as existing ones. By improving a firm's 'production function' for tangible and intangible assets, competences act as catalysts. They allow the firm to accumulate the asset stocks required to exploit cost and differentiation drivers in ways which competitors cannot. The relationships implied here are summarized in Figure 4.2.[7]

Recognition of the role of core competences as catalysts to asset accumulation has three important implications. First, the more

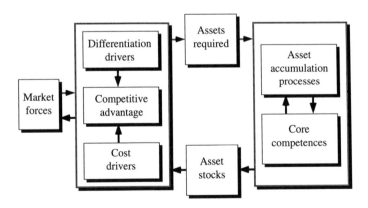

FIGURE 4.2 A 'production function' for competitive advantage

---

[7]As noted by Prahalad and Hamel (1990), core competences may be improved as a spinoff of the asset accumulation process. Experience of building a dealer network, for example, may help improve a firm's core competence in dealer management.

difficult it is to secure a particular asset through endowment, acquisition or sharing, and the more difficult it is to accumulate, other things equal, the more it will contribute to competitive advantage. Thus core competences will be increasingly valuable when they can be used as a catalyst in the process of accumulating those assets which are otherwise slow and costly to build.

Second, it is always important to recognize that the value of a core competence depends on the value of the asset it helps to create. Thus, the more unique the customer benefits the resulting asset can deliver to a market, the more valuable is a firm's competence to build that asset. The danger of a purely 'inward-looking' approach to exploiting competences is that they will be used to create assets which add little to the company's market strength (for example, an excellent repair facility when what the market demands is a more reliable product).

Third, as we move away from the concept of asset sharing towards asset building and competence deployment, the definition of 'business relatedness' changes. This helps unearth links between products like SLR cameras, fax machines, calculators, photocopiers, bubble-jet printers and cell analyzers—to name a few of Canon's businesses—despite little scope for direct asset sharing and few common components. Moreover, it challenges us to extend traditional definitions of entry barriers built around the concept of markets separated by industry-specific assets. The implications of the asset accumulation concept and its characteristics for the traditional 'structural' entry barriers have been explored elsewhere; see Verdin and Williamson, 1991 and Williamson and Verdin, 1992.

It is also worth noting that core competences may play a role in increasing the ability of a business unit to build its asset portfolio in other ways. Specifically:

1. Core competences may increase the potential for asset sharing (e.g. a company which licensed a process for manufacture of LCDs may be unable to adapt the line to produce components for a new product market in contrast, a firm with a core competence in LCD manufacturing technology may be able to successfully increase the flexibility of the line to produce the new product on the same equipment).
2. Core competences may assist a business to successfully integrate assets acquired in the external market (e.g. companies with certain organizational systems may be more successful in integrating acquisitions than others, some businesses have much

greater competences in quickly operationalizing newly licensed technologies or in bringing new plants on stream after raising additional capital).

LEVERAGING OFF THE CORE COMPETENCES OF OTHERS

It is not necessary for all the competences a firm deploys in overcoming asset accumulation barriers to be in-house, or even within a corporate group. Many companies have successfully leveraged off the competences of third parties through licensing, supply partnerships, distribution agreements and other types of alliances in order to provide catalysts to help develop the new assets they need either to maintain their competitive advantage in an existing business or to diversify into a new one.

The disappointing results of many alliances can be traced back to lack of clarity as to the precise nature of the benefits the partnership was intended to generate (Hamel, Doz and Prahalad, 1989). However, by understanding the nature of hard-to-replicate assets that will underpin competitive advantage in a market and identifying the competences which could act as catalysts to speed up the rate at which these assets could be built cost effectively, a business can precisely target the benefits it wants from each alliance relationship. These may range from product and process technology through to knowhow in developing a global brand franchise or building an effective distribution network in an unfamiliar market.

The most successful alliances, such as those used by Fujitsu and NEC in the computer industry or Ford and Mazda in automobiles, are not simply about borrowing a partner's existing assets. More importantly, they hinge on one or both partners developing new competences in order to build and improve future asset bases of their own (see Hamel, Doz and Prahalad, 1989; Lewis, 1990).

CORE COMPETENCES AND MARKET 'BREAKTHROUGHS'

From time to time 'maverick' competitors will try to change the 'rules of the game' in a market. These are often small or relatively young firms who lack the large accumulated asset bases of entrenched competitors. Because they face impediments to competing on the basis of rapid and cost expansion of existing types of assets, they seek to prosper by satisfying customers' needs on the basis of new sets of assets, unfamiliar to existing competitors. A classic example is the challenge which was presented to the traditional, large-scale film-processing laboratories by networks of 'one-hour' film-processing stations. The established film processors had perfected the assets and knowledge bases to collect exposed films from retailers, transport it to centralized processing facilities and develop films cost effectively in complex, large-scale plants without misplacing individual customers' treasured memories.

The maverick, one-hour film-processing networks served the customer on the basis of a very different bundle of assets. The competences required to put these in place were equally different to those that had been important in the past. Competences in franchising, miniaturization of equipment, materials distribution and de-skilling of the operation were critical in successfully underpinning this new way of better satisfying an existing market need.

In this new competitive game many of the existing assets of established players were rendered obsolete. In determining the right strategy to respond, however, it was critical to understand which existing competences could help put a new asset base in place as well as where new competences would be required. In the event, players like Kodak were able to draw on their core competences to build a new business centering on sales of processing equipment and supplies such as chemicals and treated papers to the 'one-hour' networks. Using these competences, augmented with additional ones, new assets from plant capacity through to sales, distribution and service networks were accumulated, along with the necessary experience to streamline the new business and improve its initial profitability.

Identification and deployment of its core competences, therefore, not only gives a company the opportunity to accelerate its rate of learning, share assets across the group, and assist it in the integration of newly acquired assets. The ability to recognize and transfer competences is also essential in allowing a firm to regenerate its asset base when faced with market 'breakthroughs' which render existing assets obsolete by changing the rules of the competitive game.

STRUCTURAL INDICATORS OF THE IMPORTANCE OF CORE COMPETENCES

Thus far we have explored the links between market forces and core competences, as summarized in Figure 4.2. But these links pose two further questions:

1. Are there structural indicators that signal which core competences are likely to be a potential source of advantage in a particular market?
2. Are there any systematic relationships between market structure and the importance of access to these competences as a source of competitive advantage?

In what follows we provide a 'first-cut' empirical test to shed some light on these questions. It is clear that not all types of firm-specific assets will be relevant for every business or market. Our hypothesis is that differences between markets in the type of asset services required, the ways in which they can be obtained and the role of core competences in this process are an important element of market structure underweighted by traditional analyses of market positioning.

Asset stocks and core competences, however, are very difficult, if not impossible, to measure directly on a consistent basis across different industries. Therefore it is useful to develop observable indicators that flag the nature of the assets required and the ease with which they can be accumulated. We discuss these under three headings: customer relationship indicators, channel relationship indicators, and indicators of the nature and importance of process experience.

CUSTOMER RELATIONSHIP INDICATORS

The first set of indicators seeks to capture the fact that the nature of interactions or 'contact points' with the customer is an important determinant of the types of assets necessary to effectively serve a market.

1. *Customer fragmentation.* The more fragmented customers are, the harder it is to reach them and the more important is a substantial

in-house distribution function. Distribution infrastructure, personnel and systems are likely to benefit from extensive operating experience, which cannot be easily compressed in time or purchased outside and therefore make entry and survival difficult for independent entrants. These assets can potentially be borrowed or shared with other business units or the corporate parent, but for many businesses a dedicated infrastructure will be required. Thus access to the parent's core competence in building up an efficient distribution function will be critical. A measure for this structural feature is *MCUST*, the percentage of product lines for which there were over 1000 customer accounts at the manufacturer level (be they users or resellers). An alternative measure is customer density, a direct indicator of the ease with which a given market may be covered.

2. *Frequency of purchase.* This variable refers to the requirement and the ease with which a relationship with the customer can be built *over time.* In frequently purchased goods, experience of a given customer with an established brand is recent. So long as the customer maintains a favorable view of their existing brand, this leads to stronger loyalty and therefore it is more difficult for a new firm to induce trial. Infrequent purchase, in contrast, tends to depreciate the value of information collected at the last purchase juncture, encouraging customers to conduct a new search. Access to core competences in rapidly building successful brands is thus likely to be more important where the product is purchased frequently. For items infrequently purchased, in contrast, the product is more likely to win customers on its independent merits since buyers' brand loyalty will have been eroded by time. Core competences in brand building will be less critical in environments where purchases are infrequent. Frequency of purchase can be measured by the proportion of product lines belonging to a given industry for which the user generally purchases with a frequency of more than once per year (*FQPUR*).

3. *Product customization (products made to order) versus standardization.* Successful made-to-order supply depends on a close relationship between manufacturer and customer with a high exchange of information. Once transactions cost investments have been made with established businesses it will be more difficult for a new business to break into such a customer relationship. Not only is this a non-tradable asset, but it is rather hard for newcomers to establish such relationships in a compressed

timescale. The importance of product customization, measured by the percentage of products classified to the industry which are made to order based on customer specifications (*TORDER*), therefore can be considered as another structural indicator for the importance of established customer contacts. However, the handicap it represents to newcomers to the industry will be significantly lower for businesses that can benefit from existing customer relationships with other units in the same company (sharing). Likewise, access to core competences in establishing, building and managing 'made to order' customer relationship will also be more advantageous when *TORDER* is high.

4. *Major purchase*. This structural indicator refers to the possibility of winning new customers, based on their risk attitude and the informational characteristics of the buyer–seller relationship in the market. The risk associated with error for a major purchase may deter buyers from trying the product of a new business unit rather than continuing with established suppliers. New firms here may face a 'chicken and egg' dilemma: customers are reluctant to buy from a supplier without a demonstrable track record, yet the new firm cannot develop that track record quickly without a rapid buildup of its installed base (cf. asset mass efficiencies). According to this argument, core competences in product launch, rapid ramp-up of production, and possibly brand creation would be especially advantageous in markets for 'major' purchases. On the other hand, the higher significance of a major purchase makes it more worthwhile to incur the costs of search rather than relying on past experience or on manufacturer's claims (see Porter, 1976), and hence the disadvantage faced by a new entrant may be reduced when purchases are major. In this case the product is more likely to stand or fall on its quality as objectively determined. Core competences would then be of less value. The relative importance of the purchase of the product or service may be measured by *MAJOR*, defined as the percentage of product lines which represented a major purchase for the ultimate buyer (more than \$100 for households, judgmentally determined for non-household buyers). Alternative indicators, for which we currently lack data, could include the perceived risk of product failure and its expected cost.

5. *Service requirement*. Good customer relationships (service reputation) and the organizational capital to provide quality service are both largely non-tradable assets which are often slow

and difficult to accumulate. They are likely to be more important in markets where the demand for service is high. Corporate affiliation might benefit a business by allowing it to draw on the service reputation of its parent or affiliated businesses and share their related market intelligence. More importantly, access to core competences in rapidly establishing an organization capable of providing quality service to the customer will offer greater advantage in 'high-service' markets. Alternatively, service may present an opportunity for startups to do better than established firms if they are able to offer new or more flexible, responsive service. In this case the deployment of corporate 'core competences' could even be a disadvantage if it constrains flexibility and innovation or leads to the imposition of inappropriate systems and definitions of 'good service' developed in the course of serving other markets. The service requirement in the industry can be measured by the percentage of product lines requiring a 'moderate to high' degree of after-sales or technical service (*HSERV*).

6. *Media advertising.* Customer assets such as brand awareness, brand loyalty, etc. (see Aaker, 1991) are often the cumulative result of media promotion over an extended length of time, rather than the flow of advertising outlays in any given period. Long-term success also depends not only on how much is spent but how effective each media campaign dollar proves to be. These considerations would argue that core competences in launching successful media campaigns would offer an advantage where brand awareness was important in underpinning competitive advantage. However, access to media advertising and advertising agencies is quite open and competitive. Advertising can be bought by independent newcomers under almost equal conditions as by established firms. Moreover, since brands can be bought and sold, it may be possible to purchase the results of successful advertising in the past, thereby compensating for lack of core competences in rapidly building a new brand. Furthermore, high advertising outlays in an industry may be a symptom of relatively high rate of brand erosion, reducing the effective impact of brands as a source of competitive advantage.[8] It is therefore unclear as to whether core competences in media promotion will

---

[8]In fact, even in the debate on the competitive impact of advertising it has been argued to be a 'gateway' to entry and evidence has been produced on either side of the issue (see e.g. Verdin and Williamson, 1991). The asset accumulation perspective, however, sheds new light on the question.

be systematically more important in advertising intensive markets which measure by expenditure on media advertising as a percentage of total sales value (*MEDIA*).

CHANNEL RELATIONSHIP INDICATORS

A second class of indicators refers to scope for building channel-related assets as a basis for competitive advantage. Such assets are likely to be more important in industries where a large portion of the products are sold through intermediaries and which rely heavily on 'push marketing'.

7. *Channel dependence.* We define channel dependence of a product as the degree to which the product requires gaining access to a distribution channel in order to reach the final customer, as opposed to the possibility of selling direct to the final user. To the extent that obtaining channel access and 'shelf space' is easier for those with an established track record, we would then expect older firms to have a greater advantage where channel dependence was high, an advantage that is hard to trade on the open market, takes time to accumulate and is subject to substantial scale and scope economies. Porter (1976), for example, has argued that 'for products sold through convenience outlets, . . . gaining access to distribution actually becomes easier as the brand image matures' (p. 28). This reflects the fact that where goods must be sold through retail conveniences stores a certain density of sales are required to make it economic to handle the brand. In 'non-convenience goods', meanwhile, the retailer, wholesaler or agent may be unwilling to carry the unknown brand of a young firm, since even a high margin cannot match the average return for a given amount of sales effort he or she receives by selling a well-established brand. In these cases, young businesses may be effectively blocked from gaining exposure to customers, or at least encounter a serious disadvantage that can only be overcome with substantial, costly sales incentives. Here corporate affiliation may be helpful because it provides opportunities to 'piggyback' off existing channel relationships (asset sharing). Corporate affiliation may also provide access to core competences in developing and managing channel relationships. Our measure for channel dependence is the percentage

of products which pass through an intermediary before reaching the final user (*CHANNEL*).

8. *Push marketing.* This refers to the importance of marketing activities through the channel and associated infrastructure and staff required to support the product. It is measured by the cost of marketing other than that spent directly on media advertising (discussed above), as a percentage of sales (*PUSH*). Since such activities are complex and require high levels of team building and staff experience, which tend to develop as a business matures, we expect industries where *PUSH* is high to display high asset barriers. As the underlying asset cannot easily be acquired or accumulated, access to a core competence in developing this asset will provide a significant advantage to newcomers in overcoming this barrier.

PROCESS EXPERIENCE AND GENERAL ASSET INDICATORS

In most industries it is important to build up relevant process experience in order to survive and be successful. However, we expect this process experience to be more critical in industries requiring large amounts of high-skilled labor and R&D capability.

9. *Labor intensity.* Firm-specific assets are most often related to experience gained by personnel and hence are 'embodied' in *human* capital. In equipment-intensive industries, in contrast, much of the learning is embodied in the capital of a particular vintage and can be easily purchased or otherwise acquired by newcomers. In addition, by setting up with new equipment, newcomers have the opportunity to capture state-of-the-art learning in their operation while older incumbents are left with less productive, earlier vintage equipment for which they cannot justify immediate replacement. Higher labor intensity will thus increase the potential importance of staff experience as an intangible asset, giving older firms more of an advantage over young businesses. However, new startups belonging to a corporate group may benefit from the accumulated experience of the parent and, more importantly, from a core competence in laborforce training and human resource development. *L/K* measures labor intensity as total employment over the total book value of plant and equipment in the industry.

10. *The skill level of the labor force.* To the extent that skills are specific to the industry, young firms will be faced with the problem of hiring the necessary specialists and forming these recruits into a smoothly co-ordinated resource. Contracting and then successfully transferring complete teams with the necessary skills is notoriously difficult, particularly for businesses who are uncertain to survive. In industries where groups of skilled staff are an important source of advantage, young businesses are likely to be at a greater handicap compared with established rivals who have gradually evolved an effective base of skilled staff with experience working together. This is not easy to acquire, given time-compression diseconomies and causal ambiguity. A core competence in developing skilled staff again may prove a great benefit, helping corporate diversifiers to overcome this potential barrier. *SKILL* measures the proportion of 'high-skilled' jobs in the industry as a percentage of total employment.

11. *R&D.* To the extent that success in R&D involves the accumulation of team experience which is largely non-tradable, we could expect new businesses to be at a greater disadvantage as R&D intensity increases. But new corporate subsidiaries may benefit from access to corporate level core competences in R&D management. Glaxo plc, for example, is often thought to have a core competence in new drug development, as noted in Table 4.2. The benefits of corporate affiliation may be offset, however, if a high R&D intensity were to signal a state of rapid technical change. In this case, the value of the existing stock of R&D would erode quickly generating opportunities for younger firms to build strong positions on the basis of new technology (often obtained via an initial endowment from an owner). The measure used is *RDSLS*, the total expenditure on R&D as a percentage of sales made by the industry.

A summary view of these structural indicators and the measures used in our empirical test below is provided in Table 4.3.

A SIMPLE EMPIRICAL TEST

Elsewhere we have presented empirical evidence that market segments with the following characteristics prove to be relatively

TABLE 4.3 Indicators of the assets required for competitive advantage

Asset type and specific asset	Structural indicator	Measure
Customer assets		
●Customer loyalty (existing)	Media advertising	*MEDIA*
●Brand recognition	Product standardization	*TORDER*
(new customers)		
●Installed base	Purchase frequency	*FQPUR*
	Major purchase	*MAJOR*
●Service network	Service requirement	*HSERV*
●Service quality	Service requirement	*HSERV*
Channel assets		
●Distribution network	Customer fragmentation	*MCUST*
●Dealer/distributor/retailer	Channel dependence	*CHANNEL*
loyalty	Push marketing	*PUSH*
Process experience		
●Technological knowhow	Capital intensity	*K/E*
●Functional experience	Skill level	*SKILL*
●R&D capability/stock	R&D requirement	*RDSLS*
General assets		
●Human capital	Labor intensity	*L/K*
	Skill level	*SKILL*

hostile to independent startups: high customer fragmentation, frequent purchase, products made to order, major purchase (signalling the importance of certain types of customer relationship assets); high channel dependence and push marketing (flagging the importance of certain types of channel relationship assets); and labor intensity (signalling the importance of human resources which the firm has accumulated) (Verdin and Williamson, 1991; Williamson and Verdin, 1992). Here we wish to begin addressing the two further questions posed above, namely: do these structural indicators also signal the importance of access to competences as a source of competitive advantage and do they help to pinpoint which core competences are most relevant to a particular market? Our test involves estimating whether new business units with access to core competences through corporate affiliation have an advantage in terms of their survival chances after entry as compared to these independent startup firms and, more specifically, whether any such advantage depends on the market environment as characterized by the structural indicators introduced above.

In estimating these effects we divided our sample into two age ranges. The first group comprises independent startups and new corporate subsidiaries which had been in business for 5 or fewer years (this partitioning reflects data availability). The second group comprises both independent firms and corporate subsidiaries which had been estabished for six or more years. In this way we can examine whether the benefits of corporate affiliation are different for a group of young firms trying to accumulate an initial base of assets compared with well-established businesses whose task is to continually improve and renew their existing asset stocks. These tests are specified in terms of two equations:

$$(SRHAZ)_i = \alpha_0 + \sum_{k=1}^{m} \beta_k AA_{ik} + \epsilon \tag{4.1}$$

$$(LRHAZ)_i = \gamma_0 + \sum_{k=1}^{m} \delta_k AA_{ik} + \omega \tag{4.2}$$

where *SRHAZ* is a measure for the short-term *relative* survival chances of young independent firms versus corporate business units into the market i, defined as the ratio of the survival rate of young (0–5 years old) independent businesses to the survival rate of corporate affiliates of the same age group, over the same time period. *LRHAZ* is a measure for the long-term relative survival chances of independent firms and corporate affiliates in market i, defined as the ratio of the survival rate of established independent businesses (over 5 years old) to the survival rate of corporate affiliates of the same age. These data on business survival rates across a set of 134, 3-digit manufacturing industries were secured for a sample of 377 000 business units extracted from the USEEM file of the US Small Business Administration covering the period 1978–94. AA_{ik} are measures for the set (k) of structural indicators in market i as defined above.[9]

---

[9]Information on the composition of these industries in terms of single-plant firms (i.e. 'independent establishments') and plants belonging to multi-plant or diversified firms ('dependent establishments') and their age class was available over the years 1978–84; establishments could be tracked over time from one point of observation to another allowing for establishment-based entry measures to be derived for each industry by identifying those firms and dependent establishments who were in existence in 1984 but not in 1978. The variables *HSERV, TORDER, FQPUR, MAJOR, PUSH, CHANNEL* and *MCUST*, as defined above, were drawn from a US survey of marketing expenditures (Bailey, 1975). *RDSLS* was taken from National Science Foundation (1978), *MEDIA* from PICA: FTC Line of Business (1976), *K/E* was calculated from BIE Capital Stock Data Base (1978) with employment data from the US SBA Data Base, *SKILL* was computed from job classifications contained in the Census of Population (1980) and *UN* from Kokkelenberg-Sockell (1985). For a full description of the data see MacDonald (1985), Phillips (1985) and Williamson and Verdin (1992).

Due to the limitations of this dataset, two caveats should be made in interpreting the results. First, we would have preferred to carry through into the empirical test our theoretical distinction between the more 'traditional' concept of asset sharing or corporate synergy (static concept), on the one hand, and the impact of core competence, on the other (enabling the development of the required industry-specific assets, a dynamic concept). Unfortunately, this was not possible with the available data.

A second complication in interpreting the results arises from the possibility that parent groups often impose 'artificial' exit barriers on their subsidiaries. This may take the form of cross-subsidization of losses from earning elsewhere in the firm in order to support a diversification drive, for example, or unwillingness to write off assets in the corporate books. This means that survival does not necessarily reflect only the competitive advantage of the business unit itself but also the impact of exogenous *corporate* objectives or other constraints. When labor is organized into a union, for example, it may be more costly and difficult for a corporation to close down one of its businesses. We tested this effect through the variable UN, the degree of unionization in the industry, measured by the percentage of total employees belonging to a union.

RESULTS

Comparing the survival rates between our samples of firms established in the past 5 years, we find that corporate affiliates enjoy almost 50% higher probability of survival than independent startups facing the same market environments. This is consistent with the hypothesis that access to the core competences accumulated within a corporate group helps a new subsidiary build its own asset base. The 'corporate nursery' seems to work.

Theoretically at least, we might expect to find this benefit of corporate affiliation to continue even after a business became well established and accumulated its own specific asset base. Continued access to the core competences of the group should help an individual business to successively improve its assets and adjust to changing market demands faster than competitors, but in our sample it does not seem to do so. The ability of corporate affiliates to withstand the rough and tumble of competition is insignificantly different from established independent firms once both samples have been in business for more than 5 years.

If there are potential benefits of continued transfer of core competences between business units within a corporate group, we are unable to find evidence that these benefits are successfully being exploited. There are many possible explanations, including the emergence of a 'not invented here' syndrome among established subsidiaries or the failure of the corporate center either to identify the core competences of the group or to provide a mechanism to transfer them between business units (Pralahad and Hamel, 1990).

In order to further explore how the benefits of access to the assets and competences of the center and sister business units varies corporate affiliation, equations (4.1) and (4.2) were estimated using ordinary least squares. The statistical results are reported in Table 4.4.[10]

TABLE 4.4   Asset accumulation, core competence and business unit success

Variable	Equation (4.1) SRHAZ	Equation (4.2) LRHAZ
INTERCEPT	0.723	0.653
MCUST	0.001	
	(1.388)	
TORDER	0.009	
	(3.294)	
MAJOR	−0.005	−0.002
	(1.673)	(2.537)
HSERV		−0.002
		(2.160)
MEDIA	0.016	
	(1.138)	
CHANNEL	0.005	
	(2.421)	
L/K	−0.001	−0.004
	(6.943)	(4.804)
UN		0.003
		(2.340)
R^2	0.370	0.345
Adj. R^2	0.328	0.322
Degrees of freedom	98	118

t-statistics in parentheses

[10]Statistical tests on these equations are based on the usual assumption that the error terms e and w are normally distributed. Theoretically we might expect a skew caused by higher hazard rates of small and medium-sized businesses. Unfortunately, the dataset does not provide the necessary information on business unit size to assess the impact of this possible distortion.

CORE COMPETENCES AND THE CORPORATE NURSERY

Looking first at our paired samples of businesses 5 or less years old, the following implications of these statistical results are notable:

1. In markets where customer relationships are important and costly to build, as signalled by a high degree of customer fragmentation and made-to-order products, access to corporate group assets and competences brings significant benefits to young businesses as they struggle to accumulate the assets necessary to compete. Independent businesses which lack access to corporate competences are at a relative disadvantage in these types of environments (positive and significant coefficients on *MCUST* and *TORDER*).

2. In markets with high channel dependence, corporate affiliates also have a substantial advantage over independent startups over the first five years after commencing operations (positive and significant coefficient on *CHANNEL*). This suggests that sharing of core competences in channel management across a corporation is important in helping new subsidiaries become successfully established in markets where the channel performance has a powerful impact on competitive advantage.

3. There is some evidence that access to corporate skills is an advantage to a young business when media advertising plays a key role in the competitive armory, but this relationship is only weakly significant (positive coefficient on *MEDIA*).

4. In markets where the product represents a 'major' spending decision for the consumer, in contrast, independent startups are relatively better off. It seems that customers discount their existing relationships affiliates within the group and access to core competences when they make a very important purchase (negative and significant coefficient on *MAJOR*). This would accord with the theory of 'non-convenience' goods which suggests that buyers will invest more in collecting objective information when they go to make such purchases (Porter, 1976).

5. In highly labor-intensive industries, independent firms have a relatively better chance to compete compared with recently established corporate subsidiaries. There are a number of possible explanations for this result. It may be that inflexible labor practices imposed by corporate group norms hamper the effectiveness of corporate subsidiaries relative to more fleet-of-foot

independent startups. This result may also reflect the exposure to cash crisis faced by independent startups in high capital intensity (hence high fixed cost) businesses, while corporate subsidiaries enjoy the protection of the parent's 'long purse'.

6. Corporate affiliation seems to play little systematic role in overcoming barriers to building effective service networks, attracting skilled labor, producing advances through R&D and developing customer loyalty for frequently purchased products. Building customer loyalty for frequent purchases appeared as a significant hurdle for independent startups in our earlier research (Williamson and Verdin, 1992). Access to the core competences of a corporate group does not appear to make it significantly easier to clear this hurdle.

CORE COMPETENCE AND LONG-TERM SYNERGY BENEFITS

As we have already noted, the advantage enjoyed by newly established corporate subsidiaries found to exist, on average, across different markets generally does not appear to be sustained. After five years in the business, the successful independent firms have generally caught up with their competitors affiliated with a larger corporate group. This lack of sustained advantage from continued access to the core competences of the group remained the case when we tested for differences between market environments (the indicators *MCUST, TORDER, MEDIA, CHANNEL* were not statistically significant in equation (4.2)).

This result leads us to suspect that reason lies in a failure of many American corporations to continue to exploit opportunities to transfer core competences between business units once these SBUs are seen as 'mature' or even well established in their own right. This finding adds to the body of evidence questioning the value-added or contribution of the corporate center to their business units (see e.g. Rumelt, 1991, showing the near-absence of any corporate factor in explaining business unit level profitability variances).[11] It is also interesting in light of the suggestion by Prahalad and Hamel, 1990, that many corporations have failed to establish organizational

---

[11]Disregarding for difference in performance indicators used (we use survival, Rumelt uses profitability). Our results on equation (4.1) then may add an interesting nuance to Rumelt's findings insofar as we did find a short-term 'startup' benefit of corporate affiliation for *young* business units.

mechanisms for the continuous transfer of their core-competences between their SBUs.

Worse still in markets where customers demand high levels of service, our results suggest that corporate affiliation can act as a long-run handicap to competitiveness (negative coefficient on *HSERV* in equation (4.2)). It may be that bureaucratic cultures in some large groups adversely show up as poor service when they establish new subsidiaries.[12]

IMPLICATIONS FOR THE PRACTITIONER

In this chapter we have sought to forge links between the core competence framework and more traditional market-competitor analysis. The nature of these links has a number of important lessons for the business practitioner which may be summarized in four maxims:

1. *Understand exactly which competences can offer competitive advantage.* Competences that are widespread among rivals will seldom offer the firm a competitive edge. Those competences which enable a company to build assets that are slow and costly for competitors to imitate are the ones that count. These include assets like an efficient network of distributors, a response system to deliver made-to-order products, or a brand-loyal customer base that competitors can neither buy off the shelf nor copy quickly; and accumulated process knowhow that equipment suppliers cannot provide. It is the competences which can be deployed as catalysts in building these kinds of assets more quickly than competitors that are core to achieving competitive advantage. This rule is also relevant to diversification. Competences will not underpin competitive advantage in a new market if the resulting assets can easily be replicated by incumbents or imitated by other entrants with similar capabilities.
2. *Start from the market in deciding how to use your core competences.* The fact that an asset is hard for competitors to imitate is obviously not enough for it to yield advantage. The market

---

[12]Our control variable of unionization confirms our expectation that organized labor may artificially prolong the life of otherwise unviable or uncompetitive businesses (positive and significant coefficient on *UN*).

must also value the services that asset can deliver. There is little point, for example, exploiting a competence in channel management if customers are increasingly buying direct from the manufacturer. There would have been limited advantage in Kodak focusing its competences on building and managing yet larger-scale, centralized film-processing facilities when customers were demanding a one-hour turnaround. The goal is to direct competences so as to harness the drivers of competitive advantage in a market. Since these drivers differ between market environments, so will the key assets required to win. Which assets are critical will also change over time. Core competences must be focused on building the right assets faster than rivals. Our results suggest a number of market indicators that are useful in deciding where to focus a firm's competences. These include the level of customer fragmentation, whether the product represents a major or minor purchase for the customer, the frequency of purchase, and the importance of offering a 'make-to-order' service. Analysis of these aspects of market structure can help determine the benefits of focusing core competences on improving 'customer relationship assets' and the right types of assets to build. The degree of 'channel dependence' is another important indicator of where existing competences should be deployed as well as the need to build new competences or lever off the core competences of others through alliances. The level of labor intensity and the role of media advertising are further indicators of where competences should be deployed. A number of these factors have received inadequate attention in the traditional competitive analysis.

3. *Look for ways to transfer core competences from one business unit to others within the group and establish processes to ensure these transfers continue, cycle after cycle, as competence levels improve.* Our results suggest that many corporations are successful at sharing their core competences with new subsidiaries in their startup phase. All too often, however, this flow of competences is not sustained as the SBU matures. Our findings indicate that too few corporations have established successful mechanisms for continually transferring improvements in the competence of one business unit to others within the group.

4. *Transfer competences from young subsidiaries back into mature ones, not just from mature SBUs to startups.* We found that mature business units do help new SBUs to build assets like an effective distribution network, powerful brands and efficient, capital-

intensive facilities more quickly and cost effectively than independent entrants who lack similar access to the core competences of a corporate group. But we were unable to detect evidence of learning flowing the other way. Mature SBUs seemed to derive no significant benefits from transfer of competences within the group. Worse still, corporate affiliation, if anything, blunted the competitiveness of established businesses in products where customers demanded high levels of service. This suggests opportunities for practitioners to improve competitive advantage by ensuring that as new subsidiaries develop new competences, they become 'teachers' within their corporate groups, not only students of established SBUs.

Exploiting core competences is not just a matter of looking inward. Just as traditional competitive strategy must identify how a recommended market positioning is to be achieved, and the assets required to do so, core competences must be assessed in terms of the market benefits they can be used to unlock. The real payoffs come from linking an understanding of competences with a rigorous analysis of market. Forging these links will enable a firm to use its core competences in order to build or leverage its strategic assets so as to become a pacesetter for cost reductions and product differentiation in the areas that really count for competitive advantage.

ACKNOWLEDGEMENTS

Helpful comments of our discussant, Mark W. de Jong, Dena Gollish and anonymous referees are gratefully acknowledged.

REFERENCES

Aaker, D. (1991). *Managing Brand Equity*. New York: Free Press.
Bailey, E. L. (1975). *Marketing Cost Ratios of U.S. Manufacturers*. Conference Board Report No. 662, New York: Conference Board, 1975.
Barney, J. B. (1986). Strategic factor markets: expectations, luck and business strategy. *Management Science*, October, 1231–41.
Barney, J. B. (1991). Firm resources and sustained competitive advantage. *Journal of Management*, **171**, 99–120.

Bogaert, I., Martens, R. and Van Cauwenbergh, A. (this volume). Strategy as a situational puzzle: The fit of components.

Conner, K. R. (1991). A historical comparison of resource-based theory and five schools of thought within industrial organization economics: do we have a new theory of the firm? *Journal of Management*, 121–54.

Dierickx, I. and Cool, K. (1989). Asset stock accumulation and sustainability of competitive advantage. *Management Science*, December, 1504–14.

Eaton, B. and Lipsey, R. (1980). Exit barriers are entry barriers: the durability of capital as a barrier to entry. *Bell Journal of Economics*, Autumn, 721–9.

Ghemawat, P. (1986). *Wal-Mart Stores Discount Operations*. Boston: Harvard Business School, Case no. 9-387-018.

Ghemawat, P. (1991). *Commitment: The Dynamic of Strategy*. New York: Free Press.

Grant, R. M. (1991). The resource-based theory of competitive advantage: implications for strategy formulation. *California Management Review*, Spring, 119–35.

Hamel G., Doz, Y. L. and Prahalad, C. K. (1989). Collaborate with your competitors—and win. *Harvard Business Review*, **67**, January–February, No. 1.

Kokkelenberg, E. C. and Sockell, D. R. (1985). Union membership in the U.S. 1973–1981. *Industrial and Labor Relations Review*, 497–543.

Lado A., Boyd, N. and Wright, P. (1992). A competency-based model of sustainable competitive advantage: toward a conceptual integration. *Journal of Management*, 77–91.

Lewis, J. D. (1990). *Partnerships for Profit: Structuring and Managing Strategic Alliances*. New York: Free Press.

Lippman, S. A. and Rumelt, R. P. (1982). Uncertain imitability: an analysis of interfirm differences in efficiency under competition. *Bell Journal of Economics*, 418–38.

MacDonald, J. M. (1985). Dun & Bradstreet business microdata. *Journal of Economic and Social Measurement*, 173–85.

National Science Foundation (1978). *Research and Development in Industry*. Technical Notes and Detailed Statistical Tables, Washington, DC.

Peteraf, M. A. (1991). *The cornerstones of competitive advantage: a resource-based view*. Discussion Paper 90–29, J. L. Kellog Graduate School of Management, Northwestern University, March.

Phillips, B. D. (1985). *The Development of the Small Business Data Base of the U.S. Small Business Administration: A Working Bibliography*. November, Washington, DC: US Small Business Administration.

Porter, M. E. (1976). *Interbrand Choice, Strategy and Bilateral Market Power*. Cambridge, MA: Harvard University Press.

Porter, M. E. (1980). *Competitive Strategy: Techniques for Analyzing Industries and Competitors*. New York: Free Press.

Porter, M. E. (1984). *Rockwell Water Meters*. Harvard Business School Case Study 9-841-060, Boston: HBS Case Clearing.

Porter, M. E. (1985). Competitive advantage: creating and sustaining superior performance. *Harvard Business Review*, May–June, 43–59.

Porter, M. E. (1990). *The Competitive Advantage of Nations*. New York: Free Press.

Porter, M. E. (1991). Towards a dynamic theory of strategy. *Strategic Management Journal*, 95–117.

Prahalad, C. K. and Hamel, G. (1990). The core competence of the corporation. *Harvard Business Review*, May–June, 71–91.

Reed, R. and DeFillippi, R. J. (1990). Causal ambiguity, barriers to imitation, and sustainable competitive advantage. *Academy of Management Review*, 88–102.

Rumelt, R. P. (1991). How much does industry matter? *Strategic Management Journal*, 167–85.

Schmalensee, R. (1985). Do markets differ much? *American Economic Review*, June, 341–51.

Stalk, G., Evans, P. and Shulman, L. E. (1992). Competing on capabilities: the new rules of corporate strategy. *Harvard Business Review*, March–April, 57–69.

US, Bureau of Census (1980). Job classification statistics. *Census of Population*. Washington DC: US Government Printing Office.

US Department of Labor (1974). *Capital Stock Estimates for Input–Output Industries: Methods and Data*. Bureau of Labor Statistics, Bulletin #2034.

US Small Business Administration (1984a). *Constructing a Business Microdata Base for the Analysis of Small Business Activity*. Washington, DC: Office of Advocacy, US Small Business Administration.

US Small Business Administration (1984b). *The Derivation of the U.S. Establishment Longitudinal Microdata USELM File*. Washington, DC: Office of Advocacy, US Small Business Administration.

Verdin, P. J. and Williamson, P. J. (1991). From barriers to entry to barriers to survival. A paper presented at the 11th Annual International Conference of the Strategic Management Society, Toronto, October 1991, forthcoming in the *Conference Proceedings*.

Wernerfelt, B. (1984). A resource-based view of the firm. *Strategic Management Journal*, **5**, April–June, 171–80.

Williamson, O. (1975). *Markets and Hierarchies: Analysis and Antitrust Implications*. New York: Free Press.

Williamson, P. J. and Verdin, P. J. (1992). Age, experience and corporate synergy: when are they sources of business unit advantage? *British Journal of Management*, **3**, No. 4, December, 221–36.

5

Core Competence and Competitive Advantage: A Model and Illustrative Evidence from the Pharmaceutical Industry

WILLIAM C. BOGNER, HOWARD THOMAS

INTRODUCTION

The competitive advantages which seem to endure through both good and bad economic times are the most prized assets of the firms which possess them, and the most frustrating challenges for competitors which do not. Frustration occurs primarily because the keys to competitive success are often difficult to determine and imitate. They lie beneath the product/market interface where firms typically compete. In particular, sustainable competitive advantage arises from the distinctive core competencies developed within the firm. Periods of economic recession and recovery highlight those

Competence-Based Competition.
Edited by G. Hamel and A. Heene.

firms whose strategies are built firmly on inimitable core competencies and those which are not. Businesses with competitive strategies grounded in core skills not only survive troubled times with less pain than their competitors, they emerge stronger still. Firms wishing to understand or emulate industry leaders and leaders wanting to maintain their competitive position need to clearly understand what the concept of a core competence is and how it relates to competitive advantages in the marketplace.

Unfortunately, core competence is often perceived as a static concept. In defining a core competence or in describing a competitor's competence at any point in time, a description is often used which implies a stable condition or relationship. Competition and the competitive environment, however, are dynamic. Therefore, firms which maintain their competitive advantages over many business cycles must have dynamic, not static, core competencies. In defining core competence in this chapter we always assume that competition and the competitive environment are fluid. We infer from this that one of the basic challenges of any general manager is the relentless pursuit of alignment between the ever-changing core competencies within the firm and the ever-changing demands of the external environment. If a manager is to accomplish this, then a clear understanding of the changing relationship between those core competencies and competitive environment is needed.

In this chapter we provide a framework to examine the relationship between core competence and competitive advantage using both conceptual models and real-world examples. The conceptual models draw on both academic and practitioner literature. Our primary intent is to capture the many elements which drive core competencies and which link them to competitive advantage. Our real-world analysis then evaluates competition in the pharmaceutical industry and assesses those factors which have historically led to success in this industry. It examines and analyzes the role which core competencies have played in the performance of both leader and follower firms and charts the effectiveness of nine firms in maintaining market alignment over a 40-year period of change.

THE CONCEPT OF CORE COMPETENCE

We propose a definition that encompasses each of the critical elements which create and sustain a core competence and which distinguishes core competence from other, related, concepts. First a formal definition:

> Core competencies are firm-specific skills and cognitive traits directed towards the attainment of the highest possible levels of customer satisfaction *vis-à-vis* competitors. Core competencies may be leveraged directly to satisfy existing customer needs or indirectly to develop a range of core products or core services. Firms with core competencies are more than just highly adapt at executing core skill sets. In addition, they have built appropriate cognitive traits which include:
>
> 1. Recipes and organizational routines for approaching ill-structured problems,
> 2. Shared value systems which direct action in unique situations, and
> 3. Tacit understandings of the interactions of technology, organizational dynamics and product markets.

Both the activity oriented and the cognitive aspects of a core competence are built up cumulatively through learning, and are constantly adapted towards applying a firm's skills so as to achieve competitive advantage.

The model in Figure 5.1 shows more clearly how cognitive traits, action-oriented skill sets and the competitive environment interact. These relationships are more fully discussed below.

CORE COMPETENCE AND COMPETITIVE ADVANTAGE

The first component of our definition is critical. It addresses the relationships at the very top of Figure 5.1. We believe that no skill, no matter how refined, can be a core competence if it does not give a firm an advantage in the marketplace by satisfying a customer need better than a competitor. Although the point seems rather elementary, it is important for avoiding both a misallocation of resources to activities which, although done well, do not lead to competitive advantage and an under-allocation of resources to those activities which, although not directly linked to the market, could lead to competitive advantage.

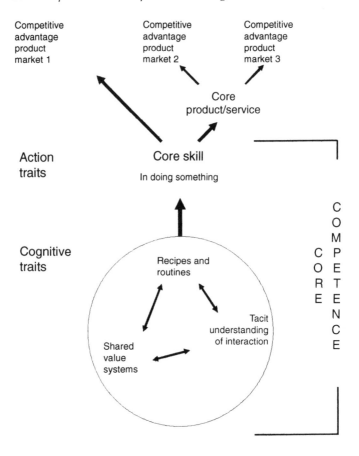

FIGURE 5.1

The distinction between core competencies and competitive advantage is important. Core competencies are internal traits of a firm. They are skills and understandings that are accumulated over time. Competitive advantage describes an edge that firm has in external market competition based on the bundle of goods and services offered for a price charged. Core competencies usually underscore competitive advantages, but they are not the same thing. For example, customers may not be concerned with, or even aware of, Honda's core skills in refining the internal combustion engine as described by Prahalad and Hamel (1990). They are motivated to purchase a Honda over a competitor's vehicle because of the perceived value which comes from a reputation for overall reliability.

The core skill in engine design underlies the ability of Honda to compete more effectively for customers, but the actual outcomes of retail competition occur on a different plane. (Competitive advantages arising from pure luck are not based on core competencies; they have neither the traits of a skill base nor replicability.)

Finally, our definition infers that a core competence must be unique to the firm. Core competencies must lead to unique, distinctive traits such that economic profit can be earned in otherwise open competition. It is based on this point that core competencies are often called 'distinctive competencies' (Andrews, 1980). Failure of the competence to be distinctive will result in the equivalent of Porter's (1980) 'profitless prosperity'.

CORE COMPETENCIES AND CORE PRODUCTS AND SERVICES

Figure 5.1 indicates that competence may not lead directly to a competitive advantage. Here the idea of a core product or service is introduced (Prahalad and Hamel, 1990). This is located on the right-side of the figure and will be referred to only as 'core product', although services clearly are major applications of competence. A core product serves as an intermediary between the core competence and a product in market competition. The core product is not the final product consumed in the market, and may not even clearly identify the market in which competitive advantage will be realized.

There is a sequence here, not unlike an activity chain, which ties the core competence to competitive advantage through the core product. Core competencies are first applied in core products and services, then other traits are wrapped around these core products to create the final product or service which will advantageously compete in the market. (Note it is assumed here that the 'non-competence' goods or services in the final product or service bundle clear a minimum threshold such that they do not detract from or offset the value added by the competence, thereby destroying the competitive advantage the competencies create.) Hence, it is through the mechanism of the core product that a single set of core competencies can be dispersed to multiple-product markets. In this respect core products and services can be the basis for successful diversification. In Prahalad and Hamel's example of Honda they show how engine competencies allowed that firm to compete successfully in the distinctive markets for automobiles, motorcycles, lawnmowers and electric generators. Packaging the core product with other traits led to successful diversification into multiple markets wherein the core product could lead to competitive advantage. In contrast, we can infer that Honda's core competencies would not lead to competitive advantage in, say, ladies' retail clothing; the core products which their core competencies produce cannot be advantageously packaged with other traits for competition in that product market.

Core Competence as both Action and Cognition

A firm's core competence exists on two levels. On one level is the active component of a core competence, the 'doing' of an activity which focuses on exploiting a skill better than the competition. For example, actually designing increasingly more efficient internal combustion engines would be a skill exploitation. Consistent with the internal orientation of core competence developed thus far, we see such core skills are meaningful *in* competition, but they need not be *the* basis of product/market competition itself. The performance of activities (skill exploitation) are tied to unique cognitive traits (skill knowledge) and is a key component of the iterative learning process (skill development) which improves both exploitation and knowledge.

The second level or component is the cognitive portion of the competence. Our model assumes all relevant actions and skills are driven by a distinctive set of cognitive traits (values, recipes, understandings) which lie behind core skills and which transform the mere doing of an act into a competence. These cognitive traits may be shared by a group or they may be found in the mind of the single individual. It is through the effective, on-going development of these cognitive traits that skills rise to a level which is distinct from those of a competitor, leading to core products and competitive advantage. These 'soft' traits of core competence are subdivided into three parts, all of which are interrelated, as indicated by the two-headed arrows in Figure 5.1. The roles of all three are predicated on the basic assumption of a constantly changing competitive environment, where change often occurs in non-linear and unpredictable ways. Indeed, without the need for firms to cope with such on-going dynamics, the learning process would not be necessary and the concept of a core competence would revert only to the maintenance of specific, stable core skills.

The discussion of cognitive traits in the model begins with the parallels in the dynamic process of competition. Mintzberg (1978) makes the point that competitive strategy 'emerges' over time, in contrast to being a rationally executable fixed plan. So too, all knowledge aspects of competition (e.g. technology, management skills) develop sequentially over time. Unknown as well as unknowable information, along with cognitive process constraints, limit understanding, requiring an on-going processing of information (Quinn, 1980). As information emerges, existing 'recipes or routines' (Nelson and Winter, 1982) play an important role in further competence enhancement. They embody the way in which the firm organizes stimuli as they come from the environment. These stimuli carry important information about the future effectiveness of a core competence in providing competitive advantage, but because of the unpredictable nature of emergent events, organizational routines have to be flexible in collecting and interpreting this information. Therefore, the dynamic process of maintaining core competence must contain routines for efficiently and effectively attending to external events, and recipes for integrating relevant changes into the set of core skills.

The cognitive traits of a core competence also include a shared value system (Ouchi, 1981; Peters and Waterman, 1982) among key decision makers. It is the shared vision of those who hone the core organizational skills which gives the appearance of singular action to a multi-person effort. For example, Intel has been described as a decentralized and ill-structured organization. But its strong shared value system uses this as a strength, enabling a large organization to respond smoothly and quickly to the fast-changing environment for microprocessors (Hof, 1992). The shared understanding of what the core skills are and how they relate to competitive advantage drives team efforts in salesforces, research labs, and the like. Such a shared vision ties to flexible recipes and routines by allowing for the common recognition of the non-linear external changes affecting the core competence, and the quick integration of change in core activities (Eisenhardt, 1989).

The third cognitive aspect of core competence is an integrated understanding of the different aspects of competitive dynamics. The competitive advantages to which core competencies lead is a function of several forces from both the supply and the demand side. Environmental events directly and indirectly impact several of these factors simultaneously (Bogner, Thomas and McGee, 1992). Responses to changes in the external environment must be formulated based on the totality of the competitive situation. These actions require deep understandings of how the various components of supply and demand relate to the core competence and the competitive advantage it produces. For example, a change in the regulatory environment may significantly effect a firm's ability to bring new products to market. But it also interacts with the functions of the firm's research team and the application of its marketing skills, among others. It is the combined impact of the change in technology with all these other factors that will determine the actual impact of the environmental change on the firm's competitive posture. Therefore, maintaining core competencies requires an understanding of the interaction of a change in one aspect of the environment with other aspects of the organization. Kotter (1982) identifies such rich cognitive understandings as one of the traits of effective top managers. Here the roles of shared values and established recipes and routines facilitate the process.

CONTINUOUS LEARNING

There is more to the dynamics of maintaining a core competence than just responding to the environment. Organizations must learn. By learning, we refer to the acquisition of new and unique knowledge through experimentation. Competencies evolve through an iteration of doing, learning and doing some more. Each sequence expands knowledge and enriches core competence. Clearly, this process will occur more often as organizations digest change from their external environment, but organizations which nurture their core competencies tend to continue their internal learning processes even in the absence of external motivation. Indeed, one of the shared values of organizations which have maintained long-term competencies is a belief in the continuous refinement of their core skills. Senge (1992) states that this process of experimentation and improvement is the key to competitive success. For example, Mintzberg and Waters (1982) identified it as the process by which Steinberg Inc. of Canada shifted from a traditional grocery to a self-service operator. Similarly, the late Sam Walton describes his organization's two decades of experimental learning about discount retailing prior to the explosive growth of the Wal-Mart chain (Walton, 1992). The dynamic environment, and the ability to experiment and improve, are seen here as competitive opportunities for the competence leaders to be entrepreneurial—to stay ahead of competitors, not just keep up. The flow of learning from the experimental doing phase to the cognitive traits which make a shared sense out of the competitive market is a critical part of our model in the context of a dynamic world.

THE TOTAL MODEL AND A CAVEAT

The firm's goal of earning economic profit inexorably ties the demands of the competitive environment to the core competence of the firm. We should re-emphasize the point that all the activities which take place in the lower part of Figure 5.1 are still performed in the context of the larger product/market relationship and the pursuit of competitive advantage. The concept of critical success factors in an industry (Bullen and Rockart, 1986) indicates that there are key areas which any firm must address in order to compete in an industry. Indeed, a firm which wishes to earn sustainable profits from competition must address at least one of these success factors better than the competitors if there is to be a basis for earning an economic profit. In this respect the market determines what core a competitor may have. Similarly, firms that have developed competitive advantages in the market have predetermined for themselves which core competencies must be maintained.

This is not to say that purely entrepreneurial activity does not take place. Indeed, the examples of Steinberg and Wal-Mart mentioned above indicate that what is often considered entrepreneurial behavior actually involves the development of a new set of core skills which became critical to success in the next stage of industry competition. Just as no one entrepreneur can create demand for non-existent needs, so too, no firm, no matter how skilled, can respond to major competence-destroying shifts in the environment (Tushman and Anderson, 1987). The very processes set up to handle change and manage core competencies assume some underlying basic structure of demand, and of how that demand is satisfied by the supply side. The core competencies which will retain competitive advantage in the future are built on the core competencies of today. In competence-destroying change those relationships are fundamentally altered. The quantum change destroys any competitive advantages that firms once enjoyed. It is not that underlying competencies have been imitated or that the firm has fallen behind a competitor on the competence's evolutionary trajectory, rather, the change has rendered them useless. The speed and scope of such environmental change presents a situation which is more than just evolutionary, it is revolutionary.

For example, in the 1950s many firms had developed high skill levels in the manufacture and refinement of the vacuum tube. Environmental monitoring kept labs on the edge of new knowledge in vacuum tube technology. As the technology evolved, skills and knowledge needed to maintain competitive advantage evolved as well, consistent with our model. Experimenting and learning helped leading firms push their underlying competencies outward and kept them ahead of competitors. Still, when the transistor was developed none of these evolutionary systems could save the vacuum tube market. Like buggy whips and butter churns before them, they maintained their distinctive skills but lost their competitive advantage. Importantly, no competitive advantage can exist here because no demand exists—because all the skills and competencies built up will produce neither sales nor economic profits. We therefore have to limit the scope of the model to exclude the case of a dynamic environment which undergoes competence-destroying change. (The learning portion of the model may provide a basis for understanding the evolution of newly emerging markets and develop insights into how new skill sets may lead to the development of wholly new firm-level core competencies.)

RESEARCH QUESTIONS DRAWN FROM THE MODEL

The model just described presents some assumptions about the relationships between core competencies and the market. They lead to three more formal research questions to be considered in an analysis of the pharmaceutical industry which follows.

RESEARCH QUESTION 1

The model presented here distinguishes between a core competence and a product/market relationship. We have said that core competencies and core products must address the most basic questions of any business if they are to lead to a competitive advantage: the who, what and how of customer needs (Abell, 1980). When the competence enables a product or service to satisfy some fundamental point of customer need better than the competition it will yield economic profits for the firm. We suggest that how and where core competence translates into a competitive advantage will be determined by how the customers and other environmental factors define the product/market relationship. This leads to the first research question:

> *Research Question 1* Is the determination of which competencies are 'core' and will lead to competitive advantage made by the competitive environment or the firm?

If in fact the competitive environment provides the basis on which competencies can be built, then an industry analysis should allow for a clear identification of the core competencies on which industry members will compete. Stated another way, we should not expect to find any firms in an industry competing on a base competence which is not predetermined by the competitive environment.

RESEARCH QUESTION 2

In the discussion of how core competencies related to competitive advantage we required that any competence be firm-specific. We are assuming that competencies, no matter how skillfully developed and executed, will not provide competitive advantage if they are held by more than one competitor. Similarly, those core competencies which will lead to a competitive advantage cannot be quickly acquired or purchased in an open market by a competitor. Thus, competence should have the potential to provide a firm with a long-term source of economic profit. We expect that only significant environmental change, a competitor's development of alternative skills or failure to maintain one's own competence should underlie a loss of competitive advantage.

> *Research Question 2* How do firms with established core competencies lose competitive advantage over time?

In examining changes in industry leadership over a sufficient period of time an analysis can be made of overall trends in the industry environment and the changes in the competitive positions of individual firms to see if failure to maintain core competence was responsible for the performance shift.

RESEARCH QUESTION 3

A key concept in our model is the role of organizational learning. In the model competencies are based on developing firm-specific knowledge and skills. The firm-specific nature of the knowledge enables the firm to stake out a unique competitive position. One of our key points is that learning is a two-pronged process when related to core competencies. First, a firm must constantly be *collecting* information from experimentation and from the external environment. Second, the firm must be *refining* this information internally—it must develop it to a level beyond that of competitors such that the firm retains its edge even as the competitive demands of the industry change. It is this second type of learning which Senge (1992) sees as critical to maintaining competitive advantage and we agree. This can be analyzed by looking at how firms lost their competitive edge.

Research Question 3 What role do learning processes play in maintaining core competence in a dynamic environment?

Here the interaction between the scope of the change, discussed in question 2, and the speed with which the firm can learn new skills can also be examined.

CORE COMPETENCIES AND THE PHARMACEUTICAL INDUSTRY

SELECTION OF INDUSTRY AND FIRMS FOR ANALYSIS

The pharmaceutical industry provides an excellent industry to use in studying the applicability of our model. First, this industry has been extensively studied by both academics and regulators. These discussions have led to a strong consensus about its core competencies. Second, a broad base for differentiation among therapeutic classes of drugs provides numerous opportunities for competence building and hence situations in which to observe dominant firms rising and falling over the industry's history. Finally, the industry is made up of corporations which are generally dominated by their pharmaceutical units. This allows the researcher to get a clear view of business-level competition largely unencumbered by other corporate business units.

The modern pharmaceutical industry is generally dated from the end of the Second World War. There were, however, many firms conducting drug research prior to the war and some significant products had been developed (Sneader, 1985). These pre-war operations were often greatly overshadowed by the larger chemical and dyestuff operations of many firms, particularly in Europe. In the USA almost no new ethical drug research was undertaken in the pre-war era. The war saw the shift of penicillin research from Oxford, England, to Peoria, Illinois. There a consortium of US firms developed the deep-tank fermentation techniques which allowed for the mass production of penicillin. Armed with competencies in soil screening for antibiotic action (and the fact that several European rivals were reduced to ruins) these firms expanded their efforts in pharmaceutical research. The granting of patents by the US Patent Office for artificial antibiotics in 1948 guaranteed profitable returns from pharmaceutical research. Together these events created firms whose dominant business was the pursuit of ethical drugs, independent of larger chemical of dyestuff operations.

An overall analysis of the pharmaceutical industry was completed first, including an analysis of the 41 largest firms in the USA and Western Europe. In a prior study we have looked at how the relative competitive postures of these firms changed in the US market between 1969 and 1988 (Bogner and Thomas, 1991). The nine firms which make up the primary focus of our discussion are presented in Table 5.1 together with a brief description of their competitive skills. We focus primarily these firms, although the competencies of other firms are also discussed.

CORE COMPETENCIES IN PHARMACEUTICALS

Core competencies in pharmaceuticals have traditionally been based on the skills involved in R&D, marketing and promotion. Our

TABLE 5.2   Firm's/sample analysis

Merck	Fine chemical firm, a few, key non-antibiotic products in the 1960s/jumped into rational drug design to take R&D lead in the 1980s/responded to Glaxo with broader, deeper, detailing/ 'knows' the FDA/ #1 firm in the world (1990).
Glaxo	History of focused research (cephalosporins, Zanax, new migraine drug)/developed 'blockbuster marketing' concept, first in Italy, then in the USA/ #2 firm in the world.
Bristol Myers-Squibb	Two firms with narrower product backgrounds merge to try to match Merck in product scope and R&D focus/have they matched the competence/or do they continue to lag?/ #3 firm in the world.
Hoechst	Largest corporation among top drug producers/deep skill in organic chemistry/source of many pre-Second World War breakthrough drugs/marketing skills still deficient outside of Western Europe/ #4 Rx firm in the world.
Eli Lilly	Traditionally considered an antibiotic house/major shift diversifies sales and products over broader range of therapeutic classes/marketing also reorganized to fit different physician profiles/ #9 firm in the world.
Hoffmann-LaRoche	Once the leading firm in the world/narrow focus on psychotropic drugs and related discovery in 1960s and 1970s/acquisition of Genentech (60%) in 1989/ #11 in the world.
Schering-Plough	Medium-sized firm, but much smaller than the largest ones here/focuses on a major potential product line—interferon-related cancer products/slow to pan out/limited internal scope/ #15 in the world in 1988.
Burroughs-Wellcome	Medium-sized firm/focused on major potential product line-antiviral products/success with herpes and HIV treatments in the 1980s/can this single competence support the firm?/ #23 in the world in 1988
Marion	'Search and develop' strategy not distinctive/no long-term 'distinctive' competence/ #33 in the world in 1988/acquired by Dow in 1989.

research shows, however, that these broad descriptions are much too general. Core R&D skills have to be interpreted relative to the various therapeutic classes of drugs which exist. These classes recognize not only the different pockets of demand for drugs but also the different bases of R&D skills. For example, the skills needed to develop antibiotic drugs are different from those which produce psychotropic drugs. Moreover, these therapeutic classes have shifted in their relative importance in the overall drug market over the years. In the 1940s, and 1950s antibiotics were the primary new drugs. In the 1960s a wave of psychotropic drugs provided significant advances in dealing with mental and emotional problems. In the 1980s a new generation of cardiovascular drugs replaced older therapies.

A second observation with respect to R&D skills addresses the changing character of the research methodology required to identify new drug compounds. Prior to the Second World War skills in molecular manipulation and mass-assay testing drawn from the organic chemistry of the dye trades dominated R&D. These skills retained their dominance until quite recently. The soil screening and fermentation skills of the antibiotic firms in the 1950s provide an alternative research base for some firms, primarily from the USA. Later a major shift from large-scale trial-and-error techniques occurred when developments in the life sciences of biology and chemistry advanced to the point where researchers could develop drugs based on knowledge of how the body's systems operated. This 'rational drug design' allowed for more concentrated research. The increased knowledge of biology, however, eventually led to a more radical change in the 1980s with the emergence of biotechnology as an alternative to organic chemistry as the general base for drug research. A summary of the changes in R&D and other areas of competence is provided in Table 5.2.

Similar patterns of competence changes occurred over time in the area of marketing and promotion. Prior to the 1950s direct selling to physicians did not exist. However, the creation of 'prescription-only' drugs in the USA prior to the Second World War, along with the increased flow of new synthetic antibiotics, brought about the need to develop skills for influencing the physician (Temin, 1990). In the USA the physician occupies a unique position as a gate-keeper who, in fact, purchases the drug for the patient with little regard to price. Through the decades since, firms have built detailing salesforces directed at the physicians which fit into the medical cultures of the various countries in which they sell.

TABLE 5.2   Core competencies in the Rx industry

Competencies in R&D

Technology	Impact and nature	Firms/role
Organic chemistry 1870s–present	Established Central European dye firms through molecular manipulation, trial and error.	Hoechst, Ciba-Geigy: sustained competence in product development for over a century.
Fermentation and soil screening 1940s–present	Established antibiotic firms in the USA. Narrow competence not widely transferable to other drug classes.	Lilly, Squibb: dominant products brought industry leadership for 20 years, then began to lag.
Rational drug design 1970s–present	High-cost drug development driven by advances in biochemistry.	SmithKline, Merck: able to develop drugs, requires cutting-edge research across classes.
Biotechnology 1980s–present	Non-organic approach to drug therapy. Focus now moving from protein manipulation to receptor antagonists.	Genentech, Amgen: specialized, cutting-edge research, knowledge and insight.

Competencies in marketing and promotion

Skill	Impact and nature	Firms/roles
Direct selling to physicians 1950s	Allowed for the effective marketing to gatekeepers in economic transactions.	Pfizer, Lederle: created effective differentiation of products among gatekeepers.
'Blockbuster' marketing early–mid-1980s	Single-product focus of entire detail force and promotion. Effective with narrow product line.	Glaxo: created a new way to sell; through selling, gave blockbuster potential to a chemically indifferent drug.
Specialized selling	Specialized salesforces for different therapeutic classes/medical specialties. More focus with broad product line.	Merck: specially trained and focused units in cardio, hospital, etc.
Handling regulatory requirements	Speeds drugs to market expanding time available under patent for economic profits.	Merck, Marion: of limited value without competence in acquiring new drugs.

However, at least two major shifts have occurred in that dominant selling pattern over the last 15 years as indicated in Table 5.2. These new competitive postures created new bases for the development of selling competencies. Similarly, they rendered older ways of selling ineffective.

Finally, our review indicated a new and growing source of competence: the ability to cope effectively with regulatory agencies. Again this was not always a source of competitive advantage. Only in 1962 did the USA establish pre-market approval requirements. During the 1960s most Western countries established similar administrative procedures for new drug approval. The next two decades saw these procedures become more and more onerous. Particularly in the USA large sums of money and, more importantly, over half of the product's patent life are now sacrificed in order to comply with drug-approval processes. It is clear, however, that significant variation exists in the amount of time different firms spend in the approval process. Firms aim to be 'first-to-market' so as to establish drug-of-choice status and build up switching costs with respect to subsequent entrants. Effectiveness (and speed) in dealing with regulatory agencies may lead to competitive advantages within therapeutic classes.

FIRM ANALYSIS

Nine firms which reflect the range of competitive positions in the industry were selected for intensive case study treatment. In particular, the case studies sought evidence on relationships between core competence and competitive advantage. Based on the case-study observations made here, conclusions about the research questions will be drawn. Recent sales figures for the nine firms are presented in Table 5.3. These data include only pharmaceutical drugs. Note that in the following the universal chemical names of specific drugs are generally used. The brand name used in the USA is often given in parentheses.

MERCK

Merck is the largest seller of pharmaceutical drugs in the world (1990). This is a position which Merck has held for the better part of a

TABLE 5.3   Ethical prescription sales levels (millions $)

Firms	1990 sales[a]	Rank	1988 sales[b]	Rank	1977 sales[c]	Rank
Merck	6365	1	4240	1	1261	5
Glaxo	6063	2	3160	2	621	17
Bristol-Myers Squibb	5261	3				
Bristol-Myers			2010	12	698	13
Squibb			1710	14	660	15
Hoechst	4992	4	2700	4	1882	1
Eli Lilly	3700	9	2090	11	912	10
Hoffmann-LaRoche	3463	11	1940	13	1571	3
Schering-Plough	NA	NA	1670	15	640	16
Burroughs-Wellcome	NA	NA	1340	23	NA	NA
Marion[d]	NA	17	730	33	NA	NA

[a]Top 15 firms as reported in *PMA Newsletter*, 13 January 1992, p. 3.
[b]Top 35 firms as reported in *Financial World*, 30 May 1989, p. 77.
[c]Top 25 firms as reported in *European Chemical News*, 21 July 1978, p. 8; sales figures converted from £m.
[d]Acquired by Dow Chemical in 1989, actual pharmaceutical sales not reported.
NA = firm's sales not sufficient to be ranked.

decade now, but they did not occupy it during the middle years of this industry's brief history. It was, however, the technological base which Merck brought into the industry at the outset which would be the key to their latter success.

Merck was a 'fine chemical' producer prior to the Second World War. As such, Merck did not sell proprietary remedies, rather they sold chemicals and chemical compounds to 'professionals': doctors, researchers and pharmacists. Merck participated in antibiotic research during the war and emerged with streptomycin, an important early drug. Merck, however, gave the patent to Rutgers University and allowed it to be freely licensed (Temin, 1980). As a result, Merck seems to have missed being a major player in antibiotics (which dominated the industry for 20 years). Merck did, however, stick to its skills in organic chemistry.

When rational drug design created the opportunities for firms with broad chemical backgrounds to exploit their skills more advantageously Merck's management seized the opportunity. Emphasizing established skills in cardiovascular drugs and rebuilding those in antibiotics, Merck was able to introduce a string of drugs in these and other areas in the 1980s. Merck's labs have always been seen as their strength. As Merck has grown larger, management of a creative laboratory environment has become more difficult. The questions which are raised about the ability of the firm to maintain its leadership now center on how management handles the dynamics and creativity in the lab (Weber, 1993).

Merck realigned its salesforce in the 1980s to reflect the move toward more targeted selling. Merck's salesforce is the largest in the USA and carries a reputation as being the best trained as well. The sales function is championed at Merck, with all potential executives spending some of their early months with the firm promoting drugs to doctors. Merck is also extremely adept at dealing with government regulators. While new biotechnology firms have had some well-publicized difficulties in gaining new drug approvals, Merck's products move through quickly, retaining more of their patent life.

GLAXO

Glaxo is in many ways the antithesis of Merck, although Glaxo is number two in world market-share (1990). While the company has other products and a promising pipeline in some areas, Glaxo is essentially a one-drug company, namely ranitidine (Zantac). Glaxo has focused on developing a few blockbuster drugs. In 1986 they had only 13 products in development compared to Merck's 89 (*Economist*, 1986). Their global rank has been achieved primarily through ranitidine and their competence in marketing it. Back in the 1970s Glaxo was perceived as a weak firm; Boots even attempted to take them over. They had no unique products and no presence in the two largest markets: the USA and Japan. In the late 1970s, however, they had forumulated a slightly different version of the emerging super-drug cimetidine (Tagamet), produced by Smith Kline & French, now SmithKline Beecham. Glaxo's version is not considered superior on any important trait for the vast majority of users and other second movers were entering the market too. Further, SK&F had established cimetidine as the most successful drug ever, with sales approaching $1 billion annually in the early 1980s.

However, Glaxo had developed a new strategy for selling ranitidine in Italy. Using what they learned there about focused selling they set their sights on the USA. Without a large US salesforce, Glaxo 'rented' the under-utilized salesforce of Hoffmann-LaRoche and put all its resources into promoting a single drug. The results were stunning. Ranitidine, not cimetidine, became the first billion-dollar drug and Glaxo has maintained its sales and profit growth ever since. Since the success of Glaxo's launch of ranitidine other large firms have redesigned their sales functions to mimic Glaxo's techniques. Whether Glaxo has retained a core competence in blockbuster marketing remains to be seen. Glaxo has yet to launch a second super-drug.

BRISTOL-MYERS SQUIBB

These two firms merged in 1989 with the intent of matching the scope in both products and research which is found in firms such as Merck and Ciba-Geigy. Bristol was an antibiotic firm through the 1960s. In 1969 they diversified successfully into cancer drugs and central nervous system drugs. However, by the late 1980s their total breadth of new products did not match that of the largest firms. A similar story characterizes the recent evolution of Squibb. Squibb also was a major antibiotic firm through the 1960s. In the 1970s they sought to branch out and were primarily successful in the cardiology market. However, they too were unable to keep up with leaders such as Merck.

Both firms were facing a permanent future in a second-tier position in the global market. Each had strong R&D skills, but not in all the major drug classes. They were also being pressed by the changes in marketing to build the extensive, focused salesforces needed to target drugs to specific physician groups. The merger of these two firms allowed them to address both weaknesses. The R&D strengths complemented themselves well. The new firm had skills across classes which could take advantage of technological opportunities whenever they occurred in the market. The combination of salesforces allowed for more product and physician specialization. Competencies, however, are built over time, and the merger requires that organizational competencies and managerial skills develop in parallel. We have noted that what makes a competence distinctive is the inability of other firms to quickly build or buy what is needed to match one's strength. Becoming third in the world resulted from merely combining products already out of the research pipeline which held established reputations among physicians. The competitive question for the 1990s for Bristol-Myers Squibb is whether they have the ability to come close to Merck in the underlying competencies of developing and promoting wholly new drugs and in fully integrating their core skills-sets across two diverse organizations.

HOECHST

Hoechst is a broad-based chemical firm with about 18% of its sales in pharmaceuticals. The firm has a very strong base in organic chemistry research which dates back to the nineteenth century. Hoechst attempted to build-up its pharmaceutical business through salesforce additions around the world during the 1970s and 1980s.

Hoechst provides a strong example of the endurance of firmly established competencies. Following the destruction of the Second World War, Hoechst was able to return to drug research and develop some key products, including frusemide (Lasix) and tolbutamide (Orinase, licensed to Upjohn). Importantly, the competence resided in the minds and the methods of Hoechst researchers, not in the bricks and mortar. During the war allied bombers destroyed assets which were *not* the basis of Hoechst's competence. Thus, the firm was able to rebound as a leading innovator. While capital and other limitations prevented the firm from taking full advantage of its research competencies for a period after the war, as long as the research competence is retained, the firm will continue to have a competitive advantage with their new products. As research shifts more toward a biology base and away from organic chemistry, the core skills (and competencies) of Hoechst must change in a relatively significant manner as well.

ELI LILLY

This firm provides a strong contrast to the Bristol-Myers Squibb strategy described above. Lilly has a very similar history to those other two antibiotic firms. Indeed, Lilly was even more centrally focused on antibiotics than Bristol or Squibb. Like the other two, Lilly was engaged in a research diversification program in the late 1970s. The firm notes that six of its top-ten products were antibiotics in 1980, but by 1990 its top ten products covered seven different therapeutic classes.

In the 1980s Lilly added a third wing to its salesforce to target hospitals more finely. Lilly led the world in hospital-setting drugs through the 1980s and it wants to maintain its position even as it grows elsewhere. The larger number of product areas and the desire to lead hospital sales while expanding retail presence is a challenge in competence maintenance for Lilly. As Lilly expands the number of therapeutic classes in which it seeks competitive advantage it takes an ever-increasing flow of resources to keep up with, and exceed, the R&D performances of firms such as Merck, Bristol-Myers and Hoechst in each class. The size of the cash flow available to sustain a competitive position becomes significant here. With pharmaceutical sales trailing the industry leaders by between $1.5 billion and $2.5 billion annually, Lilly has significantly less for a race to achieve and maintain competitive edge across multiple research classes.

HOFFMANN-LAROCHE

Our analysis of Hoffmann-LaRoche (Roche) indicates a firm with good basic competencies in organic chemistry, but with a limited product focus. Observation of the firm's sales performance and the scope of their new drug introductions reflect the slippage of a firm whose competence focus could not maintain its competitive advantage over time. In the 1960s and early 1970s Roche was a sales leader based on their development of the benzodiazepine class of psychotropic drugs. That discovery, however, was, in part, serendipitous (Sneader, 1985). Chlordiazepoxide (Librium), diazepam (Valium) and flurazepam (Dalmane) all became large-selling drugs. In the 1970s these drugs came under severe price pressure from government purchasers, particularly in the UK, and in the 1980s rapid patent expiration brought in a range of generic manufacturers and aggressive price competition. Had Roche nurtured a core competence in psychotropic drug development, then a new line of patent protected drugs would have replaced the older products as the drugs-of-choice. However, Roche had only a limited product range with which to replace their ageing lines. (Recall that the under-utilization of their US salesforce was a key element in Glaxo's launch of ranitidine in the USA.)

Roche was unable to replicate the success of the benzodiazepines, in spite of the huge cash flows and large leads in research insights which the firm possessed. It was not that there was an insurmountable technological barrier in the general environment. Bristol-Myers, Lilly and Upjohn were all able to bring out new, patent-protected drugs in the 1980s which were very successful in this drug class. Unable to match its prior success through internal development, Roche has sought to acquire a base competence in the new biotechnology by acquiring in 1990 60% of the leading biotechnology firm in the USA, Genentech, and then a key diagnostics technology from another biotechnology firm, Cetus, in 1991. Roche's ability to nurture the new competencies is even more a challenge than that of Lilly. Lilly is seeking to integrate cognitive and skill traits. Roche is attempting the more difficult task of reframing the firm around a new core skill-set.

SCHERING-PLOUGH

Schering-Plough is one of three smaller firms which this study will highlight. (This firm should not be confused with the German firm, Schering AG, from whose assets the US-based firm was formed after the Second World War.) In the 1960s and 1970s the firm was very dependent on one product, gentamicin sulfate (Garamycin). Foreseeing its inability to compete against larger antibiotic firms Schering-Plough appears to have sought out a niche position, focusing its limited research dollars on the once-promising substance, interferon. The firm acquired a large stake ($8 million in 1979) in Biogen, consistent with this focus on a leading-edge biotechnology. The interferon market, however, was slow to develop with the result that Schering-Plough produced the worst return to investors of any *Fortune 500* firm from 1975 to 1984 (Steyer, 1985). In the late 1980s the interferon market began to grow from an estimated $50 million toward an expected $500 million in 1996. Schering-Plough continued to focus its research on interferon and cancer treatments.

BURROUGHS-WELLCOME

Burroughs-Wellcome (BW) has a history of making significant contributions to drug research which dates back to the late 19th century. Like Schering-Plough, BW was a firm of limited scope and presence in the global pharmaceutical market in the 1970s. A major focus was a much-researched area which had been largely abandoned by other firms, namely, anti-virals. Anti-viral research was considered to be a research 'black hole' by many firms. In 1982 BW introduced acyclovir (Zovirax) to help control the symptoms of herpes, then the scourge of sexually transmitted diseases. Herpes was quickly overshadowed by AIDS and BW had the response for that virus too, bringing out azidothymidine (AZT) in 1986, a modification of an earlier disappointing cancer drug.

While BW has had other new products as well (most notably they fought with Genentech over tPA, the anti-clotting agent), anti-virals and their research has come to be a dominant force. The sales of anti-virals have greatly aided the development of the firm's overall size, but they still remain mid-sized. Here a new problem emerges in maintaining a successful competence: too much success brings in aggressive new competition from larger, established firms (Porter, 1980). Indeed, the potential market for AIDS drugs has almost all large firms engaging in significant levels of research, building their own firm-specific skills in the anti-viral area in general. With or without success in the AIDS area, these firms will have a stronger base from which to do more anti-viral research in the future. Where BW used to dominate the niche others avoided, they now face a range of large firms pursuing the same competence-based advantage in a mainstream area.

MARION

Marion no longer exists as an independent company. In the 1980s they were regarded as one of the top firms in America by *Forbes* and *Business Week*. In 1989 Marion was acquired by Dow Chemical and its performance since has been disappointing. The reality is that Marion achieved its accolades by being an innovative first-mover in outside drug acquisition. In the late 1970s Marion began licensing products to fill out its very limited product line. Two drugs, diltiazem (Cardizem) and sucralfate (Carafate) were licensed from Japanese firms which had no skills in testing new drugs for approval in the USA. Marion took these products through testing and regulatory approval. They were introduced by Marion in the USA in 1981 and 1982, respectively. Both were great successes, accounting for over

70% of the firm's sales by 1987. The firm boasted of being a 'search and development' company based on its searching for foreign firms' promising drugs and bringing them to the US market.

Marion's competence was not distinctive at all. It was easily copied by other firms. Moreover, many of the firms with whom Marion competed for new licenses were larger, with more experience in gaining drug approval and with bigger salesforces for post-approval promotion. This is not to say the firm had other competitive options. Even in its very successful 1988 fiscal year Marion's total pharmaceutical sales were less than $750 million. In the competitive environment of the 1960s a smaller firm such as Marion could survive. In the 1990s, with high drug research budgets and the largest firms aggressively competing in all important classes through R&D and promotion, a small firm is in need of a very unique niche to maintain long-term competitive advantage.

ANALYSIS OF RESEARCH QUESTIONS

RESEARCH QUESTION 1

With every one of the nine firms discussed above it is clear that the competencies they possess or pursue are defined by their environment. Any competitive advantage which a competence gives is determined not so much by the level of skill as by the market's demand for what that skill produces. This can be seen most graphically by comparing the two niche firms, Burroughs-Wellcome and Schering-Plough. The skills in anti-virals and interferon, respectively, are both first-rate at these two firms. Yet, in the 1980s, BW had great success while Schering-Plough did not, based on the scale of the market demand for the products of these skills.

Breakthrough products should be viewed in much the same way. The skills which the antibiotic firms developed during the Second World War proved to be profitable because of the pre-existing demand for a cure for infection. So, too, the products which came from the European-based organic chemistry firms were based on skills which were pursued because of marketplace demands for those skills in the first place. The sudden rise of the AIDS epidemic and the subsequent surge in research is evidence of the extent to which competencies are built as a reflection of market demands (i.e. demand-pull).

Conversely, the proposition that the core competencies which will lead to competitive advantage can be determined by the firm is rejected by the Marion case. Here a firm was able to achieve some unquestioned successes. However, Marion was not able to make their combination of seeking out licenses and bringing drugs to the US market into a competence. The market for these licenses did not define Marion's skill as distinctive *vis-à-vis* its competition. As a result, the firm was unable to continually replicate the success they had had with diltiazem and sucralfate. This may or may not be the case with Glaxo. When Glaxo developed the blockbuster approach to promotion they gained a short-term advantage over their rivals. Note that Glaxo seeks to outperform its rivals by limiting itself to a few big drugs *and* heavily marketing them with a distinctive marketing and promotion mix. Whether this combination of skills can lead to competitive advantage will be determined only over the next decade.

The tie between core competence and competitive advantage is reflected in the phenomenon of sustainable economic profit. Competitive advantage is the base on which economic profits can be earned, thus core skills must be built, accumulated and maintained towards that end over long periods of time. The more successful firms studied here did exactly that. In the case of Bristol-Myers Squibb the merger was driven by a desire for a mix of R&D skills across the therapeutic classes deemed critical by the market. In the cases of Lilly and Merck this same market-dictated goal was sought through internal development of core skills. In all three cases the future success of their skill bases in maintaining their competitive positions will be determined by the success of new drugs in the market (i.e. the extent to which their particular research-oriented skills give them products which command a competitive advantage).

RESEARCH QUESTION 2

The analysis now moves to firms which lost their competitive status over time. What contribution does distinctive competence and its relationship to competitive advantage make in explaining why some firms lost top-performance positions?

The first group of firms we looked at were the antibiotic firms. In the 1950s these emerged with competencies in a new technology which allowed them to produce products with high demand. Were those products a source of competitive advantage? Here the score is mixed. Some firms, particularly Lilly and Glaxo, were able to develop competencies in developing cephalosporins, broad-spectrum antibiotics which are used largely in hospitals, and continued to develop new generations of products from the 1950s through the 1980s. Other firms, however, were not so successful in continually distinguishing their products. Several firms, including Bristol-Myers, had ended up in similar competitive positions through their research, and their products became close substitutes for each other. The 'tetracycline conspiracy' represents the clearest evidence of the inability of these firms to distinguish their products in the market (Costello, 1968). In that case the firms simply agreed not to challenge each other's patents to tetracycline in exchange for promises not to license the drug beyond a small group of manufacturers nor to compete on price. These firms had difficulty using their initial R&D skills in antibiotics to develop differentiated new products over time.

The emerging market of the post-war era, however, rewarded the development of innovative marketing skills as well as those in R&D. With no technological advantages with which to develop new products, the antibiotic pioneers shifted their competitive energies to promotion. It was at this time, and with these products, that the firms began to build their advertising and promotion competencies. Pfizer is largely credited with the first advertisements directed to physicians. Lederle spent the then-unheard-of sum of $2 million to conduct promotions for chlortetracycline (Aureomycin) in 1948. In 1952 their direct-mail cost alone was $1 million for their tetracycline (Achromycin) (Measday, 1972).

What caused these firms to lose their edge in the 1960s was not the increased price competition which resulted from the end of the alleged price fixing. Unique and distinctive products would be immune to such competition. What hurt the firms was the inability to continue to develop new, distinctive, patent-protected drugs. The dynamics of distinctive competence requires continual improvement at a level which gives the firm a degree of differentiation sufficient to command super-normal profits. A few firms such as Lilly and Glaxo were able to move into second-generation cephalosporins, but the hospital market is very competitive, and in that market the firms were played off against each other by purchasing agents and the use of formularies. Further, as products increasingly moved toward commodity status, the differentiating ability brought about by marketing skills became less and less significant. When the use of generic substitutes in retail prescriptions was eased in the USA in the mid-1970s, the resulting price competition hurt these firms even more. Bristol-Myers, Lilly and Squibb all began more aggressive therapeutic class diversifications, moving their research programs away from antibiotics at about this time. Fortunately, this was also the time that rational drug design techniques began to take over in the laboratory, creating a basis for new R&D competencies. Still, these programs alone did not allow the antibiotic firms to recapture the lost prestige of the 1950s and 1960s. Interestingly, Merck was able to launch major new patent-protected antibiotics in the late 1980s, just as many of the traditional antibiotic firms were diversifying away from that class of drugs. Only through merger do Bristol-Myers Squibb hope to keep up with the pace in new research set by Merck and Glaxo.

Hoffmann-LaRoche illustrates how a single firm can gain distinctive products for a period of time, then fail to maintain a competence. A review of the technological environment for psychotropic drugs clearly indicates that there was still room for further advances beyond the drugs Roche introduced in the 1960s. Further, Roche did not lack financial resources or effort in trying to maintain its competitive position in the drug class. Their research skills simply failed to produce subsequent products needed to replace the benzodiazepines. Meanwhile, other firms, most notably Lilly, Bristol and Upjohn, were able to produce new and very successful drugs in that therapeutic class.

These two situations, antibiotics and the benzodiazepines, provide interesting examples of how competitive advantage can be lost. Many antibiotic firms had their advantages in the therapeutic class shrink as more and more firms matched the leader with similar drugs. No one could either significantly distinguish themselves from the competition or push out the technological boundary through internal research. Alternatively, in Roche's case competitors bypassed the leader with new drugs. In the first case competitive advantage disappeared, in the second it was transferred to other competitors. In both cases there was still opportunity to push out the technological horizon through new product research.

It should be noted how the technological barriers to maintaining a competitive advantage become more difficult over time. This is precisely why competitive advantages can be unique and sustainable for the few firms which can effectively maintain them through internally protected skills and knowledge. When the barriers were low in the early days of the antibiotics several firms made similar advances in skills and competencies. As a result, no advantage ensued, save through conspiracy. Over time, the increased difficulty of vaulting the higher technological barriers allowed only the most highly skilled—those with true competencies—to launch successful new products. In both antibiotics and psychotropics the analysis supports our proposition that competitive advantage which is not based on replicable and growing distinctive skills will not be sustainable over time.

Thus, we see core competence and competitive advantage as fitting tightly into the Schumpeterian system of creative destruction. Firms with a competitive product at one point in time are constantly challenged to maintain that advantage by rivals. Failure to increase core skills ahead of rivals leads to an eventual loss of an ability to earn economic profits.

RESEARCH QUESTION 3

The two prior discussions lead directly to the role of learning in sustaining competence. Two things are clear about the changes in technology, marketing and regulation discussed here. First, the environment in all three areas is constantly changing. Second, not all firms take advantage of these changes. A third point with respect to the technological and marketing areas is also important. Internally developed skills often drive the ability to meet existing demands better. Learning, particularly firm-specific learning, is therefore critical for long-term maintenance of competitive advantage. In the technology area we saw how firms in major drug classes succeed or failed based on their ability to learn about that class of drugs and its underlying biology and chemistry. Recall that we are using learning here in the sense of truly experimenting and discovering. The firms which stayed in the lead (e.g. Merck and Hoechst) were able to pursue this type of learning effectively, mixing the results of their experimentation with new public information to maintain an overall level of knowledge which was inclusive and unique. Others (e.g. Roche) were not.

The importance of staying ahead in learning can also be seen in the smaller firms examined. Burroughs-Wellcome was able to stay ahead in anti-virals for some time. However, one can ask how much of that lead was attributed to distinctive tacit skills and how much to lack of interest by the rest of the industry which considered the anti-virus area to be unprofitable. Only time will tell if BW can continue to push out anti-viral knowledge through internal learning at a pace which allows it to maintain its lead in new product introductions. Time did prove to be unfavorable in the case of Marion. Their first-mover advantages were quickly learned by others and there was no additional skill which Marion could learn to maintain their distinctiveness. In smaller markets, where competition is less vigorous, competitive advantage and economic profits may endure for some time. Yet in the light of strong competitors, a firm must lead in learning if it is to maintain its advantage in the market. Our analysis strongly underscores the role of every firm's ability to learn as a critical factor in maintaining long-term competitive advantage.

We can now turn to an important distinction about maintaining advantage in the light of aggressive competition. Acquisition is not necessarily a form of, or a substitute for, learning. The Bristol-Myers Squibb merger allowed these firms to combine their past successes. But does this mean that the new firm, at double the size of either old firm, can continue to learn in each of these therapeutic classes it now covers? Corporate strategy indicates how a firm must learn if the acquisition is to retain value (Porter, 1987). Buying one's way to the leading edge of technology should require a purchase price that reflects the present value of the expected economic profits which will accrue from the leading-edge core skill acquired. Thus, the purchasers should not receive any economic gain from their acquisition unless they can push out the technological edge further still through additional learning. In merger or acquisition, dynamic learning requires a state of knowledge which will change position, not just possession. New or combined product areas create the need for learning to continue in areas or ways the firm was not positioned to learn previously. Roche's recent acquisition of a controlling interest in Genentech is the interesting case here. Roche clearly would like to push out Genentech's leading-edge core skills; whether its acquisition will include Genentech's ability to learn in biotechnology beyond the skills already possessed is the key. Roche possessed leading-edge core skills in psychotropic drugs at one time too, but they were unable to push out that knowledge further over time.

Similarly, acquisition must not be seen as a replacement for core products as the base for growth into new markets from the existing core competence. Core products lead to new marketplace products because learning takes place in the organization through the building of core products and team-based organizational skills. Over time, the number of product/market interfaces where competitive advantage exists may increase, even while the number of core competencies which have to be nurtured by learning remains the same. Hoffmann-LaRoche was able to develop two different tranquilizers and a sleeping pill, all of which were major products, from its base discovery in the benzodiazepines.

Finally, we note that how well others can copy what a firm has learned clearly limits the firm's ability to maintain competence. Glaxo learned blockbuster marketing in Italy and employed it in the USA with ranitidine, but has it been copied? Speed and efficiency in copying what others have learned once it becomes public is the effective limit on the returns which internal learning can bring. For example, recently some biotechnology startups have been unable to develop skills in dealing with regulators and their products have been slow to reach the market. But have enough firms effectively mastered this skill such that it no longer represents a competitive advantage to a Merck or a Pfizer, only a weakness to those firms which do not have it? If internal learning is the key to maintaining competitive edges and skills, then the external dispersion of these skills so they can be learned by others is the way in which the resulting competitive advantage can be lost.

STRATEGIC GROUPS AND COMPETITIVE ADVANTAGE

Throughout the discussion of the pharmaceutical industry it is clear that the nature of the opportunity to which distinctive competence is targeted changes from time to time. Dynamic strategic group studies reflect these variations across an industry and over time (Cool and Schendel, 1987; Fiegenbaum and Thomas, 1990). The larger study of competition in the pharmaceutical industry shows that there are alternative bases on which competencies were built at different points in an industry's history. In general, the ability of firms within the same industry to choose alternative competitive postures is not new (Galbraith, 1973, Miles and Snow, 1978). In dynamic strategic group studies clusterings of firms are developed based on the patterns of resource allocations of the member firms. As industries evolve, differing competitive alternatives will appear and rivalry is anticipated within each group of similarly competing firms. Thus, core competence and competitive advantage would seem to be most significant in intra-group competition.

We suggest that competitive rivalry can build up intensely within a strategic group as an outcome of the on-going pursuit of competitive advantage through similar competence. Because groups distinguish the alternative patterns of resource allocations across an industry, each group contains firms which are attempting to build similar competencies. These rivals invest in the development of core skills and tacit knowledge over time. They develop resource bases or bundles which cannot be easily changed and which are dedicated to the pursuit of the particular strategic posture which the group represents. If a firm gains competitive advantage it will outperform its rivals. The others, however, have difficulty abandoning the trajectory which they have developed through prior resource allocation decisions. To do so requires the building of alternative core skill bases from the ground up and competing against entrenched competitors in other viable positions. Instead, followers will try harder to win in the group of which they are currently members. The fact that fellow group members are pursuing similar strategies makes them the ones most likely to figure out and copy the leader's strategy or to leapfrog the leader with new competencies. Within-group rivalry is thus driven by the pursuit of competitive advantage through distinctive competence.

Conclusions

Competitive advantage must be based on distinctive core competence if it is to be sustained over time. But such relationships are neither stable over time nor uniform at any one point in time. A core competence must continue to give competitive advantage as the demands of the environment, and hence what constitutes a competitive advantage, changes. Therefore, the skills which underlie the core products and services of the firm must be constantly changing and improving over time via learning. Those firms pursuing similar customers along similar resource trajectory are the ones most likely to push this Schumpeterian process over time.

This process of change and improvement in core skills involves decision makers who need to employ their cognitive abilities to manage this on-going change. Through an interactive process of learning, firms alter their core competencies continuously in an attempt to maintain competitive advantage in a changing environment. Our analysis of the pharmaceutical industry shows that this is the key to successful tying of core competence to competitive advantage in the long term, but it is difficult. Few (if any) firms can continuously maintain the lead position in this process over the long term. In our study we saw different firms dominating different segments of the pharmaceutical industry with different skills at different times. Those firms which consistently built on their core skills and aggressively pursued the competitive advantages that their environment made available tended to be the most successful over the long term.

REFERENCES

Abell, D. (1980). *Defining the Business: The Starting Point of Strategic Planning.* Englewood Cliffs, NJ: Prentice-Hall.

Andrews, K. (1980). *The Concept of Corporate Strategy,* 2nd edn. Homewood, ILL: Richard D. Irwin.

Bogner, W. and Thomas, H. (1991). A longitudinal study of the competitive positions and entry paths of European firms in the US pharmaceutical industry. Presented at the Academy of International Business, Annual Meeting, Miami, Florida.

Bogner, W., Thomas, H. and McGee, J. (1992). Technological forces as the source of industry change: An industry study. Presented at the Strategic Management Society, Annual Meeting, London.

Bullen, C. and Rockart, J. (1986). A primer on critical success factors. In J. Rockart and C. Bullen (Eds)*The Rise of Managerial Computing: The Best of the Center for Information Systems Research.* Homewood, ILL: Dow Jones-Irwin.

Cool, K. and Schendel, D. (1987). Strategic group formation and performance. *Management Science,* **33**, 1102–24.

Costello, P. (1968). The tetracycline conspiracy: Structure, conduct and performance in the drug industry. *Antitrust Law and Economic Review,* **1** Summer, 40.

Economist (1986). More than a one drug wonder. 20 December, 87–8.

Eisenhardt, K. (1989). Making fast strategic decisions in high-velocity environments. *Academy of Management Journal,* **32**, 543–76.

Fiegenbaum, A. and Thomas, H. (1990). Strategic groups and performance: The US insurance industry, 1970–84. *Strategic Management Journal,* **11**, 197–215.

Galbraith, J. (1973). *Designing Complex Organizations.* Reading, MA: Addison-Wesley.

Hof, R. (1992). Inside Intel. *Business Week,* 1 June, 86–94.

Kotter, J. (1982). *The General Managers.* New York: Free Press.

Measday, W. (1971). The pharmaceutical industry. In W. Adams (Ed.) *The Structure of American Industry* pp. 156–88. New York: Macmillan.

Miles, R. and Snow, C. (1978). *Organizational Strategy, Structure and Process*. New York: McGraw-Hill.

Mintzberg, H. (1978). Patterns in strategy formation. *Management Science*, **24**(9), 934–59.

Mintzberg, H. and Waters, J. (1982). Tracking strategy in an entrepreneurial firm. *Academy of Management Journal*, **25**(3), 465–99.

Nelson, R. and Winter, S. (1982). *An Evolutionary Theory of Economic Change*. Cambridge, MA: Harvard University Press.

Ouchi, W. (1981). *Theory Z*. Reading, MA: Addison-Wesley.

Peters, T. and Waterman, R. (1982). *In Search of Excellence: Lessons from America's Best Run Companies*. New York: Harper & Row.

Porter, M. (1980). *Competitive Strategy*. New York: Free Press.

Porter, M. (1987). From competitive advantage to corporate strategy. *Harvard Business Review*, May–June, 43–59.

Prahalad, C. and Hamel, G. (1990). The core competency of the corporation. *Harvard Business Review*, May–June, 79–91.

Quinn, J. (1980). *Strategies for Change*. Homewood, ILL: Irwin.

Senge, P. (1992). Building learning organizations. *Journal for Quality and Participation*, March.

Sneader, W. (1985). *Drug Discovery: The Evolution of Modern Medicines*. Chichester: John Wiley.

Steyer, R. (1985). The great wait for interferon. *Fortune*, 19 August, 50–53.

Temin, P. (1980). *Taking Your Medicine: Drug Regulation in the United States*. Cambridge, MA: Harvard University Press.

Tushman, M. and Anderson, P. (1987). Technological discontinuities and organizational environments. In A. Pettigrew (Ed.) *The Management of Strategic Change* (pp. 89–122). Oxford: Basil Blackwell.

Walton, S. (1992). Sam Walton in his own words. *Fortune*, 29 June, 98–106.

Weber, J. (1993). Merck is showing its age. *Business Week*, 23 Aug, 72–74.

Section III

Strategic Management Practice from a Core Competence Point of View

The previous sections mainly described and analyzed the theory-building aspects of 'core competence'. An equally important matter concerns the application of the core competence approach to daily managerial practice.

In preparing the International Workshop on 'Competence Based Competition', a brief inquiry among practitioners was undertaken in order to assess their concerns regarding core competence. This revealed that, in general, two questions emerge in the practitioner's mind when thinking about core competence: 'How do we identify the core competence of the company and of competitors?' and 'How do we develop core competence and link the acquisition and the development of core competence to processes of organizational learning?' Possible 'solutions' to these questions are addressed in this third section.

In Chapter 6 Hall offers a powerful conceptual framework for guiding the practitioners' perceptions in looking at their organization from a core competence point of view. In the framework he proposes that different classes of 'assets' and 'skills' are linked to different possibilities of building 'distinctive competence' towards competitors. Based on empirical findings, Hall reveals the importance of a number of 'generic' core competencies (as perceived by business people) and points out the potential pitfalls in building competitive advantage on those 'generic' competencies.

Klavans (Chapter 7) describes two methodologies to assess the competitor's core competence. The application of these assessment and 'measurement' methodologies and techniques is illustrated using data from the pharmaceutical industry, mainly taken from public sources. As such, this chapter highlights how 'external', publicly available data can—if properly analyzed—be a source of 'competitive intelligence' from the core competence point of view.

Starting from their theoretical analysis of the field of competence-based competition, Klein and Hiscocks describe and illustrate in Chapter 8 (through the use of case studies) six tools that were developed by the Scientific Generics Group in order to answer practical problems of skill-based strategies, such as: 'What exactly is my organization's core competence?' 'What new skills should we be investing in?' and 'What other products can we make using our existing capabilities?' Their approach highlights the great importance of information technology in the search for and identification of core competence. Suggestions for further development of the proposed tools and techniques are provided.

The relationship between core competence, competitive advantage and organizational learning is discussed in Chapter 9 by Helleloid and Simonin. The authors propose that an organization's ability to sustain competitive advantage requires continual development and upgrading of its core competence, which in turn depends on the organization's ability to learn. It is also proposed that different methods of learning may be more appropriate for different types of core competence. The chapter treats learning, and knowhow about how to learn best, not as a core competence *per se* but as a necessary process for any organization wishing to continually invest in and upgrade its core competence.

In Chapter 10 Turner and Crawford offer a conceptual framework for classifying and identifying the core competence required to manage existing operations and the changes needed to enhance performance. In addition, a number of 'generic' core competencies are described and clarified. This chapter thus illustrates what core competence can mean for a particular company and concludes with comments on the actions managers might take to enlarge and improve the competencies that their organization really demands now and in the future.

Based on an extensively described case study, Winterscheid addresses in Chapter 11 the very fundamental and intriguing question of how the manager's perceptions of existing core competence enhance or inhibit the development of new competence within the firm. Her research leads to the expression of four hypotheses for further theoretical and empirical research and for managerial practice in matters of innovation and new business development. Winterscheid's chapter thus highlights the very important question of how innovation and the building of core competence are or could be mutually linked.

Linking innovation management and the core competence approach of competition is also treated in Chapter 12 by Chiesa and Barbeschi. More precisely, the authors study the implications of a competence-based approach on the content and the process of innovation in technology-intensive firms. Three main points are worked out: the competence-based approach urges the development of a renewed framework for defining a knowledge-acquisition strategy, technology planning on business unit and corporate level should be redesigned and a core competence point of view forces the development of tools and methodologies to assess the innovative capabilities of the firm.

6

A Framework for Identifying the Intangible Sources of Sustainable Competitive Advantage

RICHARD HALL

INTRODUCTION:
THE MANAGEMENT OF INTANGIBLE RESOURCES

Profit is traditionally measured by valuing the difference in net assets at the beginning and at the end of an accounting period. For perfectly good reasons the accounting profession prefers to count as assets only those things whose value has been established by means of an exchange. However, it is possible to take a different view: Baxter (1984, p. 218) writes:

> A simple mind could hardly entertain the notion of intangible assets. In a child's tale wealth is castles, land, flocks, gold—i.e. physical things. It is a long step forward to realize that the essence of wealth is the prospect of benefits, not their physical source.

In a similar vein, Johnson and Kaplan (1987, p. 202) write:

Competence-Based Competition.
Edited by G. Hamel and A. Heene.
Copyright © 1994 The Strategic Management Society. Published 1994 by John Wiley & Sons Ltd.

> A company's economic value is not merely the sum of the values of
> its tangible assets, whether measurable at historic cost, replacement cost,
> or current market value prices. It also includes the value of intangible
> assets: the stock of innovative products, the knowledge of flexible and
> high-quality production processes, employee talent, and morals,
> customer loyalty and product awareness, reliable suppliers, efficient
> distribution networks and the like.

When the stock market values a company at a valuation in
excess of its shareholders' funds, which is usually the case, it
is taking a view on the wealth-creating potential of the company's
resources, particularly those that are not valued in the balance
sheet.

Itami and Roehl (1987) argue that most activities offer the potential
to either enhance or degrade the key intangible resources and that
successful businesses accumulate invisible as well as conventional
assets as they complete each turn of the business cycle. While
intangible resources such as reputation and knowhow are held by
many to be of paramount importance, these resources do not receive
the same formal attention as conventional assets. A physical
stocktake is a major activity in most companies' annual audit. A
regular audit of reputation, or employee knowhow, is a less common
occurrence.

Coyne (1986) suggests that sustainable competitive advantage has
four, and only four, sources. He calls these: 'business system gap',
'organization quality gap', 'position gap' and 'regulatory/legal gap'.
The word 'gap' refers to the capability gap which exists between
the company and its competitors in each of the four areas. This
chapter builds on this idea by linking individual intangible resources
to one or another of the four capabilities.

The resulting framework can be used as a basis for managing
intangible resources; as a means of auditing the relative contribution
which each intangible resource plays in business success; for
communicating a perspective between managers and thereby
establishing the degree of goal congruence, or dissonance, which
exists in the management team; as a means of competitive analysis;
and as a basis for planning.

The perceptions of chief executives with respect to the relative
importance of intangible resources have been determined by means
of a national survey, and the effectiveness of a new technique for
analysing the intangible sources of competitive advantage has been
tested by carrying out six case studies. The results of this empirical
work are reported in this chapter, and proposals are made with

respect to ways in which this approach can be used to formally manage key intangible resources.

INTANGIBLE RESOURCES

The expression 'intangible resources' is not in common use; for the purposes of this chapter it is used to describe the following:

- The intellectual property rights of patents, trademarks, copyright and registered designs
- Trade secrets
- Contracts and licences
- Databases
- Information in the public domain
- Personal and organizational networks
- The knowhow of employees, professional advisers, suppliers and distributors
- The reputation of products and company
- The culture of the organization; e.g. its ability to react to challenge, to cope with change, etc.

Intangible resources may be classified as 'assets' or 'competencies'. Intangible assets include the intellectual property rights of: patents, trademarks, copyright and registered designs; as well as contracts, trade secrets and databases. The intangible resource of reputation may also be classified as an asset due to its characteristic of 'belongingness', and while it may be defensible to attack with respect to libel, it cannot be said to have the property rights of, say, a trademark which can be bought and sold.

Skills, or competencies, include the knowhow of employees (as well as suppliers, advisers and distributors), and the collective attributes which add up to organizational culture. When a company is taken over the acquirer can be confident that he or she has acquired the acquiree's intangible resources such as patents, but cannot be certain that he will retain the intangible resources of knowhow, culture or networks which are people-dependent and which can potentially 'walk away'.

The intangible resources which have the nature and characteristics of assets may or may not exist in a legal context:

Intangible assets which are legally protectable	*Intangible assets which are not legally protectable*
Trade marks	Information in the public
Patents	domain
Copyright	Reputation
Registered designs	Organizational and personal
Contracts and licences	networks
Trade secrets	
Databases	

The intangible resources which are competencies or 'doing' capabilities are:

Functional skills	*Cultural capabilities*
Employee knowhow	Perception of quality standards
Supplier knowhow	Perception of customer service
Distributior knowhow	Ability to manage change
Servicers' knowhow,	Ability to innovate
e.g. advertising agencies	Teamworking ability, etc.

These classifications can be linked to the four generic capabilities and this taxonomy is presented below.

THE DEVELOPMENT OF A FRAMEWORK LINKING INTANGIBLE RESOURCES AND CAPABILITIES

A taxonomy of intangible resources in a strategic context is presented in this section by developing the notion of intangible assets and competencies, and by associating each individual intangible resource with a capability. As we are concerned with the role of intangible resources in business success, the framework will be developed by considering, in turn, sustainable competitive advantage and capabilities and then relating the different types of intangible resource to a framework of capabilities.

SUSTAINABLE COMPETITIVE ADVANTAGE

Companies have sustainable competitive advantage when they consistently produce products, and/or delivery systems, with attributes which match the key buying criteria for more of the customers in their targeted market segment than do their competitors. These attributes will include factors such as: price, specification, reliability, aesthetics, functionality, availability, image, etc.

Any company which is making sales must, logically, enjoy an advantage in the eyes of those customers who are buying from them. It is clear therefore that competitive advantage exists in the eyes of customers, and the 'recipe' of attributes which constitutes advantage in the eyes of one customer will not necessarily constitute advantage in the eyes of another. Competitive advantage is enjoyed by those companies who are appealing to a current, or emergent, majority of customers in their targeted market. In order to have *sustainable* competitive advantage Coyne (1986) suggests that not only do the product and/or delivery system attributes need to be significant to customers, to be sustainable they also need to be the result of a capability differential which will endure.

There are four, and only four, generic capabilities: 'regulatory', 'positional', 'functional' and 'cultural'. The nature of these four capabilities is as follows:

- *Capabilities based on assets.* A regulatory capability results from the possession of legal entities such as: intellectual property rights, contracts, trade secrets, etc. Some of these may be accorded a balance sheet valuation, they are all defensible, in some way in law. A positional capability is a consequence of past actions which, for example, have produced a certain reputation with customers or configuration of the value chain, etc. Positional differential is a consequence of previous actions and decisions. In some cases the defensibility of one's position may reside in the length of time it would take a competitor to achieve the same position.
- *Capabilities based on competencies.* A functional capability relates to the ability to do specific things; it results from the knowledge, skill and experience of employees and others in the value chain such as suppliers, distributors, stockbrokers, lawyers, advertising agents, etc. A cultural capability applies to the organization as a whole. It incorporates the habits, attitudes, beliefs and values which permeate the individuals and groups which comprise the organization. When the organization's culture results in, for example, a perception of high quality standards and an ability to react to challenge, to change, to learn, etc. then that culture is a contributor to competitive advantage.

In summary, therefore, positional and regulatory capabilities are related to assets which the business owns, such as brand names or patents, while functional and cultural capabilities are based on competencies, or skills, such as advertising, or zero-defect production. The first two capabilities are therefore concerned with 'having', while the second two are concerned with 'doing'.

It is clear, therefore, that competitive advantage results not only from distinctive competencies (i.e. skills) but also from intangible assets; these two perspectives can be combined within the concept of capabilities as shown in Figure 6.1. Each capability is produced by one, or more, intangible resource: e.g. a regulatory capability may result from a patent or a trademark; and a positional capability may result from reputation or an established

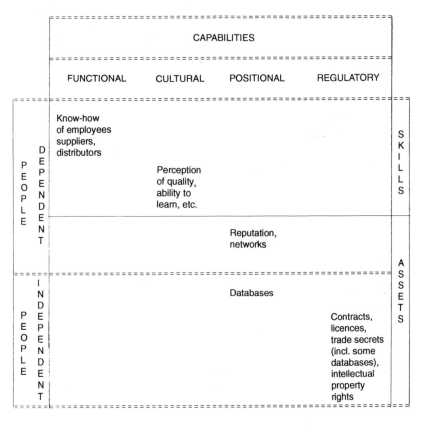

FIGURE 6.1   A framework linking intangible resources and capabilities

distribution network. Intangible resources may therefore be thought of as being the 'feedstock' of the capabilities, and each intangible resource can be uniquely associated with a capability.

The following questioning routine illustrates the way in which each intangible resource may be uniquely associated with a capability differential:

Is the resource an asset? Is it something which one 'has'? Or a competence—something which one can 'do'?

If asset: Is the resource defensible in law? If 'Yes' then the resource is associated with the regulatory differential. If it is not defensible in law then the resource is associated with the positional differential.

If competence: Is the resource a functional or professional skill? If 'Yes' then it is associated with the functional differential. If the resource is concerned with shared values and attitudes then it is associated with the cultural differential.

CHIEF EXECUTIVES' PERCEPTIONS OF THE ROLE OF INTANGIBLE RESOURCES

In order to determine the relative contribution which each intangible resource makes to success in business a national survey of executives was carried out in the UK. The results of this work were reported by the author (Hall, 1992). The detailed results are reproduced in Appendix 1 and a summary is given below.

THE CONTRIBUTORS TO BUSINESS SUCCESS

The intangible resources that were identified as making the most important contribution to business success were the people-dependent resources such as reputation, knowhow, organizational networks and culture. These factors were rated as making a more important contribution to business success than specialist physical resources by a statistically significant number of respondents.

THE MOST IMPORTANT AREA OF EMPLOYEE KNOWHOW

CEOs were asked 'Which is the single most important area of employee knowhow?' Operations was perceived as the most important area of employee knowhow by the CEOs of all sectors with the exception of 'Retailing' and 'Manufacturing Consumer Products', where in both cases sales and marketing was viewed as the most important area of employee knowhow. (It needs to be stressed that this question relates to the single most important area of employee knowhow, not the single most important function.)

INTELLECTUAL PROPERTY

All categories of intellectual property were given a low assessment with respect to the contribution they make to business success. This is held to be surprising as a brand name, or a trading name, is often the tangible embodiment of a company's reputation. If it is possible to protect this embodiment by the registration of a trademark then it would be prudent to do so.

REPLACEMENT PERIODS

The question 'Given a reasonably high priority how many years would it take to re-create the current . . . intangible resource?' resulted in reputation and knowhow being assigned the longest replacement periods. This suggests that, in addition, to making a major contribution to advantage, they also can contribute to the sustainability of that advantage by virtue of the long time it would take a competitor, starting from scratch, to match. Executives took the view that it would take significantly less time to re-create knowhow than it would to re-create reputation.

THE RESULTS OF SIX CASE STUDIES

The companies approached for the case study stage were chosen on the grounds that they would be prepared and able to test the new approach. This criterion meant that all the companies which took part in the study were successful. The six companies involved in the case studies did so on the condition that the results would be confidential and that their identity would not be disclosed in any publication. They are therefore referred to anonymously.

The six participating companies were engaged in:

Motor manufacturing
Manufacture of branded snack foods
Manufacture of branded outdoor clothing
Baking and retailing
Operation of public transport
Supermarket retailing

The average sales turnover of the six companies was US$180 million, and the executive who participated in the case study exercise was either the Managing Director or the Personnel Director.

The interviews were designed to test the new analysis technique based on the framework which links intangible resources to capabilities. The structure of the technique is shown in Appendix 2.

THE NATURE OF COMPETITIVE ADVANTAGE

This section was concerned with establishing the nature of competitive advantage by identifying a 'recipe' of product attributes. Executives had little difficulty in apportioning percentage scores across a range of product attributes as a way of defining the nature of competitive advantage. A summary of the results is given in Table 6.1. The product attribute of 'Availability/outlet location' was rated

TABLE 6.1   The 'recipes' of competitive advantage

	The % contributions to competitive advantage					
	Motor manufacturer	Packaged food	Outdoor clothing	Bakery	Transport	Food retailer
Quality/ functionality	20	30	40	25	5	20
Availability/ outlet location	15	10	10	25	90	40
Image	10	15	30	10		20
Price	20	10		20	5	15
Aesthetics	15	25	10			
Innovation	5	10				
Customer service/ after-sales service	15		10	20		5
Total	100	100	100	100	100	100

first (or first equal) by the executives from the baker, transport and retailing companies—these three companies deal directly with the public. The manufacturers deal through distributors and they rated 'Quality/functionality' as the most important product attribute.

THE CONTRIBUTION THAT EACH CAPABILITY MAKES TO COMPETITIVE ADVANTAGE

Competitive advantage can derive from one, or more, of the four capabilities (regulatory, positional, functional and cultural) but only these four. In that sense, they are exhaustive.

This section of the analysis technique was concerned with establishing the role of the four capabilities in producing a competitive advantage. In making this assessment two factors were considered: the importance of the types of feedstock resources (e.g. patents in the case of the regulatory capability) and the strength of the capability (e.g. the company's ability to pursue legal issues).

The rankings of the contributions which the different capabilities were assessed as making to competitive advantage are shown in Table 6.2. The positional, functional and cultural capabilities were all ranked high by different executives. The regulatory capability was ranked low by *all* executives. This result echoes the low rating accorded to contracts and intellectual property rights in the national survey. It would be interesting to examine whether the same perceptions hold in a more litigious business environment such as the USA.

The public transport company and the two retailers rated 'Availability/outlet location' as the most important product attributes. They also rated the positional capability as either first

TABLE 6.2   The contributions that capabilities make to competitive advantage

Capability	Number of times placed			
	1st	2nd	3rd	4th
Regulatory (e.g. patents)	0	0	0	6
Positional (e.g. reputation)	3	1	2	0
Functional (e.g. knowhow)	2	4	0	0
Cultural (e.g. ability to manage change)	3	1	1	1

Note: The rows total 6 equalling the number of case studies; the columns do not always total 6 due to the incidence of 'first equals' etc.

or second most important capability. Distribution networks, which enable availability to be achieved, are often the result of years of endeavour and it is therefore to be expected that the positional capability will be rated highly.

THE KEY INTANGIBLE RESOURCES

The purpose of this part of the analysis technique was to identify the relative importance of the intangible resources, and to compare them with the resources that were identified as key in the national survey. In summary, the resources that were most commonly identified as key in the case studies were the same as those identified by the survey, but, in addition, 'Perception of quality standards' and 'Ability to manage change' were also often identified. These subsets of culture were not included in the factors offered for rating in the survey. The intangible resources that were identified as key in the case studies and the survey are summarized as follows:

Case studies (N=6)	*National survey* (N=95) Order of ranking
Company reputation	1. Company reputation
Product reputation	2. Product reputation
Employee knowhow	3. Employee knowhow
Perception of quality standards	4. Culture
Ability to manage change	5. Organizational networks

THE SUSTAINABILITY OF COMPETITIVE ADVANTAGE

The *sustainability* of competitive advantage has two aspects; one is concerned with the sustainability of the key product attributes and the other with the durability of the superiority of the key intangible resources over those of the competition.

This section is concerned with the responses to the question 'How easy is it for the competition to match the product attributes that produce the competitive advantage?' A summary is given in Table 6.3. Some attributes were scored more than once; e.g. 'Quality' was scored 'Easy' with respect to the ability of large competitors to match, and 'Difficult' with respect to the ability of small competitors

TABLE 6.3 Summary of the rating of product attributes with respect to their sustainability

	Ability of competitor to match		
	Easy	Medium difficulty	Difficult
	Number of times identified		
Availability	2	1	4
Image	2	2	3
Quality	2	3	2
Aesthetics	1		2
Customer service			1
Price	5	1	
Functionality	2	1	
After-sales service	1	2	
Siting of outlets		1	

to match. Most of the executives assessed 'Price' as being an attribute which it is easy to match in the short term. While price is obviously a factor in the marketing mix, none of the companies held it to be of paramount importance.

The next section is concerned with the responses to the question 'How sustainable are the capability differentials?' i.e. 'How durable is the superiority of the key intangible resources?' The results of the case studies are summarized in Table 6.4. Employee knowhow (of all types) was identified as being of medium to high durability 11 times; similarly, culture (in all aspects) was identified as being of medium to high durability five times; company and product reputation, however, was only identified three times as being of medium to high durability. As one executive remarked, '. . . reputation can be lost overnight due to unforeseen circumstances . . .'

THE MANAGEMENT OF KEY INTANGIBLE RESOURCES

Five of the six executives who took part in the case studies felt that the technique described above had given them a new perspective with respect to the relative roles of the different intangible resources and capabilities. In doing so, the technique acted as a type of

TABLE 6.4 The durability of the superiority of the key intangible resources

	Durability of key intangibles		
	Low	Medium	High
	Number of times identified		
Employee knowhow[a]	5	4	7
Product reputation	1		2
Company reputation			1
Culture		1	1
Ability to innovate			1
Ability to manage change			1
Perception of quality		3	1
Distribution strategy	1		
Distribution network			1
Databases			1
Networks		1	1

[a]The interviewees cited many different areas of employee knowhow; for example one quoted his R&D knowhow as highly durable, and his information technology knowhow as of medium durability. All the subsets of knowhow (which totalled 11) have been marked against 'Employee knowhow' in this table. It was also the case that some interviewees scored one resource high *and* low, depending on the time scale involved.

audit programme. The same five executives also felt that the technique constituted an effective means of communication. It is therefore possible to use the technique to establish the degree of goal congruence, or dissonance, which exists in the management team with respect to issues such as: the ranking of the different product attributes, the roles of the different intangible resources, etc. Indeed, with respect to the issue of the key product/delivery system attributes it is clear that all companies should periodically check that their perception coincides with that of their customers.

The approach may be used for competitive analysis if, having established the importance of the product/delivery system attributes, the roles of the intangibles and the strengths of the capabilities, these are then compared with the competition. How does one's delivery performance and one's employee knowhow in lean production compare with that of the major competitor *and* how well placed is one to maintain the capability?

Finally the approach gives a framework for planning purposes. Having established the important intangibles, one needs to address the issues of: protection, enhancement and leverage. In the same way that one husbands one's tangible assets by means of insurance, maintenance and utilization one should husband one's intangible resources by appropriate means of protection, enhancement and leverage. Having identified, say, a particular area of employee knowhow as crucial to future success then it is prudent to examine the degree to which it can be protected by means of trade secrets, employment conditions, etc.; the degree to which it can be enhanced by means of training, learning by doing, etc.; and the degree to which it can be leveraged, or 'synergized'.

Clearly, managements are currently engaged in the activities described above. The recommendation of this chapter is that the approach can be formalized by means of the framework which links intangibles to capabilities, thereby allowing the same perspective to be shared by all managers concerned.

CONCLUSIONS

The identification of the intangible resources which are the most important for business success has certain implications for management practice. The importance of reputation, whether or not it is embodied in a brand name or trademark, suggests that it should receive constant management attention. Reputation, which is usually the product of years of demonstrated superior competence, is a fragile resource; it takes time to create, it cannot be bought and it can be damaged easily. The emphasis placed on this resource by CEOs suggests that a key task of management is to make sure that every employee is disposed to be both a promoter and a custodian of the reputation of the organization which employs them.

Employee knowhow was rated as one of the most important contributors to business success as well as one of the most durable resources. This emphasis on employee knowhow is in tune with the writing of Prahalad and Hamel (1990) on core competencies. They suggest that strategic thinking has been overconcerned with taking a market perspective, and too little interested in taking a core competence one. If employee knowhow is a major source of competitive advantage there is a clear requirement for the continuous enhancement of the quantity and quality of the 'stock' of knowhow. This may be by training or 'learning by doing'. The modern tendency to subcontract more and more activity does have the consequence of shrinking the area of competence to a smaller base.

It is possible that the 'mobility' of employees in the West means that the resource of employee knowhow is, generally, not as durable as the managers who participated in the case studies believed it to be. It may be that in the future companies will attempt to increase the durability of this resource by changing conditions of service, invoking the legislation regarding trade secrets, etc.

Culture was ranked as the fourth most important intangible resource by the survey. The case studies identified more aspects of culture as contributing to success than did the survey. These were:

Ability to manage change
Ability to innovate
Teamworking ability
Participative management style
Perception of high quality standards
Perception of high standards of customer service

To a degree, culture is a function of the type of activity which the organization is engaged in, to a degree it is a function of the lifecycle stage that the organization has reached; but increasingly it is being recognized that an organization's culture is produced, consciously or unconsciously, by senior managements' actions, and, in particular, by those of the CEO.

Organizational networks are essentially concerned with human relations that transcend the requirements of organizational structure, commercial relationships, etc. In discussing the 'make or buy' question with the Personnel Director of the motor manufacturing company in the case study, he maintained that it made little difference whether they were made in-house or were bought in, as they treated suppliers as an extension of their factory. While this international company was very powerful, there was clearly a high degree of networking between its employees and its suppliers' employees.

We have seen that knowhow is rated as one of the most important intangible resources. Nonaka (1991, p. 97), in writing about 'The knowledge creating company', says:

> The essence of innovation is to re-create the world according to a particular vision or ideal. To create new knowledge means quite literally to re-create the company and everyone in it in a non-stop process of personal and organisational self-renewal. In the knowledge creating company, inventing new knowledge . . . is a way of behaving, indeed a way of being, in which everyone is a knowledge worker—that is to say an entrepreneur.

Nonaka's view regarding the essence of innovation echoes the sentiments of Morgan (1986, p. 128):

> In talking about culture we are talking about a process of reality construction that allows people to see and understand particular events, actions. . . .

It seems therefore that the issues of knowhow creation and culture are closely related. It can be argued that the issue of reputation, the other highly rated intangible resource, is also related to culture. While one's reputation is held by third parties, and pertains largely to the outcomes of one's enterprise, the perceptions of third parties are also influenced by the self-image and self-esteem of the organization—both of which are components of culture. It is unlikely that if an organization has low self-esteem it will be held in high regard by others. High self-esteem is therefore, at the least, a hygiene factor and is probably a driver of one's reputation.

The relationship between the intangible resource of reputation and the product attribute of image is also complex. Image, in the first instance, is influenced by reputation. The image of a Jaguar car—a certain blend of performance and luxury—resulted initially from the reputation of the early models. Once the image was established, the reputation became more an issue of quality, sometimes good and sometimes bad.

These interrelationships and ambiguities constitute the major difficulty which has been encountered in using the concepts presented in this chapter. The experience to date is that senior executives of medium to large successful companies have little difficulty in coping with this complexity; others do not find it so easy. The aim of this chapter has been to begin the process of establishing a new perspective and language relevant for this developing subject.

APPENDIX 1: CHIEF EXECUTIVES' PERCEPTIONS OF THE ROLE OF INTANGIBLE RESOURCES— THE RESULTS OF A NATIONAL SURVEY

The survey was addressed to 847 chief executives throughout the UK, representing the following sectors: manufacturing consumer products, manufacturing industrial products, retailing, transport, distribution and services. The addressees were supplied by Dun and Bradstreet Limited, who made random selections from specified Standard Industrial Classification numbers, with the sole condition that the organizations should employ more than 100 people. The composition of the 95 respondents was as follows: Manufacturing 31; Trading 14; Transport 16; Services 21; Diversified 13.

THE CONTRIBUTORS TO BUSINESS SUCCESS

The average importance weightings across all sectors which were assigned to each factor are shown in Table A.1. It is possible to compare each factor with the benchmark factor of 'Specialist physical resources' and the 95 pairs of scores for each comparison allow the use of the 'Sign test' to determine the statistical significance of the weightings assigned to the various factors compared to the benchmark factor of 'Specialist physical resources'. At a 95% significance level the resources of 'Company reputation', 'Product reputation', 'Employee knowhow' and 'Culture' are identified as making a more important contribution to business success than 'Specialist physical resources'.

When the absolute weighting scores were analysed by sector there was a surprising unanimity over the subgroups analysed, e.g. manufacturers, traders, service companies; independents, subsidiaries; and over the low, medium and high sales performance groups. This suggests that the ranking of the contributions of the different intangible resources identified by this research is predictable for the majority of companies, irrespective of sector, status or performance characteristics.

THE MOST IMPORTANT AREA OF EMPLOYEE KNOWHOW

CEOs were asked 'Which is the single most important area of employee knowhow?' The results are shown in Table A.2. It is possible that operations

TABLE A.1 The relative importance of the contribution made by each intangible resource to the overall success of the business ($N=95$)

Ranking (1 = most important: 13 = least important)	Average weighting (insignificant = 1: crucial = 10)
1. Company reputation	8.6
2. Product reputation	8.4
3. Employee knowhow	8.1
4. Culture	7.9
5. Networks	7.1
6. Specialist physical resources[a]	6.1
7. Databases	6.0
8. Supplier knowhow	5.8
9. Distributor knowhow	5.3
10. Public knowledge	5.2
11. Contracts	4.7
12. Intellectual property rights	3.2
13. Trade secrets	2.9

[a]A benchmark factor

TABLE A.2   Percentage of CEOs quoting the function as the most important area of employee knowhow

	Total sample	Manufacturing consumer products	Retailing
Operations	43	27	8
Sales and marketing	29	46	46
Technology	17	18	31
Finance	6	0	15
Other	5	9	0
Total	100	100	100

is identified as the single most important area of employee knowhow by a majority of respondents because the knowhow in this functional area has a high tacit knowledge content; i.e. the knowhow has to be acquired by experience. In contrast, the knowhow in the finance area has a high external knowledge content, which means that the skills are formalized and transferable, and can therefore be 'bought in'.

The importance attached to 'Sales and marketing' by the 'Manufacturing consumer products' and 'Retailing' companies is to be expected. In both these sectors the sentiment is inclined to meeting consumer needs effectively rather than efficiently: management emphasis is often more on 'What you make' than on 'How you make it'; or on 'What you sell' than on how 'How you sell it'.

INTELLECTUAL PROPERTY

All categories of intellectual property were given a low assessment with respect to the contribution they make to business success. It was possible to identify those respondents who were engaged in licensing, either as licensees or as licensors; not surprisingly, this 'licensing group' assigned a much higher importance weighting to all categories of intellectual property rights than did the other respondents. However, even the 'licensing group' did not give a high weighting to the rights of 'Unregistered brand names' and 'Registered designs'. It is to be expected that any brand name which can be registered will be registered by the 'licensing group' companies, and if it cannot it will not be held as important. Registered designs are probably held to be unimportant by all respondents because of the difficulty of defending this property right.

REPLACEMENT PERIODS

The question 'Given a reasonably high priority how many years would it take to re-create the current "Reputation of your company" if you had to start from scratch?' was also asked with respect to 'The reputation of product range'; 'The knowhow of employees'; 'The knowhow of suppliers'; 'The knowhow of distributors'; and 'Networks'. The average replacement period estimated for each intangible resource is shown in Table A.3. Reputation and knowhow

TABLE A.3   Replacement periods

	Average replacement period (years) ($N=95$)
Company reputation	10.8
Product reputation	6.0
Employee knowhow	4.6
Networks	3.4
Supplier knowhow	3.1
Databases	2.1
Distributor knowhow	1.6

were assigned the longest replacement periods, suggesting that, in addition, to making a major contribution to advantage, they also can contribute to the sustainability of that advantage by virtue of the long time it would take a competitor, starting from scratch, to match.

APPENDIX 2: THE FRAMEWORK OF THE STRUCTURED INTERVIEW

Stage 1: The 'recipe' of product attributes comprising competitive advantage

Price	Quality	Functionality	Aesthetics	Availability	
. . . %	. . . %	. . . %	. . . %	. . . %	
Image	After-sales service	Innovation	Customer convenience	etc	Total
. . . %	. . . %	. . . %	. . . %	. . . %	100%

Stage 2: The roles of the capabilities in producing competitive advantage (CA)

Regulatory	Positional	Functional	Cultural
Protectable in law	Due to previous endeavour	Due to skill and experience	Capabilities of the organization
(1) . . . % contribution to CA	(2) . . . % contribution to CA	(3) . . . % contribution to CA	(4) . . . % contribution to CA Total 100%

Stage 3: The role of each intangible resource within the relevant capability

	%		%		%		%
Trade secrets	. . .	Databases	. . .	Knowhow of:		Perception of:	
Contracts	. . .	Reputation of		Employees	. . .	Quality	. . .
Licences	. . .	product	. . .	Suppliers	. . .	Service	. . .
Patents	. . .	Reputation of		Franchisors	. . .	Ability to manage	
Copyright	. . .	company	. . .	Distributors	. . .	change	. . .
Trademarks	. . .	Networks	. . .	Franchisees	. . .	Ability to	
Registered		Value chain				innovate	. . .
designs	. . .	configuration	. .			Team working	
		Established				ability	. . .
		distribution				Participative manage-	
		network	. . .			ment style	. . .
Totals	100%		100%		100%		100%

Stage 4: The sustainability of competitive advantage

Stage 4.1: How easy is it for the competition to match the product attributes which produce the competitive advantage?

	Easy	Medium difficulty	Difficult
Price	☐	☐	☐
Quality	☐	☐	☐
Functionality	☐	☐	☐
Aesthetics	☐	☐	☐
Availability	☐	☐	☐
Image	☐	☐	☐
After-sales service	☐	☐	☐
Innovation	☐	☐	☐
Customer convenience	☐	☐	☐
etc.			

Stage 4.2: How sustainable are the capability differentials? i.e. How durable is the superiority of the key intangible resources?

Key intangible resources*	Low	Medium	High
4.2.1 _____	☐	☐	☐
4.2.2 _____	☐	☐	☐

*Identified from sections 2 and 3.

Stage 5: The management of the key intangible resources

How should the key intangible resources be managed with respect to:

Recognition

_____

Protection

_____

Exploitation

_____

Enhancement

_____

REFERENCES

Baxter, W. T. (1984). *Inflation Accounting*. Deddington: Philip Allan.

Coyne, K. P. (1986). Sustainable competitive advantage—what it is and what it isn't. *Business Horizons*. January/February 54–61.

Hall, R. (1992). The strategic analysis of intangible resources. *The Strategic Management Journal*, **13**, 135–144.

Itami, H. and Roehl, T. W. (1987). *Mobilizing Invisible Assets*. Cambridge, MA: Harvard University Press.

Johnson, H. T. and Kaplan, R. S. (1987). *Relevance Lost*. Boston, MA: Harvard Business School Press.

Morgan, G. (1986). *Images of Organisation*. London: Sage Publications.

Nonaka, I. (1991). The knowledge creating company. *Harvard Business Review*, November–December, 96–104.

Prahalad, C. K. and Hamel, G. (1990). The core competence of the corporation. *Harvard Business Review*, May–June, 79–91.

7

The Measurement of a Competitor's Core Competence

RICHARD KLAVANS

INTRODUCTION

What if a competitor develops a core competence that seriously threatens the survival of your firm? Will the development of your own core competence be sufficient if you do not anticipate competitive moves?

Existing literature on core competence does not address these questions. Its focus is on the firm's core competence—not the core competencies of others. This assumption might be reasonable if other firms are of little importance. It is dangerous if other firms are capable of destroying your market position, and shortsighted if they can help by forming strategic alliances.

Techniques for analyzing the core competencies of competitors (and other organizations in general) are needed. The two techniques suggested in this chapter focus on the assessment of scientific/ technical capabilities and organizational intentions, respectively. These two techniques are qualitatively different, and reflect a schism in the literature on core competence that is discussed in the following section. Capability assessment relies on 'objective' indicators, intention assessment on 'subjective' interpretation. Each technique

Competence-Based Competition.
Edited by G. Hamel and A. Heene.
Copyright © 1994 The Strategic Management Society. Published 1994 by John Wiley & Sons Ltd.

provides a complementary approach to diagnosing a competitor's core competence.

TRENDS IN THE LITERATURE ON CORE COMPETENCE

The intellectural roots of core competence research are broad. They can be found in economics (Penrose, 1959; Schumpeter, 1934; Teece, 1980; and Winter, 1988), administrative science (Barney, 1991; Selznick, 1957; Snow and Hrebiniak, 1980) and strategy (Andrews, 1971; Ansoff, 1965; Chandler, 1962; Wrigley, 1970). The following review suggests that there is a schism in the literature between technological and institutional views of core competence. The two techniques, described in the subsequent section, correspond to these different views of core competence.

One group of researchers tend to focus on science and technology. The intellectual roots of this group can be found in evolutionary views of economic growth (Schumpeter, 1934; Penrose, 1959). Core competencies tend to be viewed as 'objective' capabilities: such as Honda knowing more about small engine design or Sony knowing more about electronic miniaturization. This definition of core competency lends itself to objective measurement, such as Honda's dominant share of US patents dealing with small-engine technology or the lead time that Sony maintains in introducing advanced miniaturized equipment.

This technological orientation focuses on the ability of the firm to 'create' (e.g. innovate) and then 'capture' (e.g. gain ownership/control of) scientific and technological knowledge. The creation of knowledge is linked to technical entrepreneurship and innovation. Knowledge is captured by the firm in a variety of ways: such as complementary resources (expensive testing facilities) or special treatment of key scientists (GM's relationship with Kettering). These capabilities might also be lost by the firm if venture capital provides funding for complementary resources and/or key scientists are not given special treatment (for example, Noyce and Moore leaving Fairchield to form Intel).

Strategy researchers (such as Andrews, 1971, and Ansoff, 1965) seem to focus more on the scientific/technical roots of core competence than the institutional. Ansoff (1965) is clearly a technologist. His work experience (Lockheed Electronics), teaching experience (Carnegie Institute of Technology) and writings emphasize the role of science and technology. His decision-making frameworks do not *require* creativity on the part of senior management.

Andrews (1971) might appear more balanced because there is explicit reference to Selznick and some time spent on the discussion of values. But Andrews's view of strategy pays little heed to the role of creativity in the redefinition of corporate goals. The formation of goals is stated as a rational choice among alternatives—flavored by non-rational preferences that come into play only after alternatives are generated.

A second group of researchers focus on the formation of organizational intentions. The intellectual root of this group can be found in Selznick's (1957) work on institutional leadership. Selznick was particularly interested in a firm's critical decisions: those decisions that involve choices that affect the basic character of the firm. These decisions require creativity in the fundamental (re)definition of a firm's goals. 'In particular, if a leadership acts as if it had no creative role in the formulation of ends, when in fact the situation demands such a role, it will fail, leaving a history of uncontrolled, opportunistic adaptation behind it' (Selznick, 1957, p. 75).

This institutional orientation, as reflected in more recent work by Prahalad and Hamel (1990), focuses on the response to a fundamental question that a leader must address: what shall we be? This question strikes at the definition of the firm's character. The response tends to be embedded in language and metaphor (for example, the word 'character' assumes the organization is analogous to a person). An effective response infuses members of the organization with a sense of long-run purpose.

MEASUREMENT TECHNIQUES

The two views of core competence described above lend themselves to two measurement techniques: bibliometric (from information science) and psycho-linguistic (from competitive intelligence). The bibliometric technique is oriented toward the technological view of core competence. Emphasis is placed on objective measurement of scientific and technological activity. The psycho-linguistic approach is oriented toward the institutional view of core competence. Emphasis is placed on language statements that reflect fundamental (re)definitions of the firm's character.

BIBLIOMETRIC ANALYSIS

Bibliometric analysis is an analytical method developed in information sciences for quantitatively measuring scientific and technical activity. It involves the quantitative analysis of scientific/technical outputs (papers, patents, proceedings, etc.). These analyses take a variety of forms. As examples, there is citation analysis (analysis of the dependency between articles and/or patents to provide insights into the flow of scientific activity); co-author analysis (analysis of data on joint publications to provide insights into the social structure of research); co-citation analysis (analysis of data on pairs of citations in the bibliographies of articles to provide insights into the structure of research); and co-word analysis (analysis of data on word pair frequency and key work in context to provide insights into the cognitive structure of science).

Bibliometric analysis is particularly useful in the assessment of competencies that are based on scientific/technical activity. It can provide a structure (i.e. naturally occurring categories of scientific and technical activity) and can indicate baseline capabilities (i.e. the revealed strengths of different firms within each category of scientific and technical activity). Bibliometric analysis of upstream scientific/ technical activities (i.e. activities in basic science), the linkage between activities (such as within-firm patent citation patterns) and key words in context (a technique for analyzing language statements) also provide insights into strategic intent.

Example: Drug-discovery Capabilities

The following example illustrates how bibliometric analysis can be used to identify base-line drug-discovery capabilities among pharmaceutical firms. These firms are actively involved in the discovery process. For example, Merck introduced 10 major new drugs in the late 1980s, such as Mevacor (for high cholesterol) and Vasotec (for high blood pressure). The discovery process can come from internal R&D facilities or joint ventures. Merck has joint ventures with Repligen (for an AIDS vaccine) and a vaccine venture with Institut Merieux (France).

The bibliometric model that is used to provide estimates of drug-discovery capabilities was developed by The Center for Research Planning (CRP) to analyze the bibliographies of worldwide scientific/

technical publications. The computer algorithms draw from the theoretical insights of Price (1963), additional theoretical developments by Kuhn (1970) and the applied work of Small and Garfield (Garfield, Sher and Torpie, 1964; Small and Griffith, 1974). Recent improvements in the algorithms have overcome some of the commonly known problems associated with co-citation analysis of the scientific/technical literature (Hicks, 1987; Leydesdorff, 1986; Mombers *et al.*, 1985).

The fundamental unit of analysis in CRP's model is a research community, i.e. a group of researchers who are working on a scientific/technical problem. Each community is composed of current research papers (the papers on the problem that appear in refereed journals) and base research papers (prior papers or books that supply the foundation for the work).

The author requested data on research community involvement for 16 research-intensive pharmaceutical firms from CRP. Table 7.1 provides data on the number of research communities that the 16 pharmaceutical firms participate in and the relationship between activity and R&D expenses. Column 1 is the number of research communities where the firm has a base research paper. Column 2 is the number of research communities where the firm has a current paper. In general, column 1 indicates the degree that the firm is part of the foundational work of others and column 2 the current activity of the firm.

Two indicator variables are calculated from these data. *BASIC* is the ratio of column 1 to column 2 and represents the capabilities, of the firm, in basic research. *CURRENT* is the ratio of column 2 (the number of current research communities) to R&D (the amount spent on current research and development activities). *CURRENT* is an indicator of current scientific activity.

Figure 7.1 is a graph showing the relationship between *BASIC* (basic science) and *CURRENT* (scientific activity). According to these data, Merck has a high level of competence in the discovery process using both indicators. Upjohn (a firm that also appears to have high competence in discovery) is biased more towards current activity.

Figure 7.1 also indicates what others have tended to avoid discussing—firms with low competence in discovery. From these data it appears that Carter-Wallace and Rhône-Poulenc Rorer have low competence in the discovery of pharmaceutical drugs. Glaxo and Warner-Lambert would get a 'fair' rating on these dimensions.

TABLE 7.1   Indicators of competence in discovery

Firm	nb	nrc	rd	bsci	scird
ABT	21	333	567	0.063	0.587
BMY	32	519	881	0.062	0.589
CAR	0	2	49	0.000	0.041
GLX	17	253	694	0.067	0.365
JNJ	53	366	834	0.145	0.439
LLY	61	496	703	0.123	0.706
MKC	26	242	358	0.107	0.676
MRK	127	1039	854	0.122	1.217
NVO	7	72	207	0.097	0.348
PFE	21	267	640	0.079	0.417
RPR	1	93	350	0.011	0.266
SBH	23	308	759	0.075	0.406
SGP	29	353	380	0.082	0.930
SYN	15	269	271	0.056	0.993
UPJ	53	676	427	0.078	1.582
WLA	9	246	379	0.037	0.649

ABT	Abbott Laboratories
BMY	Bristol-Myers Squibb
CAR	Carter-Wallace Inc.
GLX	Glaxo Holdings Plc
JNJ	Johnson & Johnson
LLY	Eli Lilly & Co.
MKC	Marion Merrell Dow Inc.
MRK	Merck & Co.
NVO	Novo-Nordisk
PFE	Pfizer Inc.
RPR	Rhône-Poulenc Rorer
SBH	Smithkline Beecham Plc
SGP	Schering-Plough
SYN	Syntex Corp.
UPJ	Upjohn Co.
WLA	Warner-Lambert Co.

nb =   number of research communities where the firm has a paper in the base bibliography (source: CRP 1985 model).

nrc =   number of research communities where the firm has a paper in the current bibliography (source: CRP 1985 model).

rd =   1990 Research & development expenditures (source: Compustat).

bsci =   nb/nrc.

scird =   nrc/rd.

PSYCHO-LINGUISTICS

Psycho-linguistic analysis is one of the techniques used in intelligence gathering for analyzing decision making in secretive organizations. The assumption behind the technique is relatively

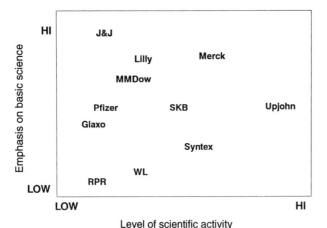

FIGURE 7.1 Competency in pharmaceutical discovery. (Source: Center for Research Planning)

straightforward—secrets 'leak out' through language statements in an unanticipated (and uncontrollable) way. These secrets can be revealed analytically if one can identify the strategic language statements.

An example from strategic management may help illustrate this technique. How can one tell that a firm was (re)defining their character along the lines of 'portfolio investor' during the 1970s? During the 1970s there were language statements that indicated a portfolio orientation ('go for market share'; 'divest from unattractive market environments'; 'cows'; 'dogs'; 'question marks' and 'stars'). While CEOs might not state that the institutional strategy was 'portfolio investor', the character of the firm is reflected in language statements emerging from the CEO ('being number one in all our markets') and divisional managers in low-growth industries ('being milked').

Firms following a strategy based on a particular view of their core competency are supposed to communicate these language statements throughout the firm (Prahalad and Hamel, 1990). If this occurs, one can expect managers to use language statements that reflect the nature of the firm's core competence (Fiol, 1991). If the language statements are considered secrets, they would not be revealed through published material. But even if an organization is secretive (e.g. not communicating the core competence outside the firm), the secrets tend to 'leak out' in normal discourse.

Example: Language Statements of Core Competence

One method for identifying language statements of a firm's core competence is to (1) conduct a role-playing exercise to generate possible language statements and (2) analyze symbolic language from the target firm for the appearance of these language statements. The role players need to be well versed in the history of the target firm and each business in the firm. The analysis of symbolic language from the target firm can use techniques from psycho-linguistics (see, for example, past issues of *The Journal of Psycholinguistic Research*) and/or cultural-linguistics (see, for example, Fiol, 1991).

The following examples are based on analysis done by students at Temple University in a competitive analysis course. Students played the role of divisional managers. Each role player would advocate a different core competence matrix—a different definition of the firm's core competence that would place them (the divisional manager) in a more favorable position if the firm followed this logic of diversification.

The role players were provided with a variety of alternative logics for developing their arguments. The logics are based on techniques for identifying corporate strengths (Stevenson, 1976); distinctive competencies (Andrews, 1971); synergies (Ansoff, 1965); relatedness patterns (Lemelin, 1982; Klavans, 1989); core competencies (Prahalad and Hamel, 1990) and commitments (Ghemawat, 1991).

Figures 7.2 and 7.3 are examples of the core competency matrices and types of language statements that emerge from this role-playing exercise. The core competence matrices are two-dimensional and each dimension represents a different competence. Divisions that draw from both competencies are in the most favorable (upper right-hand) position. Divisions or businesses that draw from neither competence are in the least favorable (lower-left) position.

One set of language statements for Upjohn (Figure 7.2) suggests that Upjohn has two competencies (biotechnology and human health). The students characterized the firm as highly focused (most businesses were close to the upper right-hand section of the core competency matrix). This firm could easily follow a core competence strategy and, if so, might (1) divest the cosmetics business (the health care services businesses were kept on the chart even though this division was divested in 1990) and (2) use language statements about their corporate strategies that were associated with biotechnology and human health.

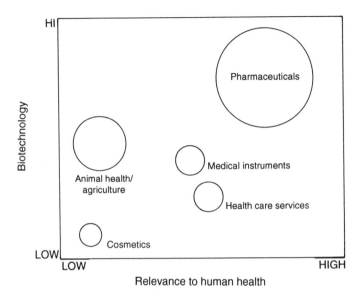

FIGURE 7.2   An example of a core competency map (Upjohn). (Reproduced by permission from Kelly *et al.*, 1991)

In Figure 7.3, Warner-Lambert was also characterized as a firm with two competencies: one centered on pharmaceuticals (which only benefited the pharmaceutical division) and one centered around 'mouth-related' (a characterization by the students of a competence dealing more with marketing/distribution capabilities of consumer products that relied on taste and tended to focus on mouth-related functions). But in this case, there was no business that drew upon both competencies. There was no 'core business', and the students concluded that the firm could not easily follow a core competence strategy. The students suggested that the firm was 'split'. Language statements consistent with this orientation would stress the independent relationships between divisions (portfolio management; short-term financial performance, etc.).

SUMMARY

Two methods for measuring core competence are suggested. The first is based on a technological orientation. Firms gain competitive advantage by gaining ownership/control of product- and process-

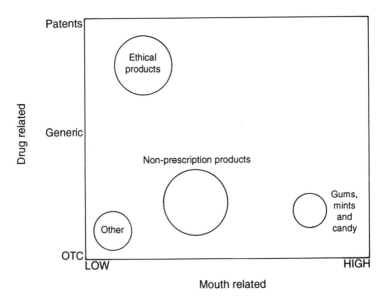

FIGURE 7.3   An example of a core competency map (Warner-Lambert). (Reproduced by permission from Kelly *et al.*, 1991)

related scientific and technological knowledge. Publication analysis is appropriate if the knowledge is 'science' (publication is part of the requirements for participating in worldwide scientific progress). Patent analysis is appropriate if the mechanism for gaining ownership/control is patents. Other objective measures could be used if the mechanism for gaining ownership/control of scientific/ technological knowledge is lead time or learning-curve effects.

The second method is based on an institutional orientation. Top executives creatively (re)define the fundamental character of the firm. An in-depth knowledge of the history of the competitor and the backgrounds of the top management team is needed. A role-playing exercise can generate language statements that suggest what these top executives might create and which become a referent point for examining the language and behavior of the firm.

REFERENCES

Andrews, K. R. (1971). *Concept of Corporate Strategy*. Homewood, ILL: Dow Jones-Irwin.

Ansoff, H. I. (1965). *Corporate Strategy*. New York: McGraw-Hill.
Barney, J. (1991). Firm resources and sustained competitive advantage. *Journal of Management*, **17**, 1, 99–120.
Chandler, A. D. Jr (1962). *Strategy and Structure: Chapters in the History of the American Industrial Enterprise*. Cambridge, MA: MIT Press.
Fiol, M. (1991). Managing culture as a competitive resource. *Journal of Management*, **17**, 1.
Garfield, E., Sher, I. and Torpie, R. J. (1964). The use of citation data in writing the history of science. Philadelphia: Institute for Scientific Information.
Ghemawat, P. (1991). *Commitment: The Dynamic of Strategy*. NY: The Free Press.
Henderson, R. (1992). Flexible integration as core competence: architectural innovation in cardiovascular drug development. Paper presented at the 1992 Academy of Management National Meetings.
Hicks, D. (1987). Limitations of co-citation analysis as a tool for science policy. *Social Studies of Science*, (17), 295–316.
Kelly, J., Price, M., Kaplan, L. and Putney, C. (1991). *Pharmaceutical Industry*. Final Report for BA950, Temple University.
Klavans, R. (1989). A measure of technology relatedness for businesses in diversified firms. FTC Line of Business Working Paper 83.
Kuhn, T. (1970). *The Structure of Scientific Revolutions*. Chicago, IL: University of Chicago Press.
Lemelin, A. (1982). Relatedness in the patterns of interindustry diversification. *Review of Economics and Statistics*, **64**, 646–657.
Leydesdorff, L. (1986). The development of frames of references. *Scientometrics*, (9), 103–25.
Mombers, C., von Heeringer, A., van Venetie, R. and le Pair, C. (1985). Displaying strengths and weaknesses in national R&D performance through document cocitation. *Scientometrics*, **7**, 341–56.
Penrose, E. T. (1959). *The Theory of the Growth of the Firm*. London: Basil Blackwell.
Prahalad, C. K. and Hamel, G. (1990). The core competence of the corporation. *Harvard Business Review*, May–June.
Price, D. J. deSolla (1963). *Little Science, Big Science* (pp. 63–91), New York: Columbia University Press.
Schumpeter, J. A. (1934). *The Theory of Economic Development*. Cambridge, MA: Harvard University Press.
Selznick, P. (1957). *Leadership in Administration*. New York: Harper & Row.
Small, H. G. and Griffith, B. C. (1974). The structure of scientific literature I: identifying and graphing specialties. *Science Studies*, 4.
Snow, C. and Hrebiniak, L. (1980). Strategy, distinctive competence, and organizational performance. *Administrative Science Quarterly*, June.
Stevenson, H. J. (1976). Defining Corporate Strengths and Weaknesses. *Sloan Management Review*, **17**, 3.
Teece, D. J. (1980). Economies of Scope and the Scope of the Enterprise. *Journal of Economic Behavior and Organization*, **1**, 3.
Teece, D. J., Pisano, G. and Shuen, A. (1990). *Firm capabilities resources, and the concept of strategy*. University of California at Berkeley, CCC Working Paper No. 90–8.

Winter, S. (1988). Knowledge and competence as strategic assets. In D. J. Teece (Ed.) *The Competitive Challenge* (pp. 159–84). Cambridge, MA: Ballinger.
Wrigley, L. (1970). *Divisional Autonomy and Diversification*. Doctoral dissertation, Graduate School of Business Administration, Harvard University.

8

Competence-based Competition: A Practical Toolkit

Jeremy A. Klein, Peter G. Hiscocks

INTRODUCTION

This chapter describes a number of structured techniques to address the practical issues of competence analysis and strategy formulation which follow from the theoretical advances discussed elsewhere. Not all business problems are amenable to such approaches, but those that are reported to be amenable include rationalization (Prahalad and Hamel, 1990), diversification (Bakker, Jones and Nichols, 1992), R&D management (Chiesa and Barbeschi, 1992), organizational development (Stalk, Evans and Shulman, 1992), mergers and acquisitions (Prahalad and Hamel, 1990) and core competence identification (Prahalad and Hamel, 1990; Bogner and Thomas, 1992).

The combination of the techniques described here is best described as a toolkit, following the view of strategy as a craft (Mintzberg, 1987). These tools, like all tools, need to be used creatively in each new assignment, perhaps being modified or used in combination with other frameworks, or changed as improvements in theory are made.

These tools will be described, the specific theory behind them explained and case studies presented. The case studies illustrate when and how the tools have been used in practice and the benefits that have resulted. Five tools are introduced here and described in detail later in the chapter.

TOOL 1: SKILL MAPPING

Skill mapping is the evaluation of an organization's skillbase and the identification of key skills. It is the first step in performing competence-based analysis or developing competence-based strategies. Organizations frequently neither know what skills they have nor how each skill compares to those of competitors.

TOOL 2: THE OPPORTUNITY MATRIX

The opportunity matrix is a way to formally identify new application, product or market opportunities for a business utilizing the skills it currently has without making large investments in new corporate skills.

TOOL 3: SKILLBASE SIMULATION

When a company is considering investments in its skills or products, skillbase simulation provides a way of working through the consequences of such an investment in advance. The opportunity matrix is built on a database structure which makes it suitable for simulation analyses to be carried out. The simulation changes the values of selected skills and reruns the database program to see if different solutions arise. It is particularly useful for 'what-if' analysis.

TOOL 4: SKILL CLUSTER ANALYSIS

Though they are important, core competences are not trivial to identify. Skill cluster analysis provides a method for seeing how skills are clustered together and therefore suggesting the constellations of skills which could constitute core competences.

TOOL 5: CRITICAL SKILL ANALYSIS

Different skills will take different lengths of time to develop, and will require different levels of investment. There is also a trade-off between investment and time: it is generally possible to speed up the acquisition of a skill by investing more in it. Critical skill analysis is an approach to identifying the interactions and trade-offs involved in the acquisition of the skills required for a product.

THEORY

DEFINITIONS

The terminological confusion surrounding the resource-based perspective has been described by many authors, including Bogaert, Martens and Van Cauwenbergh (1992) and Grant (1991). The terms in use include capabilities (Stalk, Evans and Shulman, 1992), core competences (Prahalad and Hamel, 1990), intangible assets (Hall, 1991), invisible assets (Itami, 1987), resources (Grant, 1991) and skills (Klein, Edge and Kass, 1991). Such terminological confusion is particularly problematic when using tools, where confusion in the inputs leads automatically to confusion in the meanings of the outputs and invalidates the whole process.

In this chapter, therefore, we have needed to settle on some definitions which, while not intended as final, at least allow the tools to be used and the results interpreted. The notions of *asset* and *strategic asset* as described by Bogaert, Martens and Van Cauwenbergh (1992) are good starting points, but here we also wish to make a distinction based on the level of aggregation. We will use the term *competence* to denote an aggregated asset, following Prahalad and Hamel (1990), in which major multinationals were described as having just a handful of core competences. Thus, a competence is a broad and aggregated resource, and an organization typically has only a few competences.

Other researchers have identified more specific—and therefore more numerous—aspects of firms, particularly their technologies (Klein, Edge and Kass, 1991; Miyazaki, 1991). We denote these as *skills*. An organization may have hundreds of skills, each one being narrowly defined and disaggregated.

Having defined competence and skill, we now need to define types of competence and skill which have special significance for a firm, those which are strategic in the sense outlined by Bogaert, Martens and Van Cauwenbergh (1992). We follow Prahalad and Hamel's definition: a *core competence* is one that has wide applicability, contributes to perceived customer benefit and is difficult to imitate.

At the disaggregated level some skills are more critical than others. We have found the concept of a strategic skill to be useful. A *strategic skill* is one which underpins the advantage of a company's products in the market.

THE PRINCIPLE OF LAYERED CAUSALITY

Firms may be represented as layers of skills and attributes, each layer being causally linked to the next.

Theories of resource-based competition have generally been single-layer. In the principle of layered causality, the thinking is extended to multi-layer theories. *Single-layer theories* assert a correlation between the possession of a strategic asset to performance in business, as shown in the influence diagram in Figure 8.1. Examples of this concept of causality from papers in this field include:

- Canon's success in the photocopier market being explained by its possession of 'core competences' in precision mechanics, fine optics and microelectronics (Prahalad and Hamel, 1990)
- Wal-Mart's success in discount retailing being explained by its possession of certain 'capabilities' (Stalk, Evans and Shulman, 1992).

Strategic assets can be of different types (Grant, 1991; Bogaert, Martens and Van Cauwenbergh, 1992; Turner and Crawford, 1992). Some are all-purpose, others are situation-bound, some are knowledge-based, others are activity-based; some are individual centred, others are organizational; some are tangible, others are

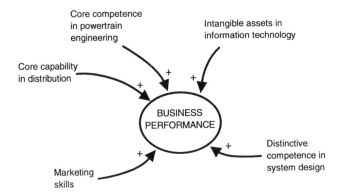

FIGURE 8.1   Example influence diagram for single-layer theories of resource-based competition

intangible; some are long-term, taking years to build up, others are almost ephemeral. This diversity of resource types is not generally recognized in single-layer models, and indeed, there is debate about precisely which sort of strategic asset should be modelled (Figure 8.1). The debate is occurring because too much is being collapsed into a single layer, resulting in inconsistencies and confusion.

To tackle this problem, *two-layer theories* recognize two types of strategic asset. It was suggested in an earlier paper (Klein, Edge and Kass, 1991) that a two-stage approach to causality could be taken, whereby a special class of skills called 'meta-skills' govern the way in which a firm acquires and deploys skills. The paper asserted that at least four fundamental meta-skills exist:

1. *Learning*: The process of building up an organization's skills from those which are used in a dedicated way in projects is a learning process. It involves pulling together the experiences gained in individual projects, recognizing the common themes and organizing them both intellectually and institutionally for future use. This is a narrower definition of learning than is often found in business literature. As an example consider a company that finds that in the course of a number of recent product development programmes, computerized project planning tools were successfully used to speed up the development process. Because of these experiences, the company sets up a working party to evaluate the computer packages and recommend which one should be used in future projects. Having made the decision, the company holds workshops to educate its staff in how to use

the package, and creates an in-house support team. In this example of learning, the company has been able to abstract from experiences, come to a conclusion and institutionalize the result.

2. *Innovating*: The process of using skills in creative ways is the essence of innovation. Often it involves applying skills in new combinations, making links across and between skills boundaries, making links that competitors either do not see or see but cannot achieve. Consider, for example, a company which has built up a skill in an aspect of electronics in one part of its business. One of the experts in this aspect of electronics happens to hear of an unsolved technical problem in another part of the company and realizes that the branch of electronics in which his part of the company is expert can be used to solve the problem. He is encouraged to transfer between the two divisions, and this results in a product being launched which is the first to use this type of electronics. This is an example of corporate innovation.

3. *Skill categorizing*: Combining and structuring a forward-looking set of skills is a crucial and creative process. Skill categorizing governs how an organization learns, how it distinguishes its own world view from the received wisdom of the outside world. Examples of skill categorizing occur in all fields where technologies are converging or diverging. In the computing industry, not all companies realized that communications was converging with computing. Those that did, and organized to take maximum advantage of the convergence, were at an advantage to those that maintained an organization which impeded the synergy of the converging technologies. Companies which ensure that they track the evolution of the technologies they use are more likely to be good at the skill-categorizing meta-skill than those that do not.

4. *Embedding*: Organizations must find ways to preserve skills to prevent their leakage. Leakage occurs through staff turnover, through teams being broken up and dispersed, through facilities falling into disrepair and through skills and knowledge simply being forgotten. Leakage can never be prevented totally, but it can be slowed by policies which limit staff turnover and by the documentation of procedures so that they are not dependent on oral transmission.

This more complex view of causality is consistent with the concepts of system dynamics, with its close attention to the nature of causality within a business situation (Senge, 1990).

Subsequent work has suggested that *multi-layer theories* are required in order to define more precisely the causal processes. It appears probable that there is another type of skill underlying these four meta-skills which may be called the *time orientation meta-skill*. This is the most fundamental meta-skill of all because it governs the way in which an organization balances its current needs and its prospective future needs. The tension between present and future has been noted by Leonard-Barton (1992, p. 111) and Turner and Crawford (1992). If markets and companies were static, competition would have ensured that each organization would be perfectly focused around its operational objectives. However, because firms exist in a dynamic disequilibrium with one another, and there are any number of exogenous influences, it is necessary for companies to defocus themselves from purely static efficiency in order to cater for the future.

A common defocusing activity is research and development. By its nature, it does not benefit current products; it is always a cost. However, without some form of R&D, a company would find its products becoming outdated in the marketplace. It is generally appreciated that either too much or too little R&D leads to corporate decline: achieving a balance is governed by the firm's time orientation meta-skill.

There are many other manifestations of the time orientation meta-skill. Organizational designs which are too statically focused will fail to allow enough slack to enable future-oriented activities to take place. Thus, many of the old machine bureaucracies were so focused on achieving static efficiency (mainly through economies of scale) that they failed organizationally to read and respond to critical signals from the environment, and suffered as a result.

The four meta-skills are all dependent on the time orientation meta-skill. Innovation and learning are both concerned with developing strategic assets for the future. Skill structuring is a matter of developing and implementing a taxonomy of skills which is neither so forward-looking as to be inefficient to apply in the present nor so static as to be a constraint. Skill embedding is the mechanism whereby skills are transmitted from the present to the future.

This approach therefore implies a layered model in which the flow of causality is as shown in Figure 8.2. More generally, firms can be seen in their environment as layers of attributes. (The term 'attribute' includes all layers of the diagram—skills, meta-skills, products, etc.) Each layer affects the behaviour of the next layer in the chain. For example, meta-skills affect the way in which skills

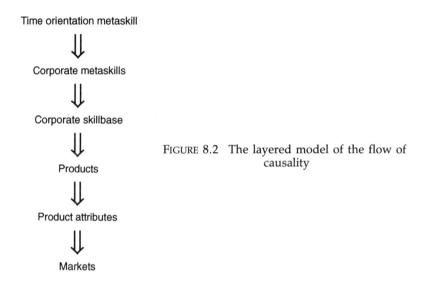

Time orientation metaskill

Corporate metaskills

Corporate skillbase

Products

Product attributes

Markets

FIGURE 8.2   The layered model of the flow of causality

are acquired. There are additional inputs into each layer, so a firm's meta-skills do not determine absolutely the skills it will have, but they do determine the way in which the firm will behave if a management decision to acquire a particular new skill is made.

The earlier in the chain of causality an attribute occurs, the wider its potential influence. Thus, the extent to which an organization is able to learn has ramifications for all its activities, whereas whether or not it has a particular skill is likely to affect a relatively small number of products. The deeper attributes are also slower to change, compared with the more superficial attributes. This ordering of attributes in sequence of their speed of change is because slow-to-change attributes must influence fast-to-change ones rather than the other way round, in the same way that climate can influence weather but weather cannot influence climate.

THE DATABASE MODELLING PRINCIPLE

A relational database can be used to model the causal relationships between layers of attributes.

A particular type of computer database—a relational database—is most suited to modelling the causal relationships between layers of attributes. A detailed understanding of relational databases is not necessary to understand this chapter, but a few key concepts are useful. While all databases allow data to be held and accessed, a relational database also allows the links between different data sets to be expressed and manipulated easily. Furthermore, a relational database overcomes the frequently encountered problem in strategy analysis that only two dimensions of a business decision can be drawn on paper.

The database approach may be understood using a simple example of the relationship between technological skills and the products that can be made using those skills. Consider two technical skills: say, 'electronic engineering' and 'mechanical engineering'. A company can possess these skills to various degrees, from 'no capability' to 'world-class'. A pair of axes can be set up and onto these axes, both products and companies can be positioned. First, the products. To develop and produce industrial robots requires high skill levels in both electronic and mechanical engineering. Local area computer networks, on the other hand, require electronic and not mechanical engineering skills; and materials handling systems require skills in mechanical engineering but not electronic. These products are plotted in Figure 8.3.

Now companies can be added. Each company can be plotted according to the skills it possesses. Any product which is enclosed by the rectangle from the skill point to the origin can plausibly

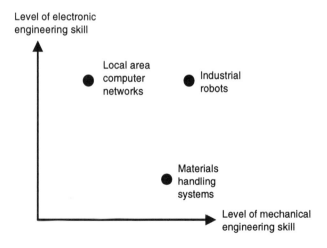

FIGURE 8.3 Products plotted on a two-dimensional skill diagram

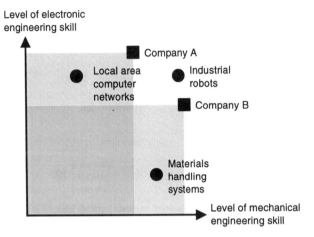

FIGURE 8.4   Products and companies plotted on a two-dimensional skill diagram

be produced. These are the shaded areas in Figure 8.4. For the two companies plotted, the overlapping area will contain the products for which they are directly in competition. Using this diagram, it is possible to:

1. Determine which products could be made by a company.
2. Determine potential competitors by virtue of their skillbase.
3. See the effect of combining skills, either across divisions of a company or between companies, in a joint venture or acquisition.
4. Show what skills need to be built up in order to access particular product sectors.
5. Show which skills are most cost-effectively built up.

These questions can be answered easily when there are just two skills under consideration, but in practice, it is necessary to take account of tens of skills, each one defined narrowly, for example: 'high-speed digital switching engineering'. This means that rather than having two axes, as in the figure, many tens are necessary. It is not possible to physically represent more than three axes, so to manage and manipulate these data an alternative approach is required. A computer database is configured so that it performs analogous calculations to the ones described. This is done when using the opportunity matrix and skill-simulation tools described in the next section.

More generally, the underlying theory assumes that each layer of attributes defines its own vector space. A vector space is a formal mathematical concept in which each axis is one component of a vector. Thus, in a vector space defined by skills, different companies can be represented by different vectors according to their different skill profiles. Figure 8.4 is a two-dimensional vector space, but vector spaces can have unlimited dimensions.

The idea of representing business characteristics in vector spaces was exploited powerfully by Lancaster (1971), in which he represented products as bundles of characteristics. Lancaster argued that the behaviour of a product in the market (one vector space) was related to its representation in another (characteristics space).

Vector spaces can be related to each other by mathematical operations known as transforms. These take the data from one vector space and project them forward into another. These transforms can easily be set up in a relational database. Thus, the causality implied by the layers of causality can be represented in vector spaces and made operational by a relational database.

THE TOOLKIT

TOOL 1: SKILL MAPPING

Description

Skill mapping is the evaluation of an organization's skillbase and the identification of strategic skills. It is an essential first step in performing competence-based analysis or developing competence-based strategies, since organizations frequently neither know what skills they have nor how each skill compares to those of competitors, nor which skills are key to the commercial success of the organization's products.

Although organization charts will provide some information on skill grouping, they frequently fail to identify all the skills in a business and rarely focus on strategic skills. For these reasons, the identification of an organization's skillbase is itself a skilled activity.

There are three stages to skill mapping. The first is to identify the individual skills an organization has, the second is to benchmark their degree of excellence and the third is to determine which ones are key to competitive advantage. Skill mapping is a precursor to the use of the other tools.

Method—Stage 1

The purpose of stage 1 is to develop a list (or taxonomy) of an organization's skills. An important consideration in this task is the level of aggregation used. If the skills are all too specific and disaggregated, then the list becomes long and uninformative; if the skills are too aggregated, then the list is short and equally uninformative. The most useful skill maps are those which are tailored to the particular organization rather than being generic. To create such skill maps requires four sources to be used:

1. The skills highlighted in the organizational structure; for example, if an organization has a 'market research' department then it is almost certain to have market research skills.
2. Skills which are identified during interviews with relevant staff members, or in large organizations, with group leaders or department heads.
3. The skills evident in the organization's products and services.
4. The skills evident to customers and market watchers.

The skills highlighted in the organizational structure are used as the starting point. They are then supplemented using fieldwork interviews within the organization; skills are frequently discovered which are not explicitly recognized in the organizational structure.

Next, the product characteristics which provide competitive or market-beating features are identified. For example, if a particular company's products are more reliable than those of competitors, it indicates that skills exist within the organization to provide the superior reliability.

Finally, detailed discussion with customers in the marketplace about the important features of a product will give further data about the product characteristics that provide long-term competitive advantage and the skills of the organization.

At the end of this stage a set of skills will have been identified which are required generically for the company's products, recognized in the organization, required specifically for important product features, or perceived by the market.

Method—Stage 2

The second stage is to benchmark each skill. We have argued previously (Klein, Edge and Kass, 1991) that corporate skills are not identical to individual skills but rather, are a systemic property which arises from human resources, from capital equipment and from organizational structure and culture. Leonard-Barton (1992) takes a similar view, arguing that core capabilities have four dimensions, namely technical systems, managerial systems, skills and knowledge, and values/norms. Thus, skill benchmarking requires these several factors to be independently investigated. This is done by interviewing within the organization, identifying capital equipment, looking at culture and management control systems, evaluating intellectual property, comparing product features with competitors' products, and by speaking with industry watchers. Only where a company has the people, the resources and the culture necessary for a skill can it be judged as having that skill. It is effective to use a five-point scale to record the results of the evaluation:

1. No capability
2. Some capability
3. Reasonable capability
4. Strong capability
5. World-leading capability

If the skills are in different parts of the organization, then it is desirable to collect the skill information separately for each part. This leads to Table 8.1.

Method—Stage 3

The final stage is to determine which skills are strategic, as shown in Table 8.2. The skill axis is on the left-hand side and other columns incorporate the importance of each skill to the capabilities of products

TABLE 8.1   Skill table showing divisional capability levels and the maximum capability

Skill		Skill capability levels	
	Maximum	Division A	Division B
Skill 1	1	1	1
Skill 2	5	5	2
Skill 3	4	1	4
. . .			
Skill n	4	4	1

TABLE 8.2   Identifying strategic skills

Skill	Maximum skill capability level	Importance to products	Importance to markets
Skill 1	1	Low	Low
Skill 2	5	Low	Low
Skill 3	4	High	Low
. . .	. . .	. . .	. . .
Skill n	4	Low	High

and to the marketplace. The 'strategic skills' are those which are the strongest (the 4s and 5s) and also particularly important to the competitive advantage of the company, reflected in its products or the market. The table shows that skills 3 and n are strategic skills by virtue of their importance.

Outputs

The skill axis and capability scores, once complete, are precursors to other tools described in this chapter. The identification of strategic skills provides a basis for opportunity development. These ideas are illustrated by the case study.

Case Study: Kollmorgen EO

Kollmorgen EO is a company whose business was focused almost exclusively on defence systems; its products were submarine periscopes, vehicle gunsights and infra-red imagers. In the early 1990s, Kollmorgen wanted to diversify away from defence and to identify new business opportunities in the commercial sector. Skill mapping was used to determine the key areas of competitive strength within Kollmorgen, and this was the basis for identifying new business.

The first stage was to identify the skill areas in Kollmorgen. Kollmorgen has a relatively compact development and engineering group so it was feasible to interview all members of staff. The products were studied, and selected customers were interviewed. This process highlighted 34 technical skill areas within the company—rather more than the Kollmorgen managers had originally imagined. The second stage was to score them on the 1 to 5 scale.

It was found that there were three skills at levels 4 and 5. These were 'analogue and digital circuit board design', 'diamond machining' and 'opto-electromechanical integration'. The third stage was to determine which of these skills was strategic. Although Kollmorgen had excellent diamond machining skills that were important in producing the optical components in their products, the market opportunity for this skill in other areas was limited. Analogue and digital circuit board design, while relevant to the company's products, are commodity skills which do not require world-class excellence in the markets in which Kollmorgen operates. Opto-electromechanical integration, however, was important to almost all of the product range, and was perceived by the market to deliver performance benefits relative to competitors' products. This is shown in Table 8.3. It was concluded that the key technical skill within Kollmorgen was opto-electromechanical integration.

This suggested that the skill on which future businesses should be built was opto-electromechanical integration, possibly by designing and manufacturing small integrated opto-electromechanical devices for civil markets. This led to a joint development with a Japanese company to design and manufacture a novel type of printing and scanning engine for high-end printing machines and, potentially, for office laser printers. Thus, skill mapping had enabled Kollmorgen to stretch beyond the confines of its defence markets, yet retain its competitive advantage. This result may not have occurred if more traditional strategy approaches were followed because the end market was so far from Kollmorgen's previous experience.

TABLE 8.3 Identifying Kollmorgen's strategic skills

Skill	Maximum skill capability level	Importance to products	Importance to markets
Analogue and digital circuit board design	4	Low	Low
Diamond machining	5	Low	Low
Opto-electromechanical integration	5	High	High

TOOL 2: THE OPPORTUNITY MATRIX

Description

The opportunity matrix is a technique which will formally identify new application, product or market opportunities for a business utilizing the skills it currently has without making large investments in new corporate skills. It is valuable in making diversification decisions, particularly in large companies which find it difficult to decide the feasibility and priority of opportunities. It does this using the database modelling principle. The database compares the skills available within the organization with the skills necessary to address specific applications and yields an accurate list of potential opportunities.

Method—Stage 1

The first stage is to define the skills axis and score the organization's skills. This is achieved using skill mapping (as described above in Tool 1). The axis is then entered into a computer database. This can be a truly relational database such as dBase or Paradox, or on a spreadsheet with a database facility, such as Excel or Lotus 123, in which relational features can be simulated.

Method—Stage 2

The second stage is to define the product axis. The products will not only be in markets the company already addresses, but also, in new markets that, *prima facie*, have similar skill requirements. Each product is then scored for the level of each skill required in order to produce and market the product effectively. The same five-point scale is used:

1. No capability required
2. Some capability required
3. Reasonable capability required
4. Strong capability required
5. World-leading capability required.

Method—Stage 3

The final stage of using the opportunity matrix is the analysis of opportunities. For this stage, the database is programmed to select those opportunities where the skills of the business are greater than, or equal to, those required for the product. This threshold relationship between products and skills is mathematically equivalent to the shaded rectangles of Figure 8.4. It can also identify products which can 'nearly' be addressed by using a suitable relationship in the database. For example, the database could be programmed to identify products where no more than two skills are just one unit too short. These opportunities could be addressed with relatively low levels of investment.

Outputs

The opportunities identified in this way are latent products in that they could be produced using the existing skillbase. The reason that the products are not currently being produced may be due to the firm's failure to realize it had the potential, or could be through a conscious decision not to. Alternatively, it could be due to the skills being separated organizationally so that a process of reorganization would be required to bring the skills together.

Case Study: Engelhard

The opportunity matrix has been used to identify new opportunities for many companies, including ICI Electronics, ICI Advanced Materials, Engelhard, and GAF Corporation. This case study describes the process and some of the detail as applied to Engelhard.

Engelhard is a specialty chemicals company with a leading market position in precious metal catalysts. The requirement was to find new business development opportunities for the company's existing skillbase. Engelhard was particularly keen to find opportunities in the environmental field, but it did not want to make substantial new investments in technology skills.

The first stage was to analyse the skills and levels of these skills within relevant parts of Engelhard. These skills were mapped in accordance with the skill mapping process, and were scored (Tool 1).

TABLE 8.4 Engelhard's main skill categories

Chemistry	Chemical Processes	Management
Fundamentals	Reactions	Marketing
Material types	Separations	Finance
Chemical engineering	Materials handling	Organization
	Mass transfer	Legal

The skills identified were principally technical; however, other areas such as marketing, distribution and finance were also included. The major skill categories are shown in Table 8.4; each of these was further sub-divided in order to be scored. This analysis produced about 120 skill areas within Engelhard Environmental Division and Central R&D relating to environmental opportunities, each of which was scored to show Engelhard's skill level.

The next stage was to determine the products that should be considered when looking at new opportunities. These were drawn not only from market areas currently addressed, such as automotive emission catalysts, but also from those that use similar skills: for example, nitrogen oxide removal from power station flue gases. Each of these sectors was considered in detail, and the result was a product axis with some 180 products (including services) relating to environmental opportunities. This led to a database with 180 products and 120 skills.

The next step was to score the level of each skill necessary for each product. The criterion used for scoring was the level of skill that would be required to be competitive. The result was a 180 by 120 opportunity matrix for Engelhard Environmental Division and a portion of this matrix is shown in Figure 8.5.

The final stage was to determine which of these opportunities could be addressed by Engelhard using its current skills. The database was programmed to compare the company's skill scores with those in the opportunity matrix (Figure 8.5), and where Engelhard's skill levels were as high, or higher, than the skills necessary for an opportunity, to highlight the opportunity. In this case, the opportunity matrix identified 15 out of the original 180 product areas that Engelhard was not addressing but by virtue of its skillbase, could address.

Clearly, skills are not the only criteria by which a company decides to invest in new opportunities. The 15 opportunities were also subjected to assessments of market attractiveness and strategic fit. This yielded two new opportunities that were attractive to the

SKILLS / APPLICATIONS	Fundamentals							Chemical Processes: Separation Technology						
	Organic	Inorganic	Physical	Catalyst	Analytical	Surface chemical	Electrochemical	Distillation	Fractionation	Crystallization	Evaporation	Condensation	Filtration	Centrifugation
Air pollution control														
• Three-way automotive catalysts	3	5	5	5	4	5	1	1	1	3	1	3	1	1
• Diesel particulate traps	3	5	3	5	4	3	1	1	1	1	1	1	5	1
• Oxidation catalysts	3	5	5	5	4	5	1	1	1	3	3	3	1	1
• Oxygen sensors	2	5	5	1	4	4	5	1	1	1	1	1	1	1
• Catalyst supports	2	5	5	4	4	5	1	1	1	3	3	1	3	1
• Electrostatic precipitators	1	1	3	1	3	3	4	1	1	2	3	3	5	1

FIGURE 8.5   A portion of Engelhard's opportunity matrix

company. One had a market potential of $250 million sales per year, the other, a potential of $100 million.

TOOL 3: SKILLBASE SIMULATION

Description

When a company is considering investments in its skills or products, skillbase simulation provides a way of working through the consequences of such an investment in advance. The opportunity matrix is built on a database structure which makes it suitable for simulation analyses to be carried out. The simulation changes the values of selected skills and reruns the database program to see if different solutions arise. These 'what-if' simulations can be carried out many times, with different changes, to look at options for a business. Because of the volume of data, such a simulation would be impossible without a computer model. The simulation analyses can be used to:

1. Identify products the business could 'nearly' address
2. Identify skill shortfalls if a particular set of products is to be addressed
3. Identify the new products which could be addressed if specific skills were enhanced, or new skills added.

Method

The stages of the method are similar to those described in Tool 2. The scope of the axes must, however, be wider. The scope of both the product axis and the skills axis must be determined in order that both potential new products and potential new skills can be plotted. This may be understood with reference to the matrix in Figure 8.6. Determining the axes is a creative process which must take account of competitors, market trends and the broad direction of the firm.

Outputs

Nearly Addressable Products

The first type of output is the products the company can 'nearly make'. The database can be programmed to identify products where the company is just a few points short of the required skill levels. For example, it could be asked to identify all products where up to two skills are one point or one skill is two points short. This would produce a list of products that could be addressed with modest investment.

Skill Shortfalls

The next type of output is a list of the skill shortfalls required for a particular product portfolio. The desired product portfolio is

	Existing products	**Potential products**
Existing skills	Current products Existing products produced using existing technologies	Latent products Products which could be produced with the existing skillbase
Potential skills	New processes Existing products using new technologies	Incremental products Products which could be produced with additional skills

FIGURE 8.6 Determining the axes

selected in advance, and the database then calculates the skill short-falls that would exist, and therefore, the skill increments required.

Once the desired skill increments for a company have been determined, a decision can be taken as to how to obtain them. One possibility is to acquire a company with these skills. The skill gaps to be filled can be compared with those available in potential acquisitions. By incorporating the skills of acquisitions into the database, the synergies can be explored. Synergies are the products that can be made by the combination of companies which cannot be produced by the individual companies.

Product Possibilities

The final type of output is the products which could be produced if the company invests in its skillbase so that certain skills are incremented. It follows from the structure of the skill–product database that different skill increments will have different effects on the portfolio of products that can be produced. An investment in one skill could allow many products to be produced whereas an investment in another might allow very few. The database can be programmed to permit 'what-if' analyses.

Case Study: A Major European Engineering Company

A major European engineering company commissioned an opportunity matrix for its whole business followed by a skillbase simulation analysis to identify 'nearby' market opportunities and their related skill gaps. This opportunity matrix covered a wide range of engineering sectors on the product axis including: automotive, aerospace, oil and gas, electrical, environmental, process and chemical, utility and power generation. Within these sectors over 400 products were selected that passed the company's strategic selection criteria in terms of market size and growth. The skills necessary to address these applications were determined and scored as in the previous case study. The major skill types used for this analysis were: materials, engineering, marketing and distribution, commercial and financial. The skills of each of the divisions of the company, and its central R&D facility, were mapped and scored and then compared with the skills necessary to address specific applications.

The simulation, or 'what-if' analysis, was carried out by searching for application areas where the company's skill capability was lacking or short on skill-score points. This simulation analysis was carried out on a division-by-division basis; for each division plus central R&D, and then for selected combinations of divisions and R&D. The following searches were made:

1. Shortfall of one skill unit in one area
2. Shortfall of one skill unit in two or more areas, up to four areas
3. Shortfall of two skill units in one area
4. Shortfall of two skill units in one area and the one skill unit in one to four areas
5. Shortfall of three skill units in one area.

This analysis has led to the identification of specific skill gaps in the company that, if filled, should enable the business to address a number of targeted new business areas.

TOOL 4: SKILL CLUSTER ANALYSIS

Description

The core competence approach has been expounded by many as a new rationale for corporate strategy. To use the approach, however, it is necessary to be able to determine what a company's core competences are. In the literature, the core competences that are normally cited are broad in nature, such as 'microelectronics' (Prahalad and Hamel, 1990), but methodologies for their determination are not given. The technique outlined here builds on the opportunity matrix to allow possible core competences to be identified scientifically by identifying the clusters of skills which exist in a company's operations.

Method

The opportunity matrix indicates which products require which skills. When just the existing products are considered, the matrix shows the way in which current skills are being utilized in combination with one another in the manufacture of products. For example, if the products which require a high level of the 'digital electronics' skill also tend to require high levels of 'miniaturization' and 'cost engineering', it is likely that the company has a core competence in low-cost digital microelectronics. However, if the company has these skills but they are not combined in the same products then it does not have this competence.

This may be made more scientific by defining the mathematical quantity called the skill clustering index, I_{ij}, which is the percentage of products in which skills i and j are both used to a high level:

$$I_{ij} = \frac{\text{Number of products using both skills } i \text{ and } j \text{ at levels 4 or 5}}{\text{Total number of products}}$$

Clear, I_{ij} is equal to I_{ji}. It is possible to calculate the matrix of skill cluster indices directly from the database using matrix multiplication. The matrix shows how each skill is clustered with each other; an example is given in Figure 8.7.

The matrix indicates that, in this instance, skills 1 and 3 are associated with each other in 60% of products, whereas skills 1 and 2 only occur together in 10% of products. However, the clustering of larger groups of skills cannot be seen directly. To identify the larger groups of skills, it is necessary to reorder the matrix by

	Skill 1	Skill 2	Skill 3	Skill 4	Skill 5
Skill 1	60	10	60	10	50
Skill 2	10	40	10	30	20
Skill 3	60	10	70	10	60
Skill 4	10	30	10	30	10
Skill 5	50	20	60	10	80

FIGURE 8.7 Raw matrix of skill-clustering indices

	Skill 4	Skill 2	Skill 5	Skill 3	Skill 1
Skill 4	30	30	10	10	10
Skill 2	30	40	20	10	10
Skill 5	10	20	80	60	50
Skill 3	10	10	60	70	60
Skill 1	10	10	50	60	60

FIGURE 8.8   Reordered skill-clustering indices showing two skill clusters

computer (Gourlay, McLean and Shepherd, 1977). The result of this process is shown in Figure 8.8. This indicates that skills 4 and 2 are clustered with each other and skills 5, 3 and 1 are clustered with each other. These two clusters represent potential core competences since they are empirically observable combinations of elemental skills.

In practice, skill cluster matrices may be complex. Figure 8.9 shows a skill cluster matrix for a medical products company. The density of shading shows the value of the skill-clustering index. The main skill cluster combines finite element analysis (FEA), bio-engineering, approvals, medical engineering, quality testing, design (CAD), polymers and polymer matrix, product development, quality control, and quality and cost engineering. This cluster may, at first, seem surprising since approvals are not always considered a core competence within this industry, but, on reflection, the results are logical.

The matrix may be recalculated to take account of new products; the new skill clusters will show the new competences which will need to be created. The emergence of a new core competence brings with it the requirement for organizational change. The skills that make up a core competence need to be institutionally linked, and possible ways of achieving this interlinkage include:

- An organizational structure which brings the skills together
- Physical co-location

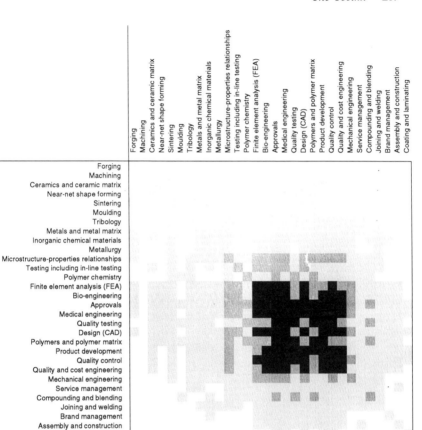

FIGURE 8.9   Skill cluster matrix for a set of medical products. The greater the skill cluster index between two skills, the denser the shading. The central cluster can be seen extending from *finite element analysis* to *quality and cost engineering*

- A philosophical interlinkage such as a revised mission statement, emphasizing their interrelatedness in pursuit of the organization's goals.

Outputs

Skill cluster analysis produces, as output, the skill clusters which exist in a company's product range. This is a valuable scientific input into the process of identifying core competences. When conducted on a company's existing skills and products, it suggests current competences; when applied to possible future skills and products, it shows how competences may need to change.

TOOL 5: CRITICAL SKILL ANALYSIS

Description

For a company to be in a position to manufacture a product it must have the skills to do so. This raises the question, what are the constraints on acquiring skills and when must a company start to acquire the skills for a specific product? This tool provides a way of answering this question, and is useful to companies considering long-term skill investments.

In general, the constraints on skill acquisition are twofold: time and money. There is a trade-off between time and cost which was termed 'time-compression diseconomies' by Dierickx and Cool (1989). A graph showing this trade-off in the acquisition of a skill is shown in Figure 8.10. The graph shows that, even if cost were unimportant, there is a minimum time to acquire a skill. Even if the skill were bought through acquisition, it could not be used instantly; this is an increasing constraint according to the level of competence required.

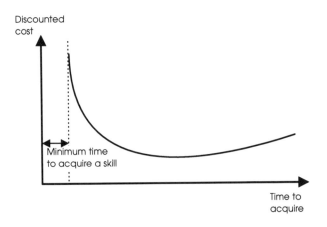

FIGURE 8.10   Time and cost of acquiring a single skill

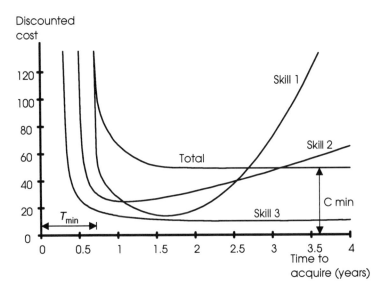

FIGURE 8.11   Time and cost of acquiring the three skills required for a product

All the skill increments required to manufacture a product may be plotted on the same graph, as shown in Figure 8.11, in which three skills are included. The x-axis is the time to acquire a skill; the y-axis is the discounted cost. The total time–cost curve has also been calculated and plotted. The graph shows that Skill 1 is the critical skill since it is governing the minimum time until the organization is able to produce the product. The total time–cost curve has been calculated for each time by determining the minimum cost required to have all the skills in place by that time. It can be seen that the minimum cost to acquire all the skills to produce the product is C_{min}. However, there are benefits to being fast to market (first-mover advantages). The financial benefit of being able to manufacture the product at each time may also be shown. This would typically be the discounted contribution to the organization of sales of the product, making assumptions for market share and price through the product's life, as in Figure 8.12.

The gap between the two curves then shows the net present value of producing the product on a specified timescale. If the product is to be produced early, there are market share advantages but the cost of forcing through the acquisition of certain skills outweighs the advantages. A much longer delay is less expensive in skill-acquisition terms but poor in terms of market share and contribution margin.

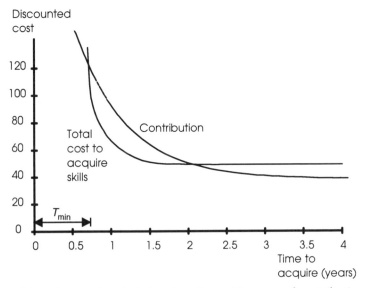

FIGURE 8.12   Time and cost of skills together with time and contribution for
product, showing window of opportunity

Method

Critical skill analysis is best applied to a product which has been
identified using the skill-simulation tool as accessible to the company,
provided a number of skills are enhanced. The required calculations
may be performed on a spreadsheet. For each skill which needs
to be enhanced (or built up from scratch) experts are asked to
estimate the minimum time that would be required to achieve the
necessary skill level, and the cost. They are then asked to estimate
how the cost changes as the time is extended. The spreadsheet can
then calculate the total cost for each time. The market share and
price behaviour can then be estimated for coming to market at
different times in the future, and thus the total contribution can
be calculated against time.

Outputs

The output from critical skill analysis is information which identifies
the most critical skill, indicates the optimal timescale for building

that skill, and provides a route map for the acquisition of the other skills involved.

CONCLUSIONS

In this chapter we have put forward a set of tools and two underlying principles that have been helpful in implementing ideas of competence-based competition. In using the tools in consulting assignments we have become acutely aware of the lack of consensus over definitions. 'Skill', 'competence' and 'capability' are terms which are used more loosely than is desirable for the construction of models capable of guiding managers on future decisions. (The literature on skills has often focused on interpretations of the past. When examined closely, these terms have often been defined, or at least used, in ways which are circular.)

We hope that the tools described in this chapter will be both useful to practitioners and helpful to theorists in teasing out more precise definitions of the entities that make up the new concepts of causality which we call competence-based competition.

REFERENCES

Bakker, H., Jones, W. and Nichols, M. (1992). Core competence and new business development. *Strategic Management Society Conference on Competence-based Competition*, Genk, Belgium.

Bogaert, I., Martens, R. and Van Cauwenbergh, A. (1992). Strategy as a situational puzzle. *Strategic Management Society Conference on Competence-based Competition*, Genk, Belgium.

Bogner, W. C. and Thomas, H. (1992). Core competence and competitive advantage: a model and illustrative evidence from the pharmaceutical industry. *Strategic Management Society Conference on Competence-based Competition*. Genk, Belgium.

Chiesa, V. and Barbeschi, M. (1992). Competence based competition and R&D organisations. *Strategic Management Society Conference on Competence-based Competition*, Genk, Belgium.

Dierickx, I. and Cool, K. (1989). Asset stock accumulation and sustainability of competitive advantage. *Management Science*, December, 1504–14.

Gourlay, A. R., McLean, J. M. and Shepherd, P. (1977). Identification and analysis of the subsystem structure of models. *Applied Mathematical Modelling*, 1, 245–52.

Grant, R. (1991). The resource-based theory of competitive advantage implications for strategy formulation. *California Management Review*, Spring, 114–35.

Hall, R. (1991). The contribution of intangible resources to business success. *Journal of General Management*, **16**, 41–52.

Itami, H. (1987). *Mobilizing Invisible Assets*. Cambridge, MA: Harvard University Press.

Klein, J. A., Edge, G. M. and Kass, T. (1991). Skill-based competition. *Journal of General Management*, **16**, 1–15.

Lancaster, K. (1971). *Consumer Demand, a new approach*. New York: Columbia University Press.

Leonard-Barton, D. (1992). Core capabilities and core rigidities: a paradox in managing new product development. *Strategic Management Journal*, **13**, 111–25.

Mintzberg, H. (1987). Crafting strategy. *Harvard Business Review*, **87**, 66–75.

Miyazaki, K. (1991). Optoelectronics-related competence building in Japanese and European firms. *Research Evaluation*, **1**(2), 89–96.

Prahalad, C. K. and Hamel, G. (1990). The core competence of the corporation. *Harvard Business Review*, **90**, 79–93.

Senge, P. (1990) *The Fifth Discipline*. New York: Doubleday.

Stalk, G., Evans, P. and Shulman, L. E. (1992). Competing on capabilities: the new rules of corporate strategy. *Harvard Business Review*, **92**, 57–69.

Turner, D. and Crawford, M. (1992). Managing current and future competitive performance: the role of competence. *Strategic Management Society Conference on Competence-based Competition*, Genk, Belgium.

9

Organizational Learning and a Firm's Core Competence

DUANE HELLELOID, BERNARD SIMONIN

INTRODUCTION

The relationship between three interrelated concepts in business—core competence, organizational learning and sustainable competitive advantage—is an increasingly relevant and underexplored area for both managers and researchers. Much has been written on each of these topics, and there is clearly an overlap between the concepts, as well as discrepancies between different authors' interpretations of the nature and interplay of the concepts. While the development of a short-term competitive advantage may be planned or fortuitous, we argue that long-term *sustained competitive advantage* requires: (1) a core competence(s) which is (2) continually upgraded and developed in advance of competitors. Sustainable competitive advantage demands that an organization possesses at least one core competence—a well of knowledge and experience upon which it can draw—which can be used to allow the organization to adapt to changing market and environmental conditions. Thus, organizations must constantly learn, and those which learn most proficiently will be most able to enhance their core competence and sustain a competitive advantage. In this chapter we look at different

Competence-Based Competition.
Edited by G. Hamel and A. Heene.
Copyright © 1994 The Strategic Management Society. Published 1994 by John Wiley & Sons Ltd.

ways organizations learn by focusing on knowledge acquisition, and propose that, over time, successful organizations learn how to learn and develop expertise in particular methods of learning. Effective learning depends upon the acquisition, processing, storage and retrieval of knowledge. The process by which the latter three stages take place is directly affected by the way the knowledge was originally acquired. Five different methods of knowledge acquisition are discussed: internal development, assisted internal development, open market procurement, inter-firm collaboration, and merger or acquisition. These methods will incur different costs each time knowledge is sought, depending upon the type of knowledge sought as well as the organization's idiosyncratic capabilities and skills in learning. Although an efficient organization will likely use all five methods at different times, it will become more proficient at knowledge acquisition in one or two methods, and will favor these methods. Other organizations faced with the need to acquire the same knowledge may use different methods. This suggests that different organizations will develop skills in different methods of learning. While consistent patterns of learning may be observed within organizations, there are differences between various organizations' patterns of learning and competence development.

The conceptual definitions and relationships between core competence, organizational learning and sustained competitive advantage, are discussed below. The following section outlines the different methods of knowledge acquisition which are available to all organizations. The implications of the method of knowledge acquisition on the later stages of learning (processing, storage and retrieval) are then discussed. Evolutionary economics and transaction cost economics-based arguments are presented for why organizations may actually specialize in only one or two of these methods of learning. The final section discusses the implications of these ideas for further research, identifies some practical problems suggested by these ideas and further outlines the relationship between organizational learning, core competence and sustainable competitive advantage.

THE RELATIONSHIP BETWEEN CORE COMPETENCE, ORGANIZATIONAL LEARNING AND SUSTAINED COMPETITIVE ADVANTAGE

Core competence reflects the specialized expertise of an organization resulting from its collective learning (Prahalad and Hamel, 1990).

Core competence has been referred to in the context of functional areas (Snow and Hrebiniak, 1980), abilities (Higgins, 1983), technologies (Prahalad and Hamel, 1990) and simply skills and resources (Reed and DeFillippi, 1990). Although most writers tend to focus on technological abilities as the basis for a core competence, other knowledge-based or experiential assets may underlie core competence. For instance, regulatory experience is critical in fields such as biotechnology (Shan, 1987), and maintaining friendly relations with governments can be essential in many international operations and regulated monopolies. Organizational culture could also be a core competence and source of sustained competitive advantage (Barney, 1986b). This diverse set of views about the nature of core competence suggests that it is, at best, difficult, and perhaps inappropriate in this chapter, to attempt to refine or redefine this list of 'things' that describe a core competence. For the purposes of this chapter we define a core competence simply as a capability which encompasses an organization's unique human, physical, organizational and co-ordinating resources (see Bogaert, Martens and Van Cauwenbergh, this volume, for a review of competing concepts). With a core competence a firm is able to respond to a variety of changing market and environmental conditions and deploy its resources in ways which can lead to a competitive advantage. Possession of a core competence does not, however, necessarily lead to a competitive advantage. An organization may not recognize how this competence may best be used, or have the organizational abilities to capitalize on the opportunities the competence makes available. While Xerox was the leader in computer user interface technologies such as pull-down menus and the mouse, it did not effectively exploit this competence. Thus, its Star computer, while possessing many technological breakthroughs which were precursors to successful products from Apple and Microsoft, never really made it out of Xerox's Palo Alto Research Center. External factors such as governmental regulations, trade barriers, industrial structures or market pressures also inhibit an organization from capitalizing on a core competence.

A competitive advantage leads to superior performance, as it allows an organization to provide high value to its customers which cannot be matched by its competition. A firm gains competitive advantage by configuring and utilizing its value chain better than its competitors (Porter, 1985). While a competitive advantage is often the outcome of tapping into a core competence, a competitive advantage may simply be the result of a fortunate concurrence of events (Barney, 1986a). While Microsoft's sustained competitive advantage is the result of several important competences, its initial success and agreement with IBM to create the MS-DOS operating system can only be described as the result of an odd and fortunate series of events. Thus, neither does competitive advantage necessarily result from a core competence, nor does a core competence necessarily lead to a competitive advantage (Reed and DeFillippi, 1990). It is our contention, however, that *sustaining* a competitive advantage over time *requires* that a firm be able to tap continuously into and utilize a core competence (or competences). At some point, luck will run out, and only those firms which have the capability to regularly update and enhance their competitive advantage by tapping into a core competence will be able to continue to earn superior returns. Some firms may sustain a competitive advantage through continually developing a core technology, others by anticipating customer demands or by fostering an innovative spirit (a unique culture) which brings new ideas to the fore and effectively introduces them to the market. Organizations are always trying to imitate the actions of other successful organizations (Lippman and Rumelt, 1982). Regardless of the nature of the core competence—the unique capability of the organization—simply having the competence attracts the attention of competitors. Thus, a core competence must be continually invested in and upgraded if it is to serve as source of sustained competitive advantage. As other organizations attempt to imitate a successful firm, not only might they catch up and surpass the firm, but, due to imperfect imitation, other organizations may create mutations which provide even greater value to customers (Hill and Helleloid, 1992). A core competence will no longer provide the organization with a sustained competitive advantage if it ceases to be unique due to the organization's failure to advance its competence ahead of its competition.

How organizations learn is a complex and poorly understood process. Although much research has been conducted on individual learning, organizational learning comprises different facets and levels of learning. It is more than the sum of the individuals at any time, as it also includes the institutionalized knowledge which transcends individuals and periods of time. Fiol and Lyles (1985), in a thorough review of the literature, cite Hedberg (1981):

> Although organizational learning occurs through individuals, it would be a mistake to conclude that organizational learning is nothing but the cumulative result of their members' learning. Organizations do not have brains, but they have cognitive systems and memories. As individuals

develop their personalities, personal habits, and beliefs over time, organizations develop world views and ideologies. Members come and go, and leadership changes, but organizations' memories preserve certain behaviors, mental maps, norms, and values over time (p. 6).

While attaining a consensus on a crisp definition of what organizational learning is and how it takes place is difficult (see Simonin, 1991, for example, for a review of different definitions and taxonomies), it is clear that each organization is likely to have its own unique style and ability to learn. Not only do organizations seek specific pieces of information to remain competitive and continue to build their core competence, they also learn how they are best able to acquire, process, store and retrieve information— they learn how to learn. Relatedly, they learn how to unlearn— when to discard information and processes which are no longer optimal and inhibit new creative approaches. Over time, effective organizations develop the ability to determine the information needed to upgrade a core competence, and devise a methodology for efficiently assimilating that information. Figure 9.1 depicts the relationships described above.

This view of how firms develop their skills in organizational learning is consistent with theories of the firm based on evolutionary economics. Nelson and Winter (1982) explain how, over time, firms develop their own distinctive organizational routines which encompasses sorting, processing and reacting to information from the environment. Each firm is viewed as unique, possessing a set of organizational routines which are the result of its own unique history, experience and administrative heritage. While these

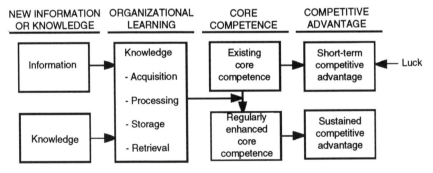

FIGURE 9.1 The relationship between organizational learning, core competence and sustained competitive advantage

organizational routines can be a core competence and source of sustained competitive advantage for some organizations (Hill and Helleloid, 1992), they can also create an organizational inertia which limits an organization's ability to fully comprehend new signals from the environment and act upon them expediently.

METHODS OF KNOWLEDGE ACQUISITION

In order to sustain a competitive advantage, organizations must continually learn and enhance their core competence. In the absence of this constant renewal, other organizations will be able to imitate or make obsolete the competence which once led to a competitive advantage. While learning consists of the acquisition, processing, storage and retrieval of information (Daft and Huber, 1987; Huber, 1989), how the latter three steps take place is affected by the way information was originally acquired by the organization. If knowledge is only acquired, but not processed, stored or retrieved, then it can do little to enhance a core competence. Organizations develop unique routines for learning that encompass all four of these steps, and create an expertise in their own style of learning. Although an effective organization will use a variety of different methods of learning as specific situations dictate, most firms will develop routines which are particularly effective for only one or two methods of learning. This section describes five methods of knowledge acquisition.

INTERNAL DEVELOPMENT

Organizations relying on internal knowledge development typically focus on advancing state-of-the-art knowledge in a key aspect of their business (that is, technologies which underlie a potentially large number of products). Some scientists, for example, may be devoted to pure research on fundamental technologies, while others are more involved in looking at the ways these technologies can be applied in commercial products. Although internal knowledge development is most commonly associated with product technologies, it is also applicable in the manufacturing and marketing functions. A core competence could be based entirely on achieving the lowest-cost (and/or highest-quality) products via a specialized expertise in manufacturing technology, as is often the case in process-intensive industries such as chemicals and paper products. The development of a particularly effective sales and marketing organization which continually provides superior market information and customer service can also be a manifestation of a core competence which is enhanced through regular internal knowledge development. A core competence based on internal knowledge development is difficult for competitors to imitate, as it not only involves an organizational culture, it is also based on a whole collection of individuals. While a competitor might be able to hire a few people away, this will not allow the competitor to replicate the competence. By continuing to learn about and further develop core competence, these internally focused firms rely on their innovative ability to stay ahead of competitors. Internally developed knowledge does not rely on my outside sources for *knowledge*, although the organization may gather a number of separate pieces of *information* from outside and bring these together to create *new knowledge*.

A danger in relying on internal knowledge development manifests itself when the organization develops skepticism for any ideas not developed internally (the 'not invented here syndrome'). When significant or unexpected changes take place in the market, or when breakthrough technologies emerge as viable substitutes, an internally focused organization can be slow to react and ill prepared to look externally for a solution. Electronic test equipment manufacturer John Fluke, a firm which had traditionally developed individual pieces of test equipment and sold them to R&D engineers, was slow to recognize that computerized test systems and modeling that combined the functions of many different pieces of equipment were eroding its sales base. Only after bringing in a new CEO and completely restructuring its organization and product lines was Fluke able to reorient itself and focus on test equipment for mobile service technicians. While the underlying technology was the same, packaging (the structural case), user interface and marketing of these products underwent significant changes as Fluke refocused on a new customer segment.

ASSISTED INTERNAL DEVELOPMENT

A variation on internal knowledge development is externally assisted internal knowledge development. Organizations which frequently utilize external sources to augment internal development take advantage of the specialized services and knowledge available from consultants or carefully focused courses. While firms may tap into these sources to extract specific knowledge, more importantly, they utilize them for assistance in refining their own processes of internal knowledge development. An organization may hire a firm with a specialized expertise in market research to better explore the potential of a new product or the needs of a particular customer segment, and use this information to validate and complement its own research or perceptions of the market. Ford, when seeking to improve its Taurus car, undertook a systematic benchmarking of some 200 features against competitors. This yielded great results for Ford, whose Taurus model became the best-selling car in the USA, surpassing the Honda Accord in 1992 for the first time. Similarly, a firm already very efficient in manufacturing may hire a consultant with specialized knowledge in machine tool group technology to improve machine usage efficiency in a particular work cell. Although the external source may itself learn from its interaction with the client organization, the flow of knowledge and information is specifically designed to go from the external source to the client organization. These sources typically have a much broader view of the environment of the organization, and can suggest avenues for learning which the organization had not considered. Organizations which regularly utilize external sources become familiar with particular expertise offered by various sources. Experience enables organizations to discern the range of services they can expect to receive and how best to tap into the sources. While the use of external sources can help diminish the risk of shortsightedness associated with a 'not invented here syndrome', these sources are also available to any other organization that contracts for their services.

MARKET PROCUREMENT

Obtaining new information from the market involves the spot purchase of particular pieces of information. While patent rights are perhaps the most obvious example, the hiring of individuals with specialized expertise or contracting with another firm to provide a turnkey facility are other instances where an organization can learn via the purchase of specific knowledge from another individual or organization. The purchase of knowledge via the market has the unusual characteristics of Arrow's paradox (Arrow, 1962), which states that it is difficult to value the worth of knowledge until it is known, but, once known, there is little incentive to buy it. Organizations which regularly utilize the market to acquire information which can enhance their core competence recognize that many useful developments take place in other organizations. For these organizations, the pace and timeliness of accessing developments taking place outside are important. Organizations which continually scan and utilize the market often have the first opportunity to learn from outside developments, and develop expertise in buying knowledge and intangible assets from other organizations. By obtaining exclusive rights or acquiring unique assets, they also pre-empt competitors. A paradoxical competence rests on the ability to bring together related developments from a variety of other organizations and develop products more quickly than competitors. Hewlett-Packard's rapid development of three-dimensional mechanical engineering design software relied heavily on its purchase of the rights to several mathematical modeling software libraries and routines. HP's success resulted from its ability to combine these underlying software routines and integrate them with a user interface it developed itself. A key limitation of this approach to learning is that much of what needs to be learned to enhance a core competence may not be available in the market, and if it is, competitors have equal access if they recognize it.

INTER-FIRM COLLABORATION

When different organizations have specialized or complementary knowledge they can often learn from each other by establishing collaborative arrangements. These collaborative arrangements could take the form of independent joint ventures, equity stake swaps, consortia or contractual agreements. Ideally, the objective of collaborations is for both organizations to benefit from a two-way flow of information, knowledge or resources. When an objective of the collaboration is organizational learning (which is infrequent), both organizations contribute expertise and may learn from the other. In reality, the transfer of knowledge is often one-sided as a result of ill-defined objectives, hidden agendas or lack of organizational resources (Hamel,1991; Simonin 1991). Specific collaborative arrangements could last for decades, or may only be used for a year or two to address a particular issue, and could be terminated by either partner. The computer industry is filled with various collaborative arrangements which address specific issues in semiconductor chip manufacturing technology, hardware standards, operating systems, software and device protocols, or marketing programs. Hewlett-Packard is known for having several very successful collaborations. When it developed the desktop laser printer it chose to work with Canon to provide the print engine even though it had developed its own laser printing capabilities independently. Canon's experience with portable and desktop 'personal' copiers was a competence that HP felt was critical to achieve first-mover advantages in personal laser printers. Similarly, HP's recent introduction of a very small hard drive for laptop computers relied on the expertise of a watchmaker (Citizen) for developing the manufacturing technology necessary for miniaturized assembly. Even though HP has a well-recognized expertise in manufacturing, it knew it could benefit from Citizen's expertise for this new product. If knowledge acquisition is a primary objective of a partner in a collaboration, once that organization has deduced that it has learned all it can from its collaborators, the lack of any additional incentives leads to the termination of the agreement. Organizations which regularly utilize collaboration to enhance competences recognize that they must not only learn from their collaborators as quickly as practical but also be careful not to develop a reputation for simply 'using' their collaborators and then 'dumping' them. While acting opportunistically is often feasible in any one collaboration, in the long run it can deter other organizations from envisioning collaborations with organizations deemed opportunistic. Opportunistic behavior can also backfire through market sanctions, as the 'Toshiba bashing' incident in the USA demonstrated in 1990. Since it is often difficult to set objectives and structure collaborative agreements, developing a reputation as a good collaborative partner both improves the willingness of other organizations to collaborate and eases the contractual problems in drafting what are often fairly open-ended agreements.

The type of competences enhanced through a collaboration does not need to be triggered by differences in the knowledge base of the partners, nor motivated by the desire to internalize a partner's expertise. Learning can occur as an unintended side-effect of a collaboration or as the result of synergism between the partners. A competence which neither organization would have been able to develop alone may be built.

MERGER AND ACQUISITION

A merger or acquisition may be the most appropriate means to attain some sorts of knowledge or competence. This is particularly the case when the knowledge is not widely available and is embodied in an indivisible part of another organization. The defense contractor Raytheon, for example, learned about the consumer appliance business via its acquisitions of Amana and Speed Queen. Likewise, rather than attempting to build a new salesforce to serve a particular customer segment or geographic region, acquiring a well-established organization or distributor is often the most viable alternative. If a new technology appears to be critically important to sustain the technical competence of an organization, the purchase of an organization which has a fully functioning R&D team may be the most expedient way to access this technology. Merger or acquisition has the additional advantage that, once acquired, no competitor can obtain this exact same competence. However, with a merger or acquisition, an organization will likely acquire many assets and resources for which it has little use. Due to culture clashes, it may also have difficulty in maintaining an entrepreneurial spirit in the acquired organization if that was an important element in the acquired organization's culture. An organization's ability to effectively internalize the learning opportunities made available by the acquisition is often undermined by problems in integrating the organizations. General Motors' acquisitions of Hughes Aircraft and EDS, for example, illustrate the inherent difficulty of opening up to contributions from outside organizations when the predominant culture was 'absorb or be absorbed'. While some organizations have made a habit of regularly acquiring and divesting other organizations, it is uncertain whether this method could be used to continually sustain competitive advantage. It is more likely that some other method of learning would have to be taking place on an on-going basis, with merger or acquisition only occasionally supplementing the learning process by allowing the organization to access competences unavailable otherwise.

IMPACT OF KNOWLEDGE ACQUISITION ON ORGANIZATIONAL LEARNING

The method by which an organization acquires knowledge has an important impact on how that knowledge is processed, stored and retrieved within the organization. Thus, decisions about how to best acquire knowledge should consider how the knowledge is to be later used by the organization. Organizations develop routines that encompass the entire learning process. Key issues concerning the processing, storage and retrieval of knowledge are discussed below. We then describe the impact of each knowledge-acquisition method on the entire learning process for upgrading core competence. Arguments based on evolutionary economics and transaction cost economics are proffered for why organizations develop unique organizational routines for learning, emphasizing one or two methods.

Processing, Storage and Retrieval

When an organization acquires knowledge to enhance a core competence, whether that knowledge can be effectively internalized by the organization depends in large part on whether the right people, and groups of people, are involved in processing and interpreting it. These people must have sufficient understanding of the core competence to comprehend fully the *depth* of knowledge acquired, and be able to ask detailed questions in order to understand how the knowledge fits with what is already known. These people must also come from diverse backgrounds so that the *breadth* of the knowledge available can be understood by the organization. Acquired knowledge from external sources is rarely available and presented in precisely the format which will be of most use to an organization, since the source has developed the knowledge for its own use and is unlikely to know exactly which pieces of information will be most important to various persons in the acquiring organization. Thus it is incumbent on the acquiring organization to make certain that the persons processing the knowledge have the necessary depth and breadth to comprehend fully the available knowledge and ask the appropriate questions so that the knowledge can be most easily assimilated into the organization and used to affectively enhance a core competence. For example, BZW, the investment banking arm of Barclays, entered a technical co-operative agreement in Thailand with Kiatnakin Finance, a Thai security and finance company. BZW (European) committed to provide research expertise in exchange for some of the privileges associated with the Thai brokerage and financial license of Kiatnakin Finance. In an effort to internalize this expertise within the organization, Kiatnakin relied on experiential learning, pairing its analysts with BZW's research analysts in the field so that they gained direct exposure to the way to handle company visits, conduct interviews and interpret the information gathered from an investment point of view. In this instance, the financial analysts (primary users of the knowledge in Kiatnakin) were on the front line of knowledge acquisition.

Once knowledge has been processed in light of a context or problem, meaning is extracted which may be directly utilized by the organization and/or stored away for future use. The key concern in storage of knowledge is the *permanence* of the storage mechanism— will the knowledge be available for later retrieval? To the extent that the knowledge can be codified and written, the storage of knowledge is likely to be more permanent than if it is stored only in individuals' minds. Since the minds walk out the door every evening (occasionally permanently), it is certainly possible that they will not be around to be accessed at a later time. A key principle of organizational learning is that organizational memory must substitute for a collection of individual memories; redundancy of information, replication of experiential knowledge and duplication of knowledge bases become valuable properties to resist accidental depletion or extensive erosion of memory. The full extent of the knowledge cannot be codified because of context-specific aspects of the knowledge which are not understood or anticipated at the time of storage. A multiplicity of depository agents will help assure that the knowledge can be accessed at a later time.

For knowledge to be later diffused within an organization, the persons who require access to the knowledge have to know of its existence and know how to retrieve it. If knowledge is not widely *accessible* or no particular mechanism exists to co-ordinate the referencing of the knowledge, those who need it may not know of its existence, or where they can access it. Consulting and market research firms often relay anecdotes about how different divisions within a single organization will contract to have essentially the same information provided to them that another division has already purchased.

Another example of the importance of knowledge accessibility relates to a large French company which had adopted APL as the programming language for its scientific applications. Given the power of the language and its intellectual appeal, scientists started to develop their own programming functions for individual use.

Without an interactive library of current and recorded functions, scientists could not assess the organizational state of the art for their programming needs, lacked the ability to identify existing solutions to their problems or to contribute to upgrading the knowledge base, and thus initiated a mass production of similar programs. In this case, the duplication of effort was truly a waste of organizational resources rather than a healthy replication of knowledge.

How the Acquisition Method Affects Organizational Learning

Internal Development

In building and enhancing core competence through the internal development of knowledge the same people or groups may be responsible for the entire learning process. In the case of a technological core competence this would likely be a small laboratory department. These people not only acquire the knowledge, they also process it within their group, store it either in written form or simply in their collective minds, and can retrieve it at any time. While this can be a very efficient way of augmenting an existing core competence, others in the organization outside the group have to know about the addition to the core competence and be able to access the new knowledge. Manufacturing, for example, may need to directly link new manufacturing technologies to the new product technology, and marketing would have to be aware of new developments if it is to identify specific product opportunities for the technology. In multinational organizations, the sharing of knowledge across international borders in order to improve operations world-wide is a very critical issue (Bartlett and Ghoshal, 1989). An innovation in one national organization may not only be useful world-wide, it may have even greater value in an operation other than the one which developed it. Internal development is particularly appropriate for building a core competence which is very tacit, as no knowledge has to flow outside the organization. However, because the entire learning process takes place among a small group of people, organizations may never be able to capitalize on core competence built in this way if others in the organization are unaware of the knowledge created. Thus, unless the knowledge is widely and readily accessible, it may not be processed by all the interested parties to truly enhance a core competence throughout the organization. Knowledge can also be lost through reorganizations and personnel turnover if it is not appropriately stored in any codified format or systematically shared across the organization. As suggested earlier, simply having a core competence does not ensure that an organization will have a competitive advantage. A number of different functions within a firm must know of and supplement a core competence if it is to be turned into products or services that provide superior value to customers. The description of Proctor & Gamble's very successful launch of Liquid Tide, a product that combined the contributions of researchers from three continents, illustrates both the challenges and the benefits from combining the expertise of different groups within the same company (Bartlett and Ghoshal, 1989).

Assisted Internal Development

When other outside individuals or groups assist in the internal development of additions to core competence the circle of individuals within the organization aware of new developments and processing the knowledge is likely to be increased. Consultants working with a development team may have contacts throughout the organization and help assure that new learning is directed at needs in other areas of the organization (i.e. marketing, manufacturing, international operations). In this regard, consultants can be agents or facilitators of knowledge diffusion. Hence, external sources can help in both the internal development and distribution of additions to core competence. External sources may also end up serving as storage mechanisms for the organization, which can make the organization dependent upon them for future access to the knowledge. When the same consultants are brought back on a continuing basis to help an organization with a particular issue (i.e. improving inventory practices and factory utilization), it is arguable whether the consultants (1) provide an expertise which is uneconomical for the organization to develop or (2) hold a great deal of pertinent knowledge about the organization (i.e. the operation of its manufacturing plant). For the second of these situations the organization must consider the potential consequences of not having these consultants available at some later time, and how this could impact the further enhancement of a core competence. External sources may also serve as a conduit for the release of information about the nature of a core competence to others outside the organization. This 'leakage' may not be intentional, as it can be difficult for a consultant not to later utilize pertinent knowledge that was developed while working with an organization. Many organizations have utilized executive education programs available at top universities to assist in the development of their managerial talent. Jay Lorsch of Harvard, however, has noted that, frequently, firms send the wrong people to these courses— managers who are not really in a position to effectively process and apply the information provided in the courses. Although information is being acquired by the members of the organization, since it is not processed by personnel who can best use it nor stored in a manner accessible to others, this form of assisted internal development does little to assist the overall organization. Thus, firms like Weyerhauser, Analog Devices, Du Pont or General Electric are increasingly tailoring programs specifically for their own needs (O'Reilly, 1993).

Market Procurement

When core competence is enhanced through market procurement of new knowledge, how the knowledge is processed, stored and retrieved in the organization depends upon whom in the organization was involved in the procurement process or had information about the contract. If a large number of individuals from a variety of functional areas were included in the search, negotiation or monitoring activities, then information about the addition to the core competence is likely to be widely held and easily accessed. Those directly involved in the processing should have the depth to understand fully what is acquired (this may also be necessary for the knowledge to be stored effectively rather than dissipated quickly) as well as the breadth to make sure the knowledge is made available throughout the organization. Market procurement of knowledge is more effective when the knowledge enhances an aspect of a core competence which has been underdeveloped by the organization, but is easily understood. Knowledge too dissimilar to the core competence may be poorly processed, and hence relatively difficult to store and retrieve. When purchasing the rights to a patent, if the patent involves a technology which is very similar to one in which an organization has a core competence, then it should be reasonably easy for the organization to assimilate the knowledge and use it throughout the organization. If, however, the patent involves a technology which is less directly related to a core competence, then it may be harder for all affected members in the organization to process fully and store the information without also having a technical assistance contract from the patent holder. While HP's ability to bring together various software libraries and routines from outside firms to develop its mechanical engineering products was described previously, its initial problems are equally illustrative. When HP first purchased the rights to a mechanical engineering product from Graftek, the company found that the software had a number of significant quality problems that were not known in advance and which it could not fix. HP also did not have enough appropriately trained people to sell and support the product successfully. After pulling the product off the market, HP spent a significant amount of time training its personnel and more carefully scanning the market for products. Its later successful products relied a great deal more on tapping into the expertise of other software developers for specific functionality, while HP took full control over final product development, quality assurance and the user interface.

Although contractual agreements may make the acquisition of knowledge available to an organization, internal procedures and incentives have to be in place for the knowledge to be fully processed, stored and retrieved. When, for example, upper management contracts for a market research study but product managers feel their abilities are being slighted and research managers question the usefulness of the study, then the study is unlikely to add to the organization's core competence. Organizations which have a not-invented-here syndrome are unlikely to learn effectively from market procurement because they will not be able to process, store and retrieve the knowledge, even if access to the knowledge is successfully negotiated.

Inter-firm Collaboration

For core competence to be enhanced through collaborative agreements, learning has to be one of the objectives behind the agreement. In addition, the organization must possess an effective learning capability. Learning could be an explicit goal of the agreement, an implicit objective or simply an anticipated side-effect. This has important implications for both the structure of the collaborative agreement and the assignment of personnel. The agreement has to be structured so that personnel directly involved in the collaboration can access and process knowledge from their collaborators. This impacts upon whom is assigned to work in the collaboration ('stars' or 'dogs' in the organization), how long they work with the collaboration before transferring back into their parent organization and whether a 'critical mass' of people are assigned to the collaboration. In the NUMMI joint venture between General Motors and Toyota, it has been suggested that GM has dispersed too thinly the knowledge it has gained from the collaboration—those who worked in NUMMI have been dispatched throughout GM and absorbed by the predominant culture. It may also be important for others in the organization who are not directly involved in the collaboration to be able to access, process and store knowledge from the collaboration. For the organization to be able later to retrieve knowledge and use it in a variety of applications, having it stored in groups not directly associated with the collaboration may be essential. Learning to enhance a core competence is often only a secondary objective of a collaboration, with the primary objective being some tangible research, manufacturing, risk sharing or marketing goal. Thus the person directly involved with the collaboration may be more focused on achieving this primary objective than transferring knowledge from their collaboration to the rest of the organization. In long-running collaborations the individuals directly involved with the collaboration may switch their loyalty from their parent organization to the joint collaboration. In other cases, new personnel hired by the joint collaboration may lack the proper incentive and motivation to serve the greater objectives of the parent organizations.

Merger and Acquisition

When core competence is built and enhanced through merger and acquisition, how well the acquired organization is integrated into the rest of the organization will have a great bearing on how effectively the knowledge is processed, stored and retrieved. If the organizations are not at all integrated, the acquired knowledge will remain entirely within the acquired organization, will not be processed, stored or retrieved by the parent organization, and will be of questionable use to the organization. Given the tendency for personnel turnover after an acquisition, the knowledge could even be dissipated before it is effectively utilized to enhance a core competence. Pushing for integration too quickly, however, could greatly disrupt the acquired organization, retard continued enhancement of the competence acquired and potentially even accelerate the turnover process. Hence a balance must be reached whereby the organizations are integrated sufficiently for knowledge to be shared and learning facilitated, but not so quickly that knowledge is lost. For an organization to build a core competence on its own from an acquired organization it has to be able either to process, store and retrieve knowledge from the acquired organization or allow the acquired organization to continue to build upon its own core competence while retrieving knowledge from it for the overall organization on a regular basis. With IBM's acquisition of Rolm, neither happened. While this acquisition was done with the goal of developing IBM's telecommunications expertise, it failed to meet this objective and also caused Rolm to lose the competitive advantage it once held. The key attributes of the five methods of knowledge acquisition are summarized in Table 9.1.

ORGANIZATIONAL LEARNING AND ORGANIZATIONAL ROUTINES

It is expected that organizations which sustain a competitive advantage use all methods at different times, since in any given situation a method which is not one of the more frequently used may be the most appropriate one (i.e. will be the lowest-cost way of acquiring the information sought). However, it requires a distinctly different organizational culture to be good at internal knowledge development than is necessary for effective inter-firm collaboration. While the former culture would stress creativity and may reject ideas 'not invented here' the latter would welcome learning from collaborative partners who possess knowledge difficult to generate internally. Hence, through experience, organizations will develop routines for learning that (1) efficiently combine the steps of knowledge acquisition, processing, storage and retrieval; (2) are consistent with the organization's culture; and (3) reflect the nature of the information sought over history. Organizations will develop unique routines, and two organizations faced with a need to acquire the same information may use very different routines. For example, most pharmaceutical firms now recognize the value of biologically engineered substances. But while some firms have

TABLE 9.1 Key attributes of the five

Method of knowledge acquisition	Internal development	Assisted internal development
Description	Relying on the internal capabilities of the firm to enhance current competences	Utilizing other firms or consultants to assist in the firm in developing its competences
Common usage	R&D, technology, customer knowledge	Marketing, Human Resource Development
Implications for processing	New knowledge must be understood and available to various people in the organization	The external sources have to be working with and have access to the right people in the firm, source must be credible and accepted
Implications for storage and retrieval	Same people typically acquire, store and process, must codify and duplicate storage to avoid loss, knowledge must be identifiable by others	Need to be certain that knowledge is stored within firm, difficult and expensive to go back to the external source
Advantages	Difficult for competitors to imitate or duplicate, potential for unique breakthrough, use of existing assets	Tap into specialized expertise, utilize specific capabilities and a broad base of experiential knowledge
Limitations	Not-invented-here syndrome, limited by the firm's capabilities, competency traps	Available to any competitor, can cause leakage of knowledge, dependency traps
Key challenges for firms which use this method to regularly enhance a core competence	Developing a culture and atmosphere which encourages creativity and new ideas, but is not closed to outside forces and inspiration	Knowing which sources are best at fulfilling particular needs, avoiding dependency, pricing the assistance

methods of knowledge acquisition

Market procurement	Inter-firm collaboration	Merger and acquisition
Purchasing specific information or capabilities in the market	Co-operating with other firms to internalize, enhance or build competences	Acquiring another firm which has a desired competence
Patents, subcontracting	R&D consortia, foreign market entry	Diversification, new businesses
Need to be certain that individuals have both the depth and the breadth to understand and gain full access to knowledge acquired	Learning should be an objective of the collaboration, need to involve the right people, open (non-arrogant) attitude	Must balance the need for integration with the risk of destroying the competence of the acquired firm
Information usually must be 'reformatted' to fit into organization's memory, firm should not have to go back to the original source	Storage should also occur in the parent firm, not just in the collaboration	Either the acquired firm must be integrated or the acquiring firm must be able to access the acquired firm's knowledge base
Get the state of the art from other firms, have access to a great variety of new knowledge, awareness of what others are doing	Transfer tacit knowledge, create knowledge synergetically, share risks, calibrate and control competitors	Obtain a functioning organization which has a critical mass of proven expertise
What is really needed may not be for sale, competitors have equal access	Vulnerable to opportunistic partners, appropriate collaborators not always available, cross-cultural conflicts	Can be difficult to integrate and obtain access to specific knowledge without destroying the firm, over-paying for a subset of the assets
Efficient scanning of the market, recognizing value before competitors, pricing the knowledge	Partner selection, negotiation, management of delicate inter-firm relationships, knowing when to exit, balancing collaboration and competition	Cultural clashes, personnel turnover, what to do with parts of the firm that are not of value to the parent, integrating the targeted resources

reacted by developing their own in-house expertise in biotechnology, others have chosen to acquire biotechnology startups while others collaborate in joint ventures with smaller biotechnology firms. When faced with the need to learn something new, the most efficient way of learning will vary across organizations as a result of the organizations' established routines.

The routines by which an organization acquires knowledge clearly affect how that knowledge is stored and later processed and retrieved. When knowledge is internally developed an organization should develop proper routines to provide a map for the future retrieval of this information. Thus, even when knowledge is seemingly no longer needed and has been eroded over time, its imbeddedness in an organization and its routines can be reconstructed. In an example of how dispersed knowledge was available throughout an organization, Lenehan (1982) describes how the knowhow necessary to build a particular Steinway piano model, which had been out of production, was reconstructed. A senior craftsman familiar with past production technologies disassembled an older model, consulted a foreman's 'black book' which had been left shelved for decades and gathered information meticulously archived at a German manufacturing factory which had also produced this model for a period of time. In this case, the routines of the organization were so established that later employees were able to re-create the knowledge base needed.

Organizational routines can both facilitate and inhibit learning. Suboptimal organizational routines can limit an organization's ability to recognize that the environment has changed and that new capabilities are required. Even if environmental changes are identified, routines may still limit the organization's ability to make necessary internal adjustments. An organization which has never acquired another organization may be loath to do so, even if that is the best method of obtaining new knowledge in a certain situation. Organizational routines, while promoting and enabling organizational efficiency, may also create inertia that limits flexibility. The existence of established organizational routines, as described in the evolutionary economics literature (see, for example, Nelson and Winter, 1982), suggests that the continual use of the same routines for learning can occur for both satisfying (rote behavior) and cost-minimizing rationales. The cost-minimizing aspect of established organizational routines is described more fully by transaction cost economics, as covered below.

ORGANIZATIONAL LEARNING AND TRANSACTION COST ECONOMICS

Any process of knowledge acquisition and competence enhancement will incur some costs, be these the time spent searching internally for solutions to problems, the cost of a patent or the price of an entire acquisition. As organizations develop routines for enhancing competences, the costs of learning via a particular method will tend to decrease when the organization regularly uses the same method. When an organization looks at adding a new competence or enhancing a current one it will consider the total costs involved with a particular method of learning. This total cost will include both transaction costs (Williamson, 1985) and direct costs. The direct costs are those that can be assigned specifically to the knowledge acquired (i.e. the price of a patent or the engineering time spent on an invention). The transaction costs reflect the costs associated with the process of learning, and should decline over time. In the case of market procurement of the rights to a patent, transaction costs would include the costs of searching among potential related patents, negotiating a price and monitoring the completeness of the patent information provided. An organization regularly purchasing patent rights to enhance a competence would become familiar with the likely sources of the relevant patents, have experience in valuing and negotiating agreements, and have established procedures for facilitating and monitoring the flow of information from the patent holder to the appropriate people in its organization. Thus, an organization with an expertise in the market procurement of patents is likely to have lower transaction costs for obtaining the patent rights, and is less likely to overpay or fail to learn from a purchased patent right. This expertise would be specific to market procurement, however, as internal development transaction costs are entirely different (i.e. the costs of time spent on unfruitful efforts). By regularly using the same method or methods, an organization will lower the transaction costs of these methods and learn how to learn. (Firms with expertise in internal development establish procedures for monitoring the progress of investigations, and may be more forceful in cutting off or redirecting efforts that appear to be going nowhere.) Hence an organization is likely to use the same method for acquiring information not just simply out of habit but because its routines allow it to learn more efficiently and enhance a competence more effectively if it consistently utilizes the same method.

CONCLUSIONS

In Chapter 3 of this volume, Bogaert, Martens and Van Cauwenbergh allude to strategic assets as the pieces of a complex puzzle game characterized by an ever-changing pattern. Along this metaphor, the constant struggle of organizations to learn how to learn can be expressed as learning how to play the puzzle game through the development of superior heuristics. Likewise, knowledge acquisition can be understood as the acquisition of a new piece for the sake of fitting an identified gap or of hedging for future gaps; memory and retrieval processes as the ability to know where the needed pieces are (in the stock of unused/unsorted pieces or in the pattern itself) to redeploy them in new, emerging gaps; processing as the ability to reshape an old piece or to combine several pieces to fit a new gap; unlearning as the propensity to discard an old piece which has become obsolete in the evolutive pattern and which can only be misleading by drawing attention to an irrelevant solution (a piece without a legitimate matching gap). The better learning organizations are not only capable of reacting quickly to changes of pattern but are also able to anticipate and to prepare for the shifts in shapes and trends with reasonable accuracy. Only firms committed to an organizational learning agenda can expect to sustain a chance to keep on playing the puzzle game. Others will be forced out of the game.

This chapter has focused on the interrelationship between the concepts of core competence, organizational learning and sustained competitive advantage, with the goal of clarifying how the concepts interact and overlap. We proposed that an organization's ability to sustain a competitive advantage requires a continual development and upgrading of its core competence(s), which in turn depends upon the organization's ability to learn. While a competence can lead to a competitive advantage, sustaining that advantage requires that an organization continually invest in and enhance its competence ahead of competitors. Different organizations will develop expertise in different methods of learning, depending upon their needs and experiences. For learning to be effective, knowledge must be acquired, processed, stored and retrieved appropriately. Five different methods of knowledge acquisition were discussed: internal development, assisted internal development, open market procurement, inter-firm collaboration, and merger or acquisition. These methods will incur different costs each time knowledge is sought, depending upon the type of knowledge targeted as well as the organization's established routines. An organization will tend to choose the cost-minimizing method of learning in each situation, and over time is likely to emphasize only one or two of the methods. Thus, the transaction costs of these favored methods will decline as the organization 'learns how to learn'. Although an effective organization will likely use all five methods at different times, it will become more proficient at knowledge acquisition in one or two methods, and will favor these methods. Other organizations faced with the need to acquire the same knowledge may use different methods. The method by which knowledge is acquired has implications for how an organization processes, stores and later retrieves knowledge, and thus affects the way core competence can be enhanced.

Our perspective on how organizational learning affects the development and enhancement of core competences has several important implications for organizations. First, the entire learning process needs to be considered when particular information is sought. While initially one method may appear less expensive for the acquisition of knowledge, unless the entire organization can efficiently process, store and later retrieve the knowledge, then the least expensive method may not be the most optimal for truly contributing to a competence. Relatedly, it is important to understand both the strengths and the limitations of established routines. Given routines can allow an organization to enhance a competence very efficiently but can also prove to be inappropriate for a particular situation, limiting the organization's ability to learn. If, for example, an organization has never previously entered a joint venture, and yet this appears to be the only way a particular knowledge can be accessed, then the organization must recognize that a number of internal procedures may have to be modified for competence to be enhanced. Although regular routines may limit flexibility, the development of routines is efficient for organizations—routines allow organizations to lower the costs of processing information. Hence the existence of consistent patterns of learning should be recognized for the strengths and benefits this consistency provides. At the same time, however, these patterns limit the ability to enhance a competence with an unfamiliar method. This places a responsibility on managers to know when existing routines may facilitate or inhibit learning, and to take appropriate actions.

In an era of intensifying global competition, the requirements for an organization to sustain competitive advantage have become more complex and unpredictable. The requisite information and knowledge necessary to continually enhance a core competence ahead of worldwide competitors may be available only from sources that are outside an organization's current realm of contact. Developing new organizational learning capabilities, and challenging existing organizational routines, is critical for guaranteeing core competence enhancement and sustained competitive advantage.

REFERENCES

Arrow, K. J. (1962). Economic welfare and the allocation of resources to invention. In National Bureau of Economic Research (Ed.) *The Rate and Direction of Inventive Activity: Economic and Social Factors*. Princeton, NJ: Princeton University Press.

Barney, J. (1986a). Strategic factor markets: expectations, luck, and business strategy. *Management Science*, **32**, 1231–41.

Barney, J. (1986b). Organizational culture: can it be a source of sustained competitive advantage? *Academy of Management Review*, **11**(3), 656–5.

Bartlett, C. A. and Ghoshal, S. (1989). *Managing Across Borders: The Transnational Solution*. Boston, MA: Harvard Business School Press.

Daft, R. and Huber, G. (1987). How organizations learn: a communication framework. *Research in the Sociology of Organizations*, **5**, 1–36.

Fiol, M. and Lyles, M. (1985). Organizational learning. *Academy of Management Review*, **10**(4), 803–13.

Hamel, G. (1991). Competition for competence and inter-partner learning within international strategic alliances. *Strategic Management Journal*, **12** (Special Summer), 83–103.

Hedberg, B. (1981). How organizations learn and unlearn. In P. C. Nystrom and W. H. Starbuck (Eds) *Handbook of Organizational Design*. London: Oxford University Press.

Higgins, J. (1983). *Organizational Policy and Strategic Management: Text and Cases*. Chicago, IL: Dryden Press.

Hill, C. W. L. and Helleloid, D. (1992). A resource based theory of the multinational enterprise. Proceedings of the European International Business Association Annual Meeting, Reading, UK.

Huber, G. (1989). Organizational learning: an examination of the contributing processes and a review of the literature. Paper presented at the May 1989 Organizational Learning Conference, Carnegie-Mellon University.

Lenehan, M. (1982). The quality of the instrument. *The Atlantic Monthly*, **250**, 32–58.

Lippman, S. and Rumelt, R. (1982). Uncertain imitability: an analysis of interfirm differences in efficiency under competition. *Bell Journal of Economics*, **13**, 418–38.

Nelson, R. R. and Winter, S. G. (1982). *An Evolutionary Theory of Economic Change*. Cambridge, MA: Harvard University Press.

O'Reilly, B. (1993). How execs learn now. *Fortune*, 5 April, 52–8.

Popper, K. (1957). The aim of science. In D. Miller (Ed) *Popper Selections*. Princeton, NJ: Princeton University Press.

Popper, K. (1959). *The Logic of Scientific Discovery*. London: Hutchinson.

Porter, M. (1985). *Competitive Advantage*. New York: Free Press.

Prahalad, C. K. and Hamel, G. (1990). The core competence of the corporation. *Harvard Business Review*, May/June, 79–91.

Reed, R. and DeFillippi, R. J. (1990). Causal ambiguity, barriers to imitation, and sustainable competitive advantage. *Academy of Management Review*, **15**(1), 88–102.

Shan, W. (1987). *Technological Change and Strategic Cooperation: Evidence from the Commercialization of Biotechnology*. Unpublished dissertation, University of California, Berkeley.

Simonin, B. (1991). *Transfer of Knowledge in International Strategic Alliances: A Structural Approach*. Unpublished dissertation, University of Michigan.

Snow, C. C. and Hrebiniak, L. G. (1980). Strategy, distinctive competence, and organizational performance. *Administrative Science Quarterly*, **25**, 317–36.

Williamson, O. (1985). *The Economic Institutions of Capitalism*. New York: Free Press.

10

Managing Current and Future Competitive Performance: The Role of Competence

DENNIS TURNER, MICHAEL CRAWFORD

INTRODUCTION

To compete over long periods of time and to create value for its stakeholders, an organization has to accomplish two interrelated tasks successfully. First, it has to manage its current operations effectively. Second, it must be able to change these operations, to meet continually shifting future demands. It attempts to do this in the context of uncertainty about what will create value in the future. It is also subject to tension between the use of effort and resources which contribute to current performance and those needed to reshape itself for the future.

Many factors bear upon an organization's ability to change its operations successfully over time. The nature and extent of change around it, the actions its competitors take and the situation or circumstances in which the organization is placed have significant effect. The fundamental health and state of the firm and actions by its people also affect its success in managing through changing circumstances.

Competence-Based Competition.
Edited by G. Hamel and A. Heene.
Copyright © 1994 The Strategic Management Society. Published 1994 by John Wiley & Sons Ltd.

This chapter focuses on an additional, but crucial, factor which affects the organization's capacity to compete successfully over long periods of time. This factor is the competences which the organization commands, not only to manage current operations but also to see the changes which should be made and to accomplish them more effectively than its competitors.

In this chapter we present a conceptual framework for such competence. We categorize aspects of its ownership, orientation, foci and structure. We discuss how competence is manifested in organizations, and in lifecycles, how it may be developed and supported, and how it impacts on competitive performance over time. We end by discussing some managerial implications of our analysis.

OWNERSHIP OF COMPETENCE— PERSONAL AND CORPORATE

One perspective of competence is captured in the notion of ownership. Firms benefit from both personal and corporate competences. *Personal competences* are possessed by one individual or, at most, a few, and are lost to the organization when they leave. For example, a newly appointed manager with high personal skills in motivation makes a major impact on a unit, but then leaves. The motivation ceases with the manager's departure. Occasionally the acquisition of a firm will be followed by the exodus of a few individuals whose departure basically destroys the value of the acquisition. In these cases the acquired firm is seen to have 'hired', not 'owned', the competences upon which its value was based.

Corporate competence consists of a combination of corporate characteristics, skills, motivations and knowledge 'owned' by the organization itself. These are embedded in its systems, mechanisms and processes and diffused in its people, technology and structures. As such, it tends to endure over time despite the comings and goings of individuals. Just as a manager may have personal competence in motivating people, so an organization may have motivational competence in the way it designs and utilizes its goal-setting, evaluation and reward systems, organizes the recognition and celebration of performance, and so on. Such competences, though implemented through people, are not dependent upon the presence or absence of a few individuals and are therefore 'owned' by the corporation.

ORIENTATION OF COMPETENCE— MANAGEMENT AND TECHNICAL

While competence may be owned by a person or by a corporation, a further important dimension is captured in the differentiation between *technical* and *management competences*. A *technical competence* is concerned primarily with technological aspects of the creation, production and delivery of the organization's products and services. Such competences relate to the technical aspects of turning inputs to the firm into outputs to its market. The ability of a person to use visual merchandising skills is an example of personal technical competence in retailing. A corporate technical competence in the same area might be based on systems and technology which distribute codified visual merchandising layouts to all the managers in a large retail chain in ways they can effectively implement. A *management competence* is concerned primarily with the direction, development, motivation, control and integration of the organization's performance. An example of a personal management competence is to be a good communicator, while a corporate management competence in communication may rest on the use of media, the institution of forums and meetings and corporate values that espouse openness and legitimize the expression of differing views.

FOCUS OF COMPETENCE— OPERATIONAL AND RESHAPING

The nature and extent of competences required by a firm to perform competitively is not static. At any time the firm will have a set of competences that, to a large degree, is appropriate and relevant to its current strategy and operations. At any future time (for example, a decade hence) it will need a set of competences appropriate and relevant to the strategy, operations and circumstances of that time. If, by then, the organization has significantly different strategies or operations then its competences are likely to have also undergone substantial change. In between, in moving forward, it will have utilized competences which have enabled it to change and reshape its activities. These latter competences we call *reshaping competences* as they are primarily relevant to creating a future for the organization. We contrast these with *operational competences*, which, while they may contribute to the future, are primarily focused on current performance. Performance management is an example of a corporate operational competence while option management is an example of a reshaping competence.

STRUCTURE OF COMPETENCE— BASAL AND DISTINCTIVE

Much of the strategy literature deals with the competitive positioning of the firm (e.g. in terms of cost position or differentiation). This perspective provides important insights about competition. A somewhat different, though not inconsistent, perspective is captured in the concept of *distinctive competence*. This can be traced from the writings of Selznick (1957), Snow and Hrebiniak (1980) and, in more recent times, Prahalad and Hamel (1990) and Bogner and Thomas (1992) writing about the *core competences* of the organization. In a more general sense competence has always been a feature of the strengths and weaknesses analysis of many earlier strategy writers. Competence can provide a basis for effective competitive positioning. Thus there is a close link between strategic positioning and distinctive competence. The latter, however, includes the important notion of the ability to deliver, which is sometimes missing from considerations of strategic positioning.

Prahalad and Hamel (1990) illustrate vividly the outcomes when a variety of essentially technological competences are established as strengths of a firm and combined as core competences to produce new products and services and break into new fields. While the focus is on the outcomes of the combination of technologies, Prahalad and Hamel raise the question of how some firms successfully combine, integrate and deliver new products and others do not. They comment: 'The real sources of advantage are to be found in management's ability to consolidate corporate wide technologies and production skills into competences that empower individual businesses to adapt quickly to changing opportunities' (p. 81).

Klein, Edge and Kass (1991) extend the position presented by Prahalad and Hamel. They argue that the basis of competition is shifting as product lifecycles become shorter, relative to skill life-cycles, and they see the development of corporate skills as the basis of competitive advantage. They identify 'meta-skills' underpinning the process of developing and deploying core competences. The four key corporate meta-skills they describe are learning, innovating, skill categorization and embedding. 'Meta-skills are about behaviour rather than knowledge' and Klein, Edge and Kass (1991) argue that 'these meta-skills help explain why some companies have been in existence since the last century' (p. 6).

While the terms 'distinctive' or 'core' competences are useful descriptors to illustrate the focus of technology, skills, motivations, resources and mindsets of a particular organization at a point of time, it is important to recognize that such competences are not monolithic. They consist of a number of constituent competences that can be seen as building blocks, or components, of the larger competence and are integral to its manifestation in action.

We use the term *basal competence* to denote any competence underlying and integral to the most important competence(s) the firm commands for its competitive performance. Such basal competences are not restricted to technological combinations but include all those aspects of competence—personal/corporate, technical/management, operational/reshaping—which we have previously described. We use the term *distinctive competence* to apply to any combination of basal competences which gives the organization a competitive advantage.

Our use of the term 'basal' is akin to the use of the term 'subatomic particle' in physics. The latter covers all particles smaller than an atom, for example molecules, protons, electrons, etc., each of which is constituted from smaller subatomic particles. Some are more 'elementary' than others. In a similar manner, but without implying the elegance and rigour of atomic physics, we use the term 'basal' to encompass all the competences upon which an organization may draw to create a distinctive competence, irrespective of how composite each competence may be.

Later in the chapter we identify a specific list of basal management competences. They are not meant to be exhaustive, nor are they very basic. For instance, one of them is performance management. This depends, among other things, on goal setting, monitoring, reward systems, etc. Each of these could be treated as a basal competence. The distinctive competence of a firm flows from the combination of basal competences. Because distinctive competence is such an aggregation it can obscure understanding of the detailed development required within the firm. On the other hand, listing all conceivable basal competences would simply swamp managers with too much detail to be of use. We have therefore sought to identify a smaller group of basal competences at an intermediate level of aggregation. The consequent set is managerially meaningful and provides a degree of richness and interconnectedness that can be used for thinking about the actual competence state of a particular organization and its reshaping over time.

The conceptual framework we have described is shown in Figure 10.1. While in practice the partitioning of competences is not as discrete or specific as this framework suggests, it provides a schema for thinking about how an organization might analyse its competences and what competences it needs to develop to compete over extended periods of time. The remainder of this chapter focuses on corporate competences, the lower half of the framework in Figure 10.1 and, in particular, on corporate management competences.

COMPETENCE LIFECYCLE

If competence underlies competitive success, the rise and fall of different firms over time indicates that either competence possessed is often lost or the relevance of some particular competence to

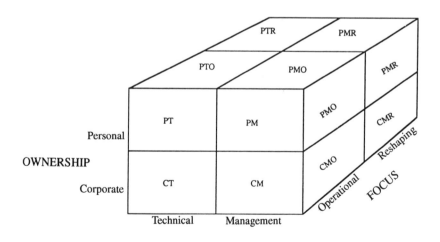

FIGURE 10.1   Basal competences

competitive advantage is not permanent. These two possibilities have different implications. If the issue is simply one of loss of competence, then management attention is needed to identify which competences are critical to success and what must be done to sustain them. This is not always as easy as it might seem. Senge and Sterman (1992) provide a compelling illustration, in the insurance industry, of practices introduced to improve performance in claims management which then caused an erosion of competence in claims adjustment and an increase in ultimate costs.

If the issue is one of competence obsolescence, other considerations come to the fore. Bogner and Thomas (1992) have described how 'core' competences have changed in the ethical drug industry over 50 years. The core R&D competences have moved in turn from those of basic organic chemistry, through fermentation and soil screening (for the development of antibiotics), to rational drug design, and recently to biotechnology. There have also been shifts in the dominant competences for marketing and promotion. In the years after the Second World War, salesforces represented a whole product range to physicians. This was succeeded by 'blockbuster' marketing (the whole salesforce focused on a single product), and, more latterly, specialized salesforces. Firms in the industry differed in the extent to which they possessed these various competences at the times each proved most potent, with consequent shifts in the competitive position of firms.

Within a few decades, the computer industry has been continuously reshaped as products and applications and markets have developed. The dominance of mainframe computers was eroded by minicomputers, then by PCs and now by networks. Concurrently, relative market value has shifted from hardware to software and to systems integration. There have been accompanying changes in distribution channels. These shifts have implied significant changes in the competences most pertinent to satisfying the market. That has led to a series of rising and falling company fortunes. IBM dominated computing in the 1970s, but ceded some position to DEC (minicomputers), then latterly to Compaq (PCs). All these have suffered in recent years relative to new competitors such as Sun (workstations). Dell (PCs), Microsoft (application and operating system software) and Novell (network software).

This dynamic is generally apparent. It leads writers in the field of competence-based competition to identify the capacity to update and form new market-relevant competences as central to continuous

TABLE 10.1 Basal

Competence name	Concept
Performance management	Goal setting within a strategic framework, with subsequent performance monitoring, and reinforcing or adjusting activities in response to current outcomes and circumstances.
Resource application	Bringing suitable resources to bear to best support the organization's strategic intent (i.e. not just resource allocation but getting the resources actually to work for and support the purpose for which they are allocated).
Motivating and enthusing	Achieving active willingness and intent to work in ways consistent with the firm's objectives, and to believe in the firm's ability thereby to achieve its objectives.
Integration of effort	Achieving co-ordinated action by members of the organization and coherence among its practices, systems and policies.
Enaction	Actually carrying decisions into action in a timely and effective way; moving from devising strategy to its implementation, and from analysis to action.
Communication	Sharing of information and understanding on matters relevant to achieving the firm's objectives, and to an extent appropriate to the circumstances of various members of the firm.

corporate management competences

Enables an organization to:	(Some) contributory competences/ mechanisms and factors
improve current performance and trigger beneficial incremental change.	Real-time monitoring of activities and outcomes linked to a theory of the business Means to reward/punish for performance Goal-setting procedures, budgets and targets with MIS providing regular feedback Performance review/appraisal systems for individuals.
maximize the benefit gain from the assets available to it.	Strategic planning systems and the communication of strategic plans Budgets and monitoring of resource use Matching managers and organization arrangements to the tasks to be done and resources assigned Project management techniques.
obtain a strong effort from its personnel, directed at doing those things supportive to its objectives.	Real recognition given to valued behaviour by personnel Celebratory functions Communicating about and endorsing champions Clarifying links between committed effort and achievement of individual aspirations Reward systems with incentive components.
act consistently and with focus in pursuit of its objectives and avoid effort that is counter-productive or wasted.	Co-ordination roles Scheduling processes Dissemination of plans and work descriptions which clarify organizational expectations Established procedures and standards Job rotation.
move quickly from perceived ability to satisfy customers, or cope with some problem, to actually serving the customers or dealing with the matter.	Corporate value that espouses action Creating and following-up on schedules for action Practice of experimentation before the 'fully thought out' idea is developed, with movement to exploit results Small groups established to solve problems, with responsibility for actioning the solutions Systems that measure outputs and results rather than inputs or energy.
have its members knowledgeable about the facts and consider-ations necessary for them to work effectively and with commitment.	Corporate value that espouses openness, consultation legitimacy of differing views Special meetings, standing committees, representative forums Standard documents to communicate common forms of information Newsletters, bulletins, circulars, etc. Electronic mail.

continued overleaf

TABLE 10.1

Competence name	Concept
Commitment formation	Achieving a coalescence of focus and support around specific options or decisions.
Pathfinding	Identification, crystallization and articulation of achievable new directions for the firm.
Development	Changing the firm's assets to enhance their relevance to its activities and directions over time.
Systems/process engineering	Progressively re-creating the systems and processes that constitute the organization, to provide effective means of carrying out its strategies
Option management	The process of developing, exploring, nurturing, and adopting or abandoning a manageable number and range of options, with timely exploitation of those that are of genuine advantage to the business.

(continued)

Enables an organization to:	(Some) contributory competences/ mechanisms and factors
move toward action and follow through in a united way because of the readiness of members to close ranks behind a chosen direction.	Consultation before decision making Representative workforce and management committees Cross-functional groupings and meetings Management of opinion leaders and linchpin members Conscious management of communications and process of reaching a decision, in order to satisfy local values that will support commitment.
find new avenues for survival and profit and means of achieving good performance in new situations.	Environmental scanning; market research Creative strategic planning, such as group sessions considering opportunities under conceivable scenarios Benchmarking of practice and performance Knowledge of the firm's assets, their abilities and their transformability.
increase its capability to perform effectively in the future, through the creation of assets well suited to its future circumstances.	Asset planning and review Strategic planning Systems for workforce skill development and workforce planning Systematic recruitment and management development practices Development of the firm's practices, technologies and operating systems.
get quality and consistency in its processes, lower the cost of what it does and introduce the capability to do new things competitively.	Systems view of the business Methods expertise IT expertise TQM methodology Change control practices.
have greater discretion in the paths open to it, while also facilitating the move from pathfinding into the development and implementation of a chosen direction.	Corporate processes to resource the development and investigation of options Personnel systems that reward those who champion successful innovations but which do not penalize those who champion options the firm chooses not to back Maintaining diverse information and contact networks Allowing selected managers to travel and seek out ideas.

competitive success (Prahalad and Hamel, 1990; Bogner and Thomas, 1992; Verdin and Williamson, 1992).

In reforming itself for the future, an organization is sometimes able to get leverage from a combination of existing competences and market circumstances. However, on other occasions competence may require quite explicit investment. It may even stipulate a reduction in the maintenance of, and importance placed on, currently relevant operational competences. In these latter circumstances the tension between current and future performance is manifest.

BASAL CORPORATE MANAGEMENT COMPETENCES

We list in Table 10.1 a number of basal corporate management competences. While it is likely that all competences in some way impact both current and future performance, the basal competences we have outlined illustrate that some are focused primarily on current operations while others relate more to shaping the future. Given this distinction, it is not hard to understand how some firms may be very successful at a point of time (their operational competences are high at that time) but later fail (their reshaping competences are not high).

Table 10.1 outlines the concept of the particular competence, its contribution and some of the underlying lower-level competences and factors that contribute to and are integral to its performance. To amplify that introduction, we describe several of them in more detail below.

PERFORMANCE MANAGEMENT

Performance management encompasses setting relevant targets for the business, tracking its performance, adjusting its activities and influencing behaviour to achieve its goals. It also involves countering factions and influences which detract from goal achievement. This competence has a strong results focus, is grounded in a theory of the business, lives very much in the present and relies on real-time monitoring. Goal-setting systems, the monitoring processes, the role of budgets, the categorization and attention given to customer complaints, and the focus of interest of top management are ways in which, among others, this competence manifests itself. Such a competence is often a force not only in achieving current performance but also in triggering incremental change.

SYSTEMS/PROCESS ENGINEERING

Much organizational change is literally re-engineering the business because it means changing the systems and processes whereby the firm produces and delivers its products and services; and monitors and controls itself and its environment. However, this essentially systemic nature of the business is often unrecognized. 'Re-engineering' occurs both consciously and unconsciously; the latter particularly when people are ignorant of the indirect impacts their actions have on the firm's processes.

A competence in systems/process engineering is the ability to progressively and beneficially re-create systems and processes that substantially constitute the organization. This competence springs partly from an understanding of the role of systems in managing activity (for example, total quality control); partly from an understanding of methods expertise and information management; and partly from a knowledge of business operations. Competence in systems engineering is not only a management competence but also a technical one with strategic implications in industries, such as banking, where managing information is a foundation of the business. This competence, which is often applied to re-creation and development of current systems, has an impact on both current operations and future performance.

PATHFINDING

This is the corporate competence to identify, crystallize and articulate achievable new directions for the firm. Part of the competence stems from an outward and future orientation of the firm's members and the intelligent use of systems and processes that empower this. Environmental scanning systems; strategic planning exercises; processes which collect competitor and market information in a systematic and disciplined way; involvement in trade and research groupings that are concerned with corporate or national development;

all foster a widespread involvement in opportunity seeking and the crystallization of informed views about new directions. Forums for discussions, with different and sometimes overlapping membership, help to sustain this competence.

Pathfinding involves a mixture of search and creativity. It also depends on self-knowledge and an understanding of the transform-ability of the firm's own assets, i.e. the degree to which it can practically apply or mould them to other uses. The paths that search reveals are only relevant to the extent that the organization is able to exploit them. This, in turn, depends to some degree on creativity in finding ways to exploit or reconfigure possibilities. This competence impacts on future performance.

LINKAGE TO OTHER CORPORATE RESOURCES AND ATTRIBUTES

In reviewing the terminology and concepts used by many recent writers on the resource-based perspective on strategy Bogaert, Martens and Van Cauwenbergh (1993, p. 7) refer to an asset (including tangible and intangible) as 'something you *have* (a brand name, a patent, access to sources of cheap energy or raw materials etc.) and to a *process* (the way something is done, such as a specific technology or team experience) as long as it has a value for some corporate purpose'. Corporate competences as they manifest themselves typically draw on combinations of assets (as described by Bogaert, Martens and Van Cauwenbergh) and on other organizational attributes. A skill, a level of energy, strong motivation, effective communication, systems and codified practices, specific knowledge, special technology or capital equipment, etc. may *all* be needed to build a particular corporate competence whether in metal fabrication, consumer advertising or systems/process engineering. It is the effective fusion or integration of these 'assets' that results in the competence and its value.

Corporate culture and values are important to competences in the way they dispose individuals to act and to draw on and apply their own skills and resources. If we compare a firm that is very effective in diffusing new information with another that is less effective, we may well find little difference in the personal communication skills of members of the two firms. However, their members may differ substantially in their disposition to communicate with others in the firm, and in their judgements about with whom they should communicate. The formal and informal communication systems and channels within the firm may also impact upon the process. Two firms that differ in the quality of their output may have little difference in their plant and facilities and in the technical skills of their personnel. The real differences may lie in members' beliefs about the potential for improvement and in their commitment to quality, and the processes or systems that empower beliefs and help structure their work.

Even where particular corporate competences are equally important to several firms, the way they are manifested is likely to differ between those firms. For example, the means of effective communication is likely to be very different in a university, a coalmine or the military, and different systems and qualities are required in order to achieve effective communication.

A sense of personal self-confidence or self-efficacy has a major impact on personal performance (Bandura, 1988). Likewise, organizations can develop in their members a sense of *esprit de corps* and confidence in the organization's ability, which is a powerful part of its competence in action and can be an important factor in its corporate performance.

Competences will often be carried in the codified and documented practices of a firm, in mechanisms for dealing with action requirements or rewards, in the formal systems and procedures, in role definitions and the effective integration of different parts of the organization and in individual skills and other resources.

DEVELOPMENT AND ATROPHY OF CORPORATE COMPETENCES

Corporate competences develop through conscious development effort and as a by-product of running the current business. Some arise through processes in which personal competences are transformed into corporate ones.

A powerful illustration of the development of a corporate competence, and of its application to corporate reshaping and change, comes from some recent perspectives which focus on the application of organizational learning skills within Japanese enterprises. Nonaka (1988a, b) has argued that the process of organizational self-renewal (i.e. major organizational change and redirection) in Japanese firms depends on the creation and management of information. The way this occurs is through the espousal of 'a challenging but equivocal vision' (Nonaka, 1988b, p. 62) by the senior management of the organization that effectively poses a contradiction when compared with the organization's existing use of resources and practices. It becomes the responsibility of less senior managers to find a resolution to this contradiction that normally results in changes to the nature of the firm's business. In doing this, they are assiduous in gathering and considering a diversity of information, and through applying it in the context of the perceived contradictions they create new information. This last is important, since it is the basis for changing the business.

The ability to do this consistently clearly constitutes a corporate competence and is partly embedded in the activities of middle and lower participants in the firm. This competence has parallels with the meta-skills of organizational learning and innovating described by Klein, Edge and Kass (1991). The meta-skills they describe of skill categorizing and embedding have parallels in the corporate competences described by Nonaka for disseminating new information and perspectives throughout the firm, particularly through the movement of people as carriers of tacit knowledge (Nonaka, 1988b).

Competences may be acquired from outside in addition to internal development (Helleloid and Simonin, 1992). This is clearly the case with personal competences but often the stimulus to mergers, acquisitions, strategic alliances, etc. is the need to add corporate competences. The current widespread interest in 'best practice management' and in 'benchmarking' practice is partly explained as a process of acquiring corporate competences which have been developed by relevant non-competing organizations and trying to transplant them. While such sought-after competences are often technical, they are not restricted to these.

Nonaka (1991) illustrates the early stages of a process in which personal competences develop into corporate competence. He describes how the tacit knowledge of an individual, specifically the kneading technique of the Head Baker at the Osaka International Hotel, was studied in depth until the stretching technique of the baker in kneading the dough could be replicated by a piece of equipment. Nonaka describes this as a move from tacit to explicit knowledge. Tacit knowledge is highly personal while explicit knowledge is formal and systematic.

However, it is not until explicit knowledge is diffused into the organization and embedded in its processes or structures that a corporate ownership and competence can be developed. While this may occasionally occur accidentally it is not until an organization develops competence or 'routines' to do this that corporate competence is developed systematically or upon any real scale.

Kay and Willman (1991), in discussing the management of techno-logical innovation, comment 'the development of an effectively innovative culture is not, therefore, a matter of finding alternatives to organizational routines for monitoring and control, but of establishing routines which stimulate appropriate innovation and achieve the integration of technology into the core activities of the business' (p. 5). They further comment 'It is the conversion of individual and external expertise into business specific know-how which is at the heart of the effective appropriation of technology by the firm' (p. 8). This process needs to be managed—it does not occur naturally. Indeed, there is often real inhibition in the transfer of personal to corporate (particularly in technology) as it involves a change in ownership and sometimes a loss of power or role. The nature of explicit or implicit contracts and the relationship of individuals to an organization is clearly involved in such transfers (Kay and Willman, 1991).

Competences atrophy as well as develop. At times, this is of no disadvantage to the organization, since the competence has lost relevance. In other cases it may be because the firm no longer perceives the relevance of the competence even though the relevance remains; or activities which sustain the competence are removed without the impact being recognized. This is most likely to occur for competences whose benefit lags the inputs required to create and sustain them.

The lending experience of banks in the USA, the UK and Australia during the 1980s is an example of this. Senior bankers are now likely to comment that they believe their banks genuinely did have high lending competence some decades earlier. However, in an era of deregulation and greater competition in financial markets, together with buoyant economies, that competence eroded and this was not generally recognized. Emphasis in training bank staff moved to sales and service at the expense of credit skills. Often credit authorization delegations were relaxed. Some of the previous checking and monitoring was abandoned or ignored because it was not providing currently relevant information. The net result was the atrophying of a corporate competence whose benefits were in the future. Now the future has come and banks are paying the cost for that deterioration.

For some banks, one response has been to recruit individuals believed to be 'good lenders' (a personal competence), with the intention of drawing on their expertise to upgrade the bank's processes and practices and the skills of existing lenders within the bank. Another response is to systematize lending decisions as much as possible, using expert systems, credit-scoring sheets, and the like. In the latter case there is the creation of a corporate competence which neither gives rise to nor depends on the existence of personal lending competence. In such cases the move substitutes a corporate competence based on procedures and systems for one based on personal competence.

In other cases corporate competences may continue to be sustained when they are no longer relevant. Because corporate competences are developed often through an accumulation of experiential processes which may involve large numbers of people, they are not easy to change. If they are inappropriate to the directions in which an organization now should go, they may well become barriers to change.

MANAGERIAL IMPLICATIONS

If competence is crucial to performance, it is the responsibility of management to increase and sustain it. Among the many actions which might be taken we single out four areas for attention, i.e.:

- Recognizing current competences and their contribution to performance
- Allocation of responsibility for competence management
- Valuing and assessing competences
- Developing competences

COMPETENCE PROFILE REVIEW

In the cut and thrust of competitive business it is easy to forget (and sometimes not to have discovered) the basal competences that combine to form the firm's distinctive competences. Aspects of identifying and measuring these can be approached from differing perspectives (Klein and Hiscocks, 1992; Klavans, 1992; Borzatta

1992). While specific competences may have been the subject of investigation, a general review of a wide range of competences may reveal strengths and weaknesses not previously apparent. The mapping of an organization's competence will benefit from a focus and a framework. The focus is probably best provided by the markets it services or aspires to serve in future. A useful framework for categorization is provided earlier in the chapter, where competence was broken down into

Personal	_____	Corporate
Technical	_____	Management
Operational	_____	Reshaping
Basal	_____	Distinctive

Listing and describing competences with such a focus and framework is likely to reveal many areas for action. Some competences will be weak and need strengthening. Some may be too dependent on particular people. Others may be relatively unimportant but absorbing heavy resources in their maintenance. The clustering of weak and strong competences in certain areas, while reflecting the firm's general orientation, needs careful review. This may apply particularly to lack of balance between operational and reshaping competences. Such a review may also reveal opportunities for the creation of new products or services with the development of relatively few new competences or by new combinations of existing ones.

ALLOCATION OF RESPONSIBILITY

Many basal competences will be clustered around what are often functionally organized activities of the firm—for example, marketing, or sales, or production or distribution. Such functions usually have a manager responsible for performance and results are usually reviewed and accountability established through some form of appraisal system.

However, many basal competences are not functionally focused, particularly those which are either essentially integrative or focused on reshaping the business over time. For example, the list of basal management competences in Table 10.1 is largely composed of competences that are essentially cross-boundary and sometimes organization-wide. Who in the firm is allocated responsibility, for example, for communication, pathfinding or options management competences; areas on which the firm's future may ultimately depend? While it may be easy to theorize and say these are either 'all managers' responsibility' or 'the general manager's responsibility', in practice they often end up as no one's responsibility and no one is held accountable for them. Allocating responsibility to specific managers for the management of competences which are not focused on specific functions or are focused on reshaping the organization is likely to result in sharper identification, development and management of these competences.

VALUING AND ASSESSING COMPETENCE

Growing interest in the valuation of intangible assets has focused on areas such as brands, market share, patents and many other items not captured in traditional balance sheets. A firm's corporate competences represent probably the largest areas of such intangible assets. Recognizing the value of these will increase the management attention to their importance and the resources that are involved in their creation and maintenance. Such attention takes place around the investment required, for example, in a new computer system but a corporate competence in motivation and enthusing or in communication (both of which may have major impact on performance) often receives little careful evaluation or quantification.

It may be argued that it is difficult to measure many competences accurately. That is true in terms of rigorous quantitative measures, but is not usually difficult to *assess* them. Indeed, a good deal of management action is based not on measurement but on assessments, (e.g. 'strong/weak', 'high/low', 'small/large') that have to be made in the ordinary course of business. The attempt to assess or, where practical, to quantify the value of some competences is likely to give managers new insights about what it costs to develop a competence in terms of both time and money and therefore what resources should be applied to maintaining or renewing them.

Developing Competences

Much of the knowledge which comes into firms arrives in individual heads and hands. Much often departs in the same way and the organization has no permanent gain. It is often the case that this possibility is not seen or voiced until a departure is imminent, by which time it is usually too late. The competence profile review mentioned earlier needs to identify specific situations where the organization is at such risk of loss. Policies and actions need to be put in place which enhance the transfer from personal to corporate competence. This may involve change in contracts or mindsets and the development of routines and methods for corporatizing personal competence and of trust and integrity between members and between them and the organization.

The development of some competences may depend upon decisions where other imperatives may overshadow the aspect of competence development. A decision to make or buy components or to outsource a particular service may be settled on aspects of price, or delivery, or speed or investment requirements, without sufficient weight being given to the competences that will develop if the firm handles the matter internally. Even some managerial competences may be imported when required rather than being institutionalized in the firm. Pathfinding is an example (often relying on the personal competence of a CEO or a few key appointees). So is systems/process engineering, where reliance may be placed on consultants. The central issue in these choices is which of the competences are likely to be most critical for competitive success, the prospect of the firm itself achieving a high standard in those competences and the extent to which the firm puts its success in the hands of others.

Developing competences always requires investment. The incentive to create corporate competences is affected by financial considerations. Firms possess a range of assets. The investment in, and use of, some of these assets, in relatively stable conditions, has a much quicker and more visible impact on the firm's profit than others. For example, the use of existing products and stock have a fairly immediate impact on the firm's bottom line. A little later in impact are the effects of investment and use of plant, labour productivity and the salesforce. Still later are the effects of budgeting and control skills, and so on. Later still in such a list would come those corporate competences (for example, pathfinding or development) which help an organization to change and adapt and thus provide the basis for competing in the future.

Assets arise principally as a consequence of investment in asset creation or asset purchase. Not only is the return quicker for investments which have early impact on profit but the relationship between the investment and ultimate financial benefit is usually clearer. Consequently, firms have a relatively weak incentive to invest in the creation and maintenance of corporate competences which relate solely or mainly to organizational reshaping and future performance. The shorter a firm's time horizon, the weaker this incentive.

Corporate competences, particularly reshaping competences, are often not only long-term investments but ones which require continuous effort to develop and maintain. When the benefits are not revealed in the short term, or not consistently judged as important for current operations, retaining a commitment to these competences is difficult. For these reasons, their development will often depend either on the composition and long-term commitment to the organization of the senior management team or on the fact that these needed competences are incidental to some other corporate activities or competences which have generally a much more immediate payoff.

Customers seek product/service attributes—which are highly dependent on technical competences. The ability efficiently to produce and deliver products currently valued by the market requires some combination of management and technical competences. The contribution of management competences in current operations is clearly important, but without some specific technical competences there is no market position. However, the nourishment and reformation of competences is fundamentally an issue of management competence, both personal and corporate. Without specific competences related to reshaping the firm's future competences, corporate survival is no more than a chance event. Understanding those competences and developing and sustaining them is therefore key to long-term survival.

REFERENCES

Bandura, A. (1988). Organisational applications of social cognitive theory. *Australian Journal of Management*, **13**(2), 275–302.

Bogaert, I., Martens, R. and Van Cauwenbergh, A. (1993). Strategy as a situational puzzle. The fit of components. Faculty of Applied Economics, UFSIA, Antwerp University, Belgium.

Bogner, W. and Thomas, H. (1992). Core competence and competitive advantage: a model and illustrative evidence from the pharmaceutical industry. International Workshop on Competence-based Competition, Genk, Belgium.

Borzatta, P. (1992). Competence based applied strategies. International Workshop on Competence-based Competition, Genk, Belgium.

Helleloid, D. and Simonin B. (1992). Organizational learning and a firm's core competence. International Workshop on Competence-based Competition, Genk, Belgium.

Kay, J. A. and Willman, P. (1991). Managing technological innovation: architecture, trust and organizational relationships in the firm. London Business School Working Paper Series, No. 102.

Klavans, R. (1992). The measurement of a firm's core competence. International Workshop on Competence-based Competition, Genk, Belgium.

Klein, J. A., Edge, G. M. and Kass, T. (1991). Skill based competition. *Journal of General Management*, **16**(4), 1–15.

Klein, J. A. and Hiscocks, D. G. (1992). Skill based competition: a practical toolkit. International Workshop on Competence-based Competition, Genk, Belgium.

Nonaka, I. (1988a). Toward middle-up-down management: Accelerating information creation. *Sloan Management Review*, **29**(3), 9–18.

Nonaka, I. (1988b). Creating organizational order out of chaos: self renewal in Japanese firms. *California Management Review*, **30**(3), 57–73.

Nonaka, I. (1991). The knowledge creating company. *Harvard Business Review*, November–December.

Prahalad, C. K. and Hamel, G. (1990). The core competence of the organization. *Harvard Business Review*, May–June, 79–91.

Selznick, P. (1957). *Leadership In Administration: A Sociological Interpretation*. New York: Harper & Row.

Senge, P. M. and Sterman, J. D. (1992). Systems thinking and organizational learning: acting locally and thinking globally in the organization of the future. International Workshop on Competence-based Competition, Genk, Belgium.

Snow, C. C. and Hrebiniak, L. G. (1980). Strategy, distinctive competence, and organizational performance. *Administrative Science Quarterly*, **25**,2 317–36.

Verdin, P. J. and Williamson, P. J. (1992). Core competence, competitive advantage and industry structure. International Workshop on Competence-based Competition, Genk, Belgium.

11

Building Capability from Within: The Insiders' View of Core Competence

BEVERLY C. WINTERSCHEID

INTRODUCTION

Despite the prominent role of individuals as the basis of idiosyncratic capital within the firm, little research has been directed to the relationship between organizational competence and individual-level perception and action. While the link between organizational knowhow and expertise and individuals as 'carriers' of such competence (Penrose, 1959; Prahalad and Hamel, 1990; Wernerfelt, 1984) is evident, it is not clear whether individuals in the firm use the concept of core competence to inform their actions, and if so, in what ways.

This chapter examines the concept of core competence from the perspective of the individuals within the firm—those persons whose thinking decisions and actions comprise strategic process. It examines one company's experience in building new competence upon a foundation of past success.

Here we adopt the 'dynamic capabilities' perspective (Teece, Pisano and Shuen, 1992). A firm's competence is defined as the

Competence-Based Competition.
Edited by G. Hamel and A. Heene.
Copyright © 1994 The Strategic Management Society. Published 1994 by John Wiley & Sons Ltd.

specific tangible and intangible assets of the firm assembled in integrated clusters, which span individuals and groups to enable distinctive activities to be performed. Obviously, competences that are required for the survival of the firm are considered core. The processes by which competences evolve are governed by dynamic organizational routines (Nelson and Winter, 1982) or capabilities that influence the rate and the direction of the evolution of a firm's competences. At the individual level, new competence for the organization is dependent upon the cognitive processes of individuals within the firm, such as the choice of logic employed in processing data (Winterscheid, 1992). Therefore strategic competence can be the possession of unique stocks within the firm, as well as organizational and individual processes that facilitate the usage of those stocks by individuals in the firm.

The chapter examines two questions. To what do insiders refer when describing core competence? How do perceptions of existing core competence enhance or inhibit the development of *new* competence within the firm? We begin with a brief description of the research context, discuss theories relevant to individual perception and core competence, present the empirical data and conclude with a discussion and critique of the findings.

THE RESEARCH CONTEXT

Thirty years ago certain executives in the Warren Corporation recognized the need to develop expertise in electronics. (All identifying references to the corporation, its divisions, product lines and employees are fictitious, as the subject company has requested anonymity.) They believed that electronics would be required in the future to sustain Warren Corporation's market leadership position in Oldbox, a profitable product line historically based in mechanical technology.

While not publicly announced, the strategic intent of developing electronic capability was adopted in the early 1960s and guided certain actions that evolved over time. Among other important management actions were the following:

- In 1970 key individuals with electronic expertise were hired.
- Throughout the 1970s and 1980s research projects were funded at the corporate and division levels to develop electronic

capabilities internally. These new applications were routinely patented.

- In the early 1980s a decision was taken to develop an electronic product for future market introduction when 'the time was right'. Multiple technical directions were pursued within different divisions.
- In 1988 the James division of Warren Corporation embarked on the Newbox product-development program. The stated objectives were to introduce a simple electronic product to customers and, in doing so, gain needed design, manufacture, customer and performance knowledge through a concrete product introduction.

This chapter examines the development of new competence in the Warren Corporation through the Newbox product development effort. Although the Warren Corporation is an American, *Fortune 500* company, it possesses certain characteristics typical to many firms world-wide faced with developing new capability from a history of past success.

1. *Warren Corporation is an established firm.* Founded in 1911, the firm has a known identity and behavior patterns with customers, competitors and employees. There are many long-tenured employees, past routines, expectations, successes and failures. In short, the firm has a history with which it must deal. Additionally, there are deeply entrenched internal practices or administrative routines to support the current success (Starbuck, 1983).
2. *Newbox represents an explicit strategy of internal product development.* The individuals responsible for past success have been called upon to develop new individual skills and to translate these skills into organizational capability. Second, Newbox is set within an existing strategic business unit structure, using standard operating procedures. Further, the technological encroachment of electronics into mechanical functions has disrupted existing functional boundaries within the firm (Quinn, 1992; Jelinek and Schoonhoven, 1990). Mechanical and electronics engineers must learn to integrate their separate areas of expertise. Marketing, engineering and manufacturing functions must also do the same if the new knowledge is to be sufficiently timely and responsive.
3. *Oldbox, Newbox's predecessor, has been a successful product of the James Division of Warren Corporation for the past 30 years.* Warren Corporation currently holds 90% market share for this product

and application. The strategic assumptions are well known (i.e. who our customers are, what product and value we provide, who our competitors are and how we compete, what internal competence is necessary to sustain and maintain current success). Individuals within the firm are now in the difficult position of assessing existing competence for its suitability in the future. These challenges are difficult, since individuals typically assume that they are on familiar ground in the same industry, as always. This assumption is often mistaken, or perhaps more precisely, the ground is the same, but the rules have changed altogether.

CORE COMPETENCE, THE MANAGEMENT PERSPECTIVE AND HIDDEN ACTORS: WHY INDIVIDUALS MAKE THE DIFFERENCE

The resource-based perspective focuses on strategies for exploiting firm-specific assets (Penrose, 1959; Rumelt, 1984; Teece, 1984) as well as strategies for developing new capabilities (Wernerfelt, 1984). It is the second dimension on which this chapter is focused, the ability of the firm repeatedly to acquire new capability through the acquisition of new skills and learning. However, this perspective encounters a problem at both the theoretical and applied levels, not widely acknowledged thus far in the literature. The problem rests with the vexing relationship between the individual and the organization, since it is only the individuals within the organization who acquire new skills and, hopefully, learn (Silverman, 1970). Of course, organizations can codify the knowledge acquired by individuals and develop institutional routines to direct the flow and interpretation of the new information acquired by them (Jelinek, 1979).

Penrose (1959) was the first to recognize the role of individual perception in shaping the strategic assets of the firm by arguing that unused productive services of resources 'shape the scope and direction of the search for knowledge' (p. 77). This notion that the firm's current resources influence managerial perceptions is a cognitive proposition that enforces the economic rationale that a firm's resource profile will influence the direction of new growth (Mahoney and Pandian, 1992; Wernerfelt, 1984).

However, literature since that time has taken a top management or at least a managerial perspective regarding the interpretation and use of existing assets within the firm, as well as the creation of new capability. A popular argument has been that the unique combinations of business experience (Huff, 1982) of the top management team creates a dominant logic (Prahalad and Bettis, 1986) that is used to develop new capability within the firm. Others note management's ability to consolidate technologies and skills into competences (Prahalad and Hamel, 1990), create and maintain organizational capabilities through periods of industry change (Chandler, 1990) and management's ability to organize and utilize the individuals' skills and capabilities to meet the 'unsteady', ever-changing demands of the market (Bogaerts, Martens and Van Cauwenbergh, this volume). Recognition of the 'unsteady' and situational nature of firm capabilities due to rapid technological or market changes is rather new, and casts those individuals within the firm who work with customers and technologies within the firm in a new light.

After all, the omission of the hidden actors, those individuals who implement the strategy through a daily, iteration of sense-making, decisions and actions (Ansoff, 1987), is curious. Firm-specific history, the choices taken by past individuals in the firm in response to their perception of competitive realities faced at the time, has been highlighted as a critical factor in explaining firm-level differences (Nelson and Winter 1982).

Second, the basis of a firm's 'dynamic capabilities' is individual learning and the organizational routines that codify and circulate such learning for use by others in the organization, independent of person, place or time. Certainly, the value of individual skills depends on the choices made by individuals to employ these skills in organizational settings. Learning processes within organizations are intrinsically a social and collective phenomenon that increasingly occurs through joint contributions to the understanding of complex problems (Teece, Pisano and Shuen, 1992). What people think about the problem at hand, what knowledge they bring to bear from past successes or failures and how they communicate that knowledge clearly matters in strategic terms. These factors affect the pace and ultimate development of the intended new competence.

Moving to the organizational level, routines are a form of organizational learning that typically contain patterns of interactions that represent successful solutions to particular problems. The literature has acknowledged that while successful patterns of interaction in group behavior are visible and can be codified, the individual knowledge embedded in those social routines cannot be fully captured (Polanyi, 1962). Alternatively, it may be that certain types of 'organizational' knowledge appear to be tacit because there have been relatively few studies of situation-specific instances of new capability development as experienced by the implementers themselves. Regardless, it is the routines within the firm and management's ability to call on individuals to perform these routines that represent a unique dynamic capability.

THE INTERPRETATION OF EXISTING COMPETENCE: CAN WE LEARN FROM ANYTHING BUT THE PAST?

Now that the link between core competence and individual sense-making has been established, let us look more closely at cognition within an organizational setting. An individual's experiences, understandings, goals and interests direct perceptual salience and establish how individuals perceive their world (Burrell and Morgan, 1979; Cyert and March, 1963; March, 1978; Kahnemann, Slovic and Tversky, 1982). The reality that individuals perceive within organizations is the product of social construction (Berger and Luckmann, 1967) due to group discourse, negotiation, values and shared language. Enacting and interpreting new data as well as acting on those perceptions appear to be difficult for individuals within organizations (Dutton and Duncan, 1987). Individuals must notice and interpret signals of change, then translate those signals into action appropriate to the new situation.

The judgment of data as new or familiar greatly affects the type of cognitive processing used to interpret the data. Research posits a significant role for past experience in cognitive processing (Kiesler and Sproull, 1982; Kahnemann, Slovic and Tversky, 1982; Daft and Weick, 1984). Individuals operate on mental representations of the world that are likely to be based on historical environments rather than on current ones (Kiesler and Sproull, 1982). Since individuals' perceptions and action choices must be the foundation of strategy, individual bias towards the past implies that interpretation of new data may be biased by pre-existing strategic categories.

New information, mildly discrepant from existing knowledge, stands a better chance of being noticed and considered than radically different information. Individuals process slightly different information more efficiently, in that subtle changes in data are more easily recognized and incorporated into current assumptions (Kiesler and Sproull, 1982). In other words, our existing 'view of the world' can be maintained with only minimal changes.

However, information that is really different from existing assumptions, strategy or organizational practices will, presumably, not be recognized at all; or, if recognized, it may be dismissed as irrelevant. Vital new information that does not fit existing strategy or assumptions may be discarded. For example, the slow response to market and/or technological changes by the American automobile industry in the 1960s and the IBM Corporation in the early 1990s support this view.

To summarize, new information faces two hazards: if it is too discrepant it may be ignored entirely as 'noise'; if it is seen as too similar, it may be approached 'mindlessly', and its discrepant nature may be unappreciated. In either case, timely change in assumptions/explanations, actions or strategy is unlikely. Not only will learning be inhibited; so, too, will perception of the need for learning.

Extending this thinking to the evolution of core competence and its learning dynamics requires little effort. Individual or shared perceptions of core competence may function in a similar fashion. Past research (Starbuck, 1983; Louis, 1980) has noted that firm processes exhibit a mindless quality when successful past practices are used for new tasks without thorough consideration of the requirements of the new task. This has been termed mindlessness (Langer, 1988). If this behavior does occur in individuals, then new information may be either ignored or interpreted as 'old'. It will be assumed to be appropriate, with minor revisions, at best. Behavior, and interpretation of that behavior, may take on the character of a routine extension of existing competence, and the need to acquire new competence will go unrecognized.

THE NEWBOX STUDY

Newbox is an automated product which links previously separate components through the integration of electronics and mechanical functions. The following intended strategy for the introduction of electronics into the Oldbox product line was developed in response to uncertainty experienced by Warren Corporation and its customers. The automation of the Newbox product line would be incremental, and the introduction into the commercial marketplace of the electronically updated Oldbox product family members would proceed only after more experience was gained, customer needs better understood, and the customer better educated regarding the benefits of switching to Newbox technology.

In other words, the intended strategy for Newbox challenged established notions within the firm of the existing product lifecycle for Oldbox-type products, and treated Newbox as a short-term vehicle to obtain marketplace knowledge regarding performance and use for future new products. This strategy was a marked change from the past.

From a managerial perspective, the technical uncertainty of integrating mechanical and electronic functions into a single product at a competitive market price posed significant engineering and manufacturing challenges for the Warren Corporation. Relevant information did reside within the organization due to Warren's longstanding strengths in these two areas. However, this expertise was in different divisions, locations and people than in past efforts, which were not integral, had little electronics or concerned different manufacturing technologies.

At the time of the research in 1989, which was part of a large-scale study on the innovation practices in established firms (Jelinek, 1990), Newbox had existed for two years as a technical program at the corporate research center and as a new product development project at James Division for 9 months. It was still approximately 6 months away from restricted quantity prototype release to a controlled set of customers.

DATA COLLECTION

Interviews were conducted with nine individuals, identified by multiple respondents within the company as those most closely involved with the Newbox project. Individuals were identified using a cascade method: those at the top of the organization identified those at the next level down whom they knew were involved in Newbox and believed could yield insight. Interviews were conducted with those individuals, who in turn identified other significant participants at their own level or the next level down. This cascade procedure continued through the organization until duplicate names emerged and, in the view of these persons, all other relevant individuals had been identified. This procedure yielded

TABLE 11.1 Description of individuals

Name[a] and level	Transcript pages
Corporate	
Art Solon	57
Middle	
Bob Quanto	81
Carl King	64
Dan Middleton	55
Ed Fox	56
Operations	
Fred Atlas	60
Gary Techman	100
Hal Barter	45
Ike Lerners	60
Location	*Individuals*
James Division	8
RDC	2
Functional area	*Individuals*
Engineering	7
Manufacturing	1
Sales/marketing	2

[a]All names are pseudonyms, in accordance with Warren Corporation's desire for anonymity and confidentiality assurance to individuals.

nine individuals summarized in Table 11.1, whose tenure with the Warren Corporation ranged from 6 months to 42 years, and represented multiple functional areas and organizational locations.

Interviews with these individuals were conducted jointly by two individuals using the following semi-structured format:

> Think back to when you first became aware of Newbox, either formally or as a perceived challenge for the company. Tell the story of Newbox development over time from your perspective.

Interviewees were probed for clarification of details and queried about elapsed time between events, and the personal significance of these events. Interviewers repeatedly fed back details of their emerging understandings of interviewees' interpretations and conclusions during the course of the interview, as an in-process validity check. Interviews were taped, transcribed and exist in written and electronic formats.

A reconstruction of the events as perceived by the individuals themselves was chosen as the main source of narrative data (Neustadt and May, 1986; Orr, 1990). This was done to put the individuals in the role of telling their version of the Newbox experience and cognitively reliving the experience in order to reconstruct key events in a manner that made sense to them (Brown and Duguid, 1990). A sense of perspective was gained on which events were personally important in the product development effort and why. Additionally, the contemporaneous, internal documents regarding the Newbox project, along with publicly available documents, were used to verify the accounts described by the insiders.

Since the purpose of the analysis was to examine insiders' descriptions of core competence while in the process of strategic activity, we chose to infer insiders' knowledge and use of the core competence concept from their accounts of the events related to Newbox (Winterscheid, 1994). The alternative, of course, was to directly inquire about core competence. However, explicit attention to the core competence concept in data collection would unduly focus insiders' attention and perhaps reveal espoused theories. Since our interest was to uncover insiders' theories-in-use regarding core competence, the inductive approach was chosen.

THE 'CONTENT' OF COMPETENCE PERCEPTIONS

Competence was coded as any statement that described being good at something, knowing something better than others or being number one in a particular area. This coding heuristic was based on the following theoretical definition of core competence: 'a set of differentiated skills, complementary assets, and routines that provide the basis for a firm's competitive capacities and sustainable advantage in a particular business' (Teece, Pisano and Shuen, 1990, p. 28). Negative statements, such as a lack of particular skill, were compared with positive statements within and across individual transcripts as a check on internal validity regarding competence. Any statements of personal or organizational learning processes or mention of explicit transfer of skills was coded as the process of capability building.

Statements in the interview transcripts regarding competence and the development of new capability at the Warren Corporation were found in discussions regarding the Oldbox product, the Newbox product development effort and remarks concerning the people involved in either activity.

Insiders at Warren Corporation perceive that their distinctive competence is derived from two types of knowledge possessed by individuals within the firm: technical competence and market knowledge. This framework is depicted in Figure 11.1. Without exception, they believe that people within Warren know their technologies and their customers better than any of the competition. Also without exception, they describe their competence in terms of the existing, market-leading product, Oldbox. Oldbox is used as the organizing framework of their descriptions, as shown in Figure 11.1. For example, insiders cite their position within the markets that they serve, which they believe is the result of complex and advanced technological expertise, as described below:

> Warren prides itself on being 1 or 2 in the markets they serve and having technologically superior products.

While 30-year sustained leadership in a market should deservedly be a source of pride, it is a result of competence, not competence itself. Another individual describes his view of what created the current competence and the market success of Oldbox:

> We spent a lot of time and money developing Oldboxes and we know just how complicated it is.

In the early years 'time and money' was translated into hiring key individuals with strategic expertise, dedicated R&D programs both

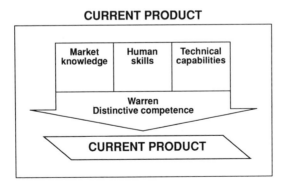

FIGURE 11.1

at the corporate research center and market-focused developmental efforts at the James Division, described at the beginning of this chapter.

Ultimately, 'time and money' provided hands-on experience with the new technology. This experience created a new competence: the unique ability to recognize technical and commercial capability:

> You might say that the Newbox is going to be a product not because it was revolutionary, but because of the recognition that we had the capability in adopting it as a product.

Insiders voice a rather Penrosian (1959) view that expertise comes from the unique ability to recognize a commercial opportunity from technical expertise. They suggested that a new commercial capability was 'recognized' once the necessary investments, technical programs and experience had been achieved. Recognition of capability occurred after hands-on knowledge was accumulated:

> And Warren introduced a product at a time that it was the 'miracle thing'. They introduced a product that had more capability, was smaller in size, had longer life and [cost] less money. So they introduced something into the market . . . that was the right product at the right time.

While the above statement may be an accurate perception of how the Oldbox product occurred on the market, at face value it describes little by way of technical capability that can be replicated for future new product introductions.

Insiders also refer to their long tenure in the Oldbox business as a source of expertise:

> If they [the competitor] take 20 years at it and just keep working and they do things better than we do they will get some business, but I don't think those people can beat us. They don't know this business like we know it. All we focus on is Oldboxes and we know the customers so intimately better than they do. Plus we don't want to be rendered a commodity product which is what [the] Newbox [technology] could literally do.

The descriptions of technical competence within the Warren Corporation are striking in their lack of specificity regarding technical matters. There is no explicit mention of particular competencies; rather, general statements of competence are attributed to past technical achievements, the recognition of 'capability' or, in other words, product potential in a guaranteed market. Warren's technical competence certainly created the smaller, more functional Oldbox, but 30 years of market success have dulled insiders' perceptions so that competence is intimately associated with their descriptions of market success.

Market competence was also linked to past years of experience with the customer. However, these descriptions revealed an interesting relationship between initial technical competence and a very unique, defensible core competence: the relationship with the customer. The initial technical and market success of the Oldbox created a two-way exchange of information regarding products, problems and people. Oldbox, the 'miracle' product, created a knowledge stream between the customer and the Warren Corporation, where valuable product performance knowledge was transferred, and close, personal relationships were developed:

> We are very close with our fleets and our end users, and when [the] engineering [department] develops a product, there is the intention that it is going into production, and so, engineering has a lot of push power [due to market knowledge].

> We're aware of sensitivities, personality problems, pricing problems, product life problems.

The insiders suggest that customer relationships, in which expertise and goodwill flow, transmit the unique character of the organization to outsiders.

> What made [the James division] what we are [today] is we listen to a user, we understand what he is saying about his needs and we put something in his hands and it works where we keep doing it until it's right.

From a core competence perspective, the 'miracle' of Oldbox was not its performance features but the product's ability to open a new link between Warren and its customers. This link was the source of technical knowledge regarding performance and need, mutual problem solving, many sales and personal relationships between Warren employees and customers.

While customer relationships of this sort can be a source of unimitable distinctive competence, a marketing manager recognized the Achilles' heel of this experience-based competence:

> They [the competitor] don't have the experience, but obviously in due time they could get it and we don't want to turn that over to anybody

else if we can control it. So there was a high motivation on my part to keep us [Warren] involved in electronics and with the end user and not turn that [experience] over to [the competitors] . . . They had never done it before, and it just takes time to develop it.

Market knowledge, derived by experience with the customer, is Warren's idiosyncratic edge over the competition. Insiders can describe what they do, how they do it and the edge it gives them over the competition. In contrast to technical knowledge, insiders describe market knowledge in tangible, dynamic terms.

The following points can be made regarding Warren insiders' theories-in-use regarding core competence. First, insiders' perceptions of core competence are based on the assumption of technical expertise that, of course has been backed by a long history of market power. Thirty years after the 'miracle' Oldbox product, Oldbox technology is still used as the point of reference and cited as a source of pride. More important, however, is that technical expertise is a precursor to the formation of mutually beneficial customer relations. Thus, getting linked to customers early in technical development enables knowledge to flow between parties, which ultimately is the source of market knowledge and relationship-based competence.

Second, technical competence is a necessary but insufficient component of competence. Personal relationships with the customers enable the flow of technical knowledge between parties. As this flow of knowledge continues, personal relationships form. These personal relationships 'humanize' information. Knowledge becomes idiosyncratic and, in turn, difficult to imitate—such as knowledge of personal sensitivities in particular companies, new customer strategies and, in general, how things get done in customer organizations. A transmission of the immutable character of the firm built over time (Penrose, 1959) occurs, as an effect of the philosophy 'we'll put it in your hands, and work until it's right' attitude. In short, knowledge becomes idiosyncratic capital.

Third, distinctive market knowledge is subject to erosion if a competitior can establish a technical relationship with the customer, as it enables technical knowledge to begin to flow to a competitor. In addition, it establishes the information channel and potential for new personal relationships between competitor and customer, which has been a distinctive competence for Warren.

Finally, Warren insiders appear to be overconfident in their estimation of their competitive position. While it is true that no one knows the Oldbox business better than they do, it is not clear that Oldbox business will remain. The new performance features and increased efficiency derived from electronics are radically shifting product standards away from Warren's current competence.

THE 'PROCESS' OF BUILDING NEW CAPABILITY

Let us now examine how Warren insiders describe the process of developing new competence in order to understand the evolution of core capability within the firm.

The strategy intent of the Newbox project was to develop two new capabilities:

1. The integration of mechanical and electronic technologies into an incremental new product with enhanced performance features; and
2. A compression of the product development process by working with different organizations within the firm.

Building new capability upon an existing base of familiar competence was important for Warren insiders:

> At that point in time [early 1970s, there] was a pretty good investment in Oldboxes and some investment in automation and electronics, so [Newbox] wasn't a case of doing something that was totally new— bringing something into the organization that was totally foreign.

'New' for this individual was considered to be 'foreign'. Top management's early role in key hires and technical investments ultimately led to the perception of electronics and automation as familiar due to hands-on experience. Employees with technical competence developed at the corporate research center as the concept of people as 'competence carriers' (Prahalad and Hamel, 1990) that form the basis of the firm's expertise, and how that new competence gets transferred is as follows:

> And then there has been some commitment by [top management] now to have bigger programs and bigger investment. [Hiring the initial people with electronic expertise] brought about the fact that [electronic] capabilities were transplanted into several different people.
> The [Newbox effort] took the people out of [RDC] who had experience, and they created [the Newbox project] at the division.

> And then there has been some commitment to have bigger programs and investments because we hired [RS] who brought automation expertise to Warren now. Hiring [RS] brought about the fact that [electronic] capabilities were transplanted into several different people.

Once knowledge of electronics was developed in key people, typically at the research center, knowledge diffusion occurred by transferring key people to operational units, in order to diffuse the new technical knowledge through multiple people and locations.

Figure 11.2 illustrates perceptions of the Newbox product development effort early in the development process. It depicts Newbox as the straightforward integration of mechanical and electronic technologies into an incremental product for a market they know well. The incremental enhancements are intended to create a better version of the existing product. Technology, product design, customer feedback and past Oldbox experience were assumed to be valid predictors for Newbox. New knowledge concerning technical and design enhancements were expected to be derived from customer feedback on Newbox prototypes and approximation from past experience and expertise. In short, Newbox

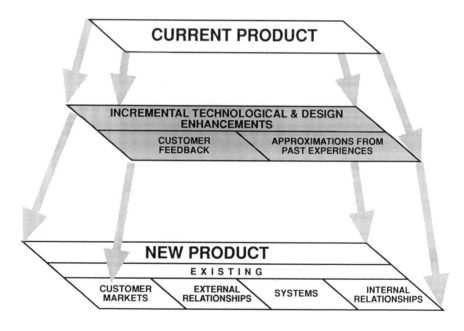

FIGURE 11.2

is a method to defend and maintain the dominant market share and product niche created by Oldbox. No data suggest that Newbox is perceived as a new product in its own right, requiring radical new learning.

Since Newbox was considered an incremental technical innovation within the firm, serious omissions may have been made in the marketing area, a source of unique competence for the organization. No mention was made of the potential changes in customer relationships precipitated by the incremental new technology. This incremental view of the capability development process confirms existing assumptions, knowledge and organizational practices within Warren Corporation. It is an excellent example of single-loop learning (Argyris and Schon, 1978).

The diffusion of new capabilities from one person to another was not a simple process, despite perceived competence in technical matters. One respondent mentioned that the technical interface between the mechanical and electronic technologies was considered unproblematic for engineers on each side as they considered the 'foreign' technology. After closer hands-on involvement, both sets of engineers discovered that Newbox would be a difficult undertaking, due to hidden complexities:

> At first, the inception of [Newbox] was really thought to be very simple for the other side of the fence, where the mechanical people said [to the electronic people] 'Well, all you're doing is putting a little controller on our Oldbox. I think by putting the two [mechanical and electronic] people on an equal level, management said "Okay, you guys battle it out and see what has to be done.".

The perception of the organizational 'fence' represents not only barriers between basic technological differences but also departmental process barriers, and barriers between the people themselves, due to training and expertise. Not the terms of condescension of the 'other' technology and possession of 'our Oldbox' by the mechanical people. The image of something foreign and new being appended to the familiar represents more than concrete technical changes. It highlights underlying technical and personal challenges involved in doing something different.

Midway through the Newbox project those closest to the action recognized that Newbox was susbtantially different from past product development processes and represented learning for everyone involved. Knowledge was gained in the midst of action, requiring a different approach to management and monitoring:

> Everybody is learning the details that are required by a manufacturing
> organization or a design services organization to release this new product
> and everybody is complaining about the detail that is required, myself
> included.

What personal challenges were faced by members of the Newbox
team? Consider that Warren was organized into separate
departments grouped by function and subgrouped by technical
expertise:

> [The mechanical and electronic manager] really, in essence, got
> themselves together as far as their interpersonal skills. They spent great
> periods of time just getting to talk to each other so that they would know
> each other on a personal level as well as a working level.

The development of personal relationships and the perception of
friendship, or at least familiarity, was essential for the technical
integration to occur. Gaps in knowledge, language and organizational
process capabilities were uncovered. Specific attempts to develop
a common language and, beyond that, common understanding
between these two groups were done daily on a personal level, and
were not anticipated by the organization, despite the stated strategic
intent of Newbox:

> You know, now [the mechanical and electronic managers] are putting
> a product together and they talk a different jargon and everything's
> different. So they have to come together in a common language and get
> some communication skills, so they understand and everyone is talking
> the same game.

Further, routine organizational procedures which served Warren
so well in the past now posed implementation problems. Existing
systems in Warren were designed for familiar, incremental
mechanical product extensions and were ill equipped to handle the
new challenges. For example, product-launch procedures such as
prediction of design milestones, termination criteria for the
milestones and budget predictions were now difficult to predict:

> The twenty milestones don't cover all of the important milestones for
> the automated products. Even the understanding of those milestones,
> they are kind of difficult sometimes to define when they've ended.

A second problem of organizational process related to the scope
and pace of needed organizational change between departments
necessary to support Newbox. While those closest to Newbox design

had already made changes in departmental systems to compensate for new learning, other departments had not:

> We have a lot of problems in the area of working with manufacturing engineering, due to the fact that they are used to working with a program that all of a sudden is a complete package. Then they can take it and run with it very well.

While Newbox was perceived as an incremental technical innovation by insiders, it was discovered *en route* that radical changes in organizational routines were required. Newbox provoked differences in language, customer and departmental relationships, and innovations to existing formal systems. Figure 11.3 shows the radical changes caused by Newbox.

New learning, new language, different relationships and potentially obsolete routines were discovered. While the strategic emphasis for building new capability was placed on technological issues, the organizational competence required to make those changes went unrecognized at the strategic level. They were treated on an *ad hoc* basis by the individuals at the project level, if those individuals had the authority or motivation.

ORDER QUALIFIERS, ORDER WINNERS AND JUST PLAIN WORDS

In the literature, knowledge in the firm can be considered a core competence when it is embodied in employee knowledge and skills and is embedded in technical systems. The processes of knowledge creation are thought to be controlled by managerial systems, and the values and norms associated with various types of embedded knowledge and processes within the firm (Leonard-Barton, 1992). It is thought that values and norms, typically ignored in the research literature, are crucial to managing new product and process development and the subsequent evolution in competence that such activities create.

Insiders within this firm primarily cited knowledge and skills relating to Oldbox, the firm's market-leading product, supporting current theory. What is new in this research were the types of competence perceived by insiders: technical capability, market knowledge and the people associated with that competence. Further, technical capability was not well articulated by insiders,

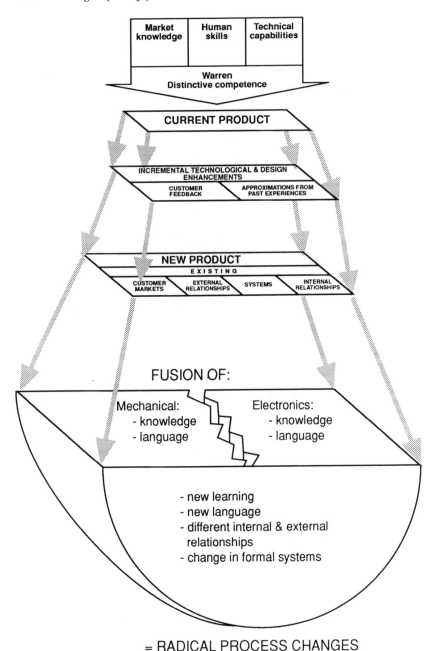

FIGURE 11.3

referring to the 'miracle product' (of course, whose functionality and size could not have been obtained without unique technical competence) or dominant market position as the source of competence. This finding is curious, given the high proportion of engineers in the research sample. After years, and perhaps managerial generations, of success in his business, insiders have lost explicit articulation of their competence.

This research has also shown that insiders consider competence more broadly than just firm-specific techniques and scientific understanding. Market knowledge, embodied by long-nurtured customer relationships, is vital. Not only are these relationships vital but they have been explicitly described by Warren insiders as the distinctive, idiosyncratic features of the organization in the marketplace. Insiders could speak of this competence in alive and dynamic terms, that is, practiced and defended as core in real-time, despite 30 years of market success. As a manager put it:

> [The competitors] don't have the experience, but . . . they could get it and we don't want to turn that over to anybody if we can control it.'

Unfortunately, in the Newbox development process at Warren these customer relationships were ignored until the scientific integration of mechanical and electronic technologies in the product was solved. Further, new capability development was explicitly directed towards technology (i.e. the merging of mechanical and electronic functions for Newbox), not the changed customer relationships' organizational routines. Relevant input by customers in terms of size, performance, and related innovations in the customer's end product were delayed due to the internal technical focus begun at first. Of course, at Warren Corporation the tech-push approach had always worked in the past. Existing capabilities in marketing, manufacturing and organizational process were assumed to be valid, despite Warren's stated intention to speed the product-development process. Obviously, insiders initially only considered the engineering aspects of the development process.

The crucial relationship between technical competence as the 'order-qualifier', that competence which is necessary merely to get into the customer's door, and market and customer knowledge, which actually is the 'order-winner', was made clear by Warren insiders. Scientific and product development competence is not enough, nor is it defensible over the long term in today's world, despite the past success of the Warren Corporation and many other corporations competing on technology today.

Shifting now to an examination of insiders' perceptions of the process of evolving new competence, this research has demonstrated the insidious power of past market success. Building upon Leonard-Barton (1992), insiders described the numerous roadblocks encountered with existing procedures and operational assumptions (established for Oldbox products and until now unquestioned). These procedures and assumptions included budgeting, planning and approval processes, milestone reviews and, most importantly for Warren's distinctive competence, when and how to interact with the customer and the type of strategic information the customer can actually provide.

What is also new in this research is the powerful effect of language recounted by Warren insiders. They were not speaking of deep-seated philosophical, international or cross-cultural differences. They were just ten knowledgeable guys who had a product-development job to do, and they had problems speaking to and understanding each other. People in different departments used different language. Even the same words used by people in different departments or functions had different meanings. The standard operating procedures usually triggered by those words, and even the assumptions behind those words, had to be acknowledged, re-examined and then debated for the success of the project. These actions were not planned by the organization or anticipated by the individuals. This social reconstruction of meaning had to occur before the project could go forward.

EVOLVING COMPETENCE: NEW VIEWS, NEW CHALLENGES

So what can be learned from the Newbox experience of value to other successful, established organizations evolving core competence towards new competitive realities? We will first present some general hypotheses regarding the evolution of core competence within the firm and conclude with recommendations for management.

HYPOTHESIS ONE

Individuals who perceive the organization to be competent in a particular area will perceive the *new* competence required in terms of their existing core competence. Little attention will be devoted to discovering the required new capability in areas that they do not know, or take for granted, in the first place.

Insiders' discussions of existing competence was in terms of Oldbox, the current mechanical product. Competence in the areas of technology, marketing and people was derived from past achievements of the organization, and there is little evidence to suggest active re-evaluation in any systematic way. In particular, existing competence was attributed to market position rather than the specific actions taken to generate that market position.

Since this market position is currently under threat due to technological change, Warren faces rapid deterioration of competence, not only in technology but also in the quality of thinking that surfaced in this research—the benchmarks used by individuals to gauge their competence. This finding could be due to Newbox's early strategic positioning as an incremental product innovation. Confirming cognitive psychological research (Kiesler and Sproull, 1982; Langer, 1988), Newbox individuals expected that their existing knowledge base was valid for the task, with only incremental additions to knowledge. People had predetermined expectations regarding new learning and the early knowledge gained from Newbox confirmed expectations. These discoveries generate Hypothesis Two.

HYPOTHESIS TWO

The expectation of a competence-evolving task as incremental innovation will initially confirm existing assumptions and practices in the firm. The new information gained from the innovation will initially be interpreted using long-held personal cognitive categories and strategic assumptions. Prolonged hands-on experience in a new development effort in which failure or other threat is confronted will provoke a re-examination of existing organizational assumptions.

The people in the Newbox team simply did not change until they were forced to. Finally, the Newbox case highlighted the problems associated with the unintended consequences of developing new capability. All insiders reported the anticipation of incremental change during early stages of Newbox development. Once further experience was gained, the multiple discoveries of the necessity of radical change in organizational routines was reported. These discoveries were made by individuals at the project level. To accomplish Newbox, the Warren Corporation was forced to change after individual discoveries of dysfunction. The Warren management simply did not anticipate the individual and organizational problems provoked by the Newbox effort.

HYPOTHESIS THREE

Content competence is a necessary but insufficient source of competitive advantage, because process competencies flow new knowledge through the firm and affect its use of such knowledge by individuals within the firm. Perhaps, similar process competencies generated the initial market success for the Warren Corporation which they have sustained for the past 30 years. However, the process competencies that initially generated success have become so deeply embedded within the organization that they are taken for granted by individuals and are assumed to be a permanent feature of the organization. As a consequence, process competencies are not easily scrutinized for potential change and learning.

Examples of emergent process competencies provoked by Newbox were the customer relationships and interactions necessary to the development of new products, the new relationships with people inside the organization, new organizational routines to track and measure Newbox progress and the development of a new language between Warren employees. Process competencies were the real-time discoveries made by Newbox insiders depicted in Figure 11.2.

The Newbox case indicates that individuals deal with process issues on the run while pursuing new technical competence. In fact, evidence in this case suggests that currently successful organizations will not confront changes in organizational routines unless forced by competitive threat.

HYPOTHESIS FOUR

The words that individuals use in an organization contain deep-seated assumptions about reality perceived by the individual. This study has begun to uncover the organizational implications of personal meaning. The first roadblock encountered in the Newbox project was that of personal communication. This problem was unexpected by individuals, and the time to construct new meaning was not planned for at the organizational level. In other words, to evolve new competence in an organization, first examine the language in use by individuals in it.

FINAL THOUGHTS FOR MANAGEMENT

Based on this research, certain prescriptions for management can be offered.

1. Organizations that choose a strategy of internal competence generation, in contrast to acquisition, should scrutinize existing competence carefully and begin to build a new competence from some aspect of the old. This is not as easy as it sounds, as described by the Newbox team. Build from a base of familiarity, but realize, anticipate and plan for the cognitive risks that the firm will run in perpetuating old knowledge.
2. Pay attention to the words used by people within your firm and what they mean when they use those words. Firms can conduct an audit of the language-in-use by key groups within the organization (Winterscheid, 1992) upon whom you depend for existing or future competence. An audit of this sort can uncover differences in personal logic or approach as well as roadblocks at the organizational level.
3. Historically successful firms should explicitly recognize the unintended consequences of new-capability generation. This research demonstrated the difficulty of learning to do something new—learning new technical skills, working with new people in different relationships, using new language or redefining familiar terms in new ways. These unintended consequences take additional time, which is difficult to anticipate beforehand. Acknowledging and creating explicit activities to expose

individuals to continuous novelty of data and the questioning of widely held organizational assumptions will encourage flexible and timely response to new challenges.

4. Firms should also develop routines to collect, organize and make available the unintended, spontaneous learning of individuals involved in doing something new within the organization. In the cognitive psychology literature this process has been termed 'meta-cognition'. Meta-cognition is defined as the awareness of using cognitive processes and the knowledge that certain cognitive strategies are useful (Brown, 1978).

One recommended meta-cognitive routine is the explicit capture of midstream discoveries made by individuals. This capture could take the form of a personal 'issue diary' designed to record insights, problems or discoveries. Electronic capture of these data could further improve their analysis and subsequent organizational value. Other meta-cognitive tactics could be regular project issues meetings with all relevant individuals to capture similar data as in the issue diary. Logs of this type of meeting would be helpful for future projects elsewhere in the organization. Debriefing meetings could also be held at the conclusion of various phases of key projects.

In conclusion, this research has identified a crucial extension to the thinking of Prahalad and Hamel. They have argued that the real sources of competitive advantages are to be found in management's ability to consolidate corporate-wide technologies and production skills into competences that empower individual businesses to adapt quickly to changing opportunities (Prahalad and Hamel, 1990, p. 90). Based on the evidence presented here, the real sources of competitive advantage are to be found in management's ability to craft technologies, production skills and organizational routines into organizational competences that empower individuals within the businesses to adapt quickly to changing opportunities.

ACKNOWLEDGEMENT

The author gratefully acknowledges the support of the Center for the Management of Science and Technology, Weatherhead School of Management, Case Western Reserve University.

REFERENCES

Ansoff, I. (1987). The emerging paradigm of strategic behavior. *Strategic Management Journal*, **8**(6), 501–15.

Argyris, C. and Schon, D. (1978). *Organizational Learning*. Reading, MA: Addison-Wesley.

Berger, P. and Luckmann, T. (1967). *The Social Construction of Reality*. New York: Anchor Books.

Brown, A. L. (1978). Knowing when, where and how to remember. A problem of metacognition. In R. Glaser (Ed.) *Advances in Instructional Psychology*, Vol. 1. Hillsdale, NJ: Erlbaum.

Brown, J. S. and Duguid, P. (1990). Organizational learning and communities of practice: towards a unified view of working, learning and innovation. *Organization Science*, **2**(1), 40–57.

Burrell, G. and Morgan, G. (1979). *Sociological Paradigms and Organizational Analysis*. Portsmouth, NH: Hienemann Books.

Chandler, A. D. (1990). *Scale and Scope: The Dynamics of Industrial Capitalism*. Cambridge, MA: Belknap Press.

Cyert, R. M. and March, J. G. (1963). *A Behavioral Theory of the Firm*. Englewood Cliffs, NJ: Prentice-Hall.

Daft, R. L. and Weick, K. (1984). Towards a model of organizations as interpretation systems. *Academy of Management Review*, **9**(2), 284–95.

Dutton, J. and Duncan, R. (1987). The creation of momentum for change through the process of strategic issue diagnosis. *Strategic Management Journal*, **8**(3), 279–96.

Hall, R. (1991). The strategic analysis of intangible resources. *Strategic Management Journal*, **13**(2), 135–4.

Huff, A. (1982). Industry influence on strategy reformulation. *Strategic Management Journal*, **3**, 119–31.

Jelinek, M. (1979). *Institutionalizing Innovation*. New York: Praeger.

Jelinek, M. (1990). Strategic innovation in established firms. CMOST Working Paper, Case Western Reserve University.

Jelinek, M. and Schoonhoven, W. (1990). *The Innovation Marathon*. Oxford and Cambridge, MA: Basil Blackwell.

Kahnemann, D., Slovic, P. and Tversky, A. (1982). *Judgment under Uncertainty: Heuristics and Biases*. Cambridge: Cambridge University Press.

Kiesler, S., Sproull, L. (1982). Managerial response to changing environments: perspectives on problem solving from social cognition. *Administrative Science Quarterly*, **27**, 548–70.

Langer, E. (1988). *Mindfulness*. Reading, MA: Addison-Wesley.

Leonard-Barton, D. (1992). Core capabilities and core rigidities. *Strategic Management Journal*, **13**, Summer, 111–26.

Louis, M. R. (1980). Surprise and sensemaking: what newcomers experience in entering unfamiliar organizational settings. *Administrative Science Quarterly*, **255**, 225–51.

Mahoney, J. and Pandian, J. (1992). The resource-based view within the conversation of strategic management. *Strategic Management Journal*, **13**(5), 363–80.

March, J. G. (1978). Bounded rationality, ambiguity, and the engineering of choice. *Bell Journal of Economics*, 587–608.

Nelson, R. and Winter, S. (1982). *An Evolutionary Theory of Economic Change.* Cambridge, MA: Harvard University Press.

Neustadt, R. E. and May, E. R. (1986). *Thinking in Time: The uses of history for decision-makers.* New York: Free Press.

Orr, L. (1990). Sharing knowledge, celebrating identity: war stories and community memory in a service culture. In D. S. Middleton and D. Edwards (Eds) *Collective Remembering: Memory in Society.* Beverly Hills, CA: Sage Publications.

Penrose, E. (1959). *The Theory of the Growth of the Firm.* London: Basil Blackwell.

Polanyi, M. (1962). *The Tacit Dimension.* New York: Doubleday.

Prahalad, C. and Bettis, R. (1986). The dominant logic: a new linkage between diversity and performance. *Strategic Management Journal*, 7, 485–501.

Prahalad, C. and Hamel, G. (1990). The core competence of the corporation. *Harvard Business Review*, May–June, 79–91.

Quinn, J. B. (1992). *The Intelligent Enterprise.* New York: Free Press.

Rumelt, R. P. (1984). Towards a strategic theory of the firm. In R. B. Lamb (Ed.) *Competitive Strategic Management*, Englewood Cliffs, NJ: Prentice-Hall.

Silverman, D. (1970). *The Theory of Organizations.* London: Heinemann.

Starbuck, W. (1983). Organizations as action generators. *American Sociological Review*, 48(2), 91–102.

Teece, D. J. (1984). Economic analysis and strategic management. *California Management Review*, 26(3), 87–110.

Teece, D. J., Pisano, G. and Shuen, A. (1992). Dynamic capabilities and strategic management. Working Paper, University of California at Berkeley, CA.

Wernerfelt, B. (1984). A resource-based view of the firm. *Strategic Management Journal*, 5, 171–80.

Winterscheid, B. C. (1992). *Strategic Innovation in Established Firms: The Intersection of Parallel Logics.* PhD dissertation, Case Western Reserve University.

Winterscheid, B. C. (1994). Nodes and codes: are words a window to the mind? In C. Stubbart, J. Porac, and J. Meindl (Eds), *Advances in Managerial Cognition and Information Processing.* Greenwich, CT: JAI Press.

12

Technology Strategy in Competence-based Competition

VITTORIO CHIESA, MAURIZIO BARBESCHI

INTRODUCTION

Recent studies have identified the competence of the corporation as a source of sustainable, long-term competitive advantage. In strategic management this has led to a line of thought that can be traced back to the *resource-based view* of the firm. An analysis of some cases of competence-based competition shows that competencies can reside in superior technical leads (Prahalad and Hamel, 1990), managerial capabilities or world-class practices or disciplines (Stalk, Evans and Shulman, 1992), but are often a combination of these. Generally, a *competence* can be defined as a unique mix of knowledge, skills and technologies leading the generation of a series of profitable innovations. This approach suggests that the firm should be viewed as a dynamic system (Bertelè, 1991), the key resources of which are embedded in the organization as the result of a cumulative process. Beside this, it has been stressed that competence building requires a 'strategic architecture', a sort of roadmap that establishes objectives and then identifies the core competencies to build and their constituent technologies. Competence building can, therefore, be viewed as a guided process of resource accumulation. An analysis of the literature on this topic

Competence-Based Competition.
Edited by G. Hamel and A. Heene.

suggests that the blocks for competence building are: (1) committing the organization to long-term objectives (Hamel and Prahalad, 1989, 1993), (2) accumulating resources; and (3) enhancing the bases of knowledge and skills through learning cycles (Dodgson, 1991; Pavitt, 1991).

In this chapter we will focus on competencies based on technological capabilities or, at least, those in which the technological side of the competence is relevant. After introducing the concept of core competencies and identifying the related building blocks, we will study the implications of a competence-based approach for the content and process of technology strategy. We will argue that:

1. A technology strategy should be viewed as the definition of a trajectory for technological resource acquisition and internalization rather than as a support activity consonant with the generic strategy that is being pursued.
2. The process of technology strategy is central to the definition of the content. Therefore, it is relevant to identify the characteristics of good practice in technology strategy processes.

We will subsequently propose a framework to formulate a technology-acquisition strategy in a competence-based approach (in this chapter technology acquisition includes both internally generated R&D and external sourcing) and identify the characteristics of successful technology strategy processes. The analysis and the proposed framework draw on a review of well-known cases of competence-based firms and on the results of an empirical study on the processes of technology acquisition in a sample of twelve multinational companies operating in the electronics, telecommunications and mechanical industries.

THE CONCEPT OF CORE COMPETENCE

Many recent studies have shown that sustainable competitive advantages are often based on the distinctive core competencies developed within the firm. In strategic management this has led to a line of thought that adopts a resource-based view of the firm. Wernefelt (1984) stated that advantages in markets may exist where a firm's resources are superior to those of competitors. Collis (1991) defines the core competencies as a 'vector of irreversible assets along which the firm is uniquely advantaged'. Prahalad and Hamel (1990) have defined the core competencies as 'the collective learning in the organization, especially how to co-ordinate diverse production skills and integrate multiple streams of technologies'.

Other authors have stressed the role of the business processes as the building blocks of a corporate strategy. They have argued that competitive success depends on transforming a company's key processes into strategic capabilities (in the view of Stalk, Evans and Shulman, 1992, 'core competence emphasizes technological and production expertise at specific points along the value chain, capabilities are more broadly based, encompassing the entire value chain'), or on redesigning the core processes (Kaplan and Murdock, 1991), or on implementing disciplines enabling the company to deliver a product faster and better (Hamel, 1991).

Leonard-Barton (1992) proposes that core capability is 'a knowledge set comprising four dimensions: (1) employee knowledge and skills, that are embedded in (2) technical systems. Its processes are guided by (3) managerial systems and (4) values and norms (. . .) associated with the processes of knowledge creation and control.' Examples of competence-based strategies show that competencies are not identifiable with one dimension but are often a combination of various elements. In the case of Honda, scholars have been witnessing a passionate debate on what Honda's core competencies actually are: engine technology, dealer relationship management, or the product development process. Stalk, Evans and Shulman (1992) recognized that 'as the Honda sample suggests, competencies and capabilities represent two different but complementary dimensions of an emerging paradigm for corporate strategy.' In the case of 3M (which produces 60 000 products), the technical competence in sticky products is combined with a culture fostering innovation at all levels of the organization and with procedures for developing innovative ideas.

Whatever the typology of the competence, the key characteristics is that it is the result of a cumulative resource development process that leads to a build-up of firm-specific competencies. Ultimately, these are based on an organization's *skills* and *knowledge* (Hedlund and Rolander, 1990). Knowledge and skills which are hard to imitate are a source of lasting advantage. These are 'embedded in the organization, in its ability to develop series of advances, matched by commercial skills. . . . Skills are built incrementally via a series of short-term learning cycles within a long-term process of accumulating capabilities' (Grindley, 1991).

It has been stressed that competence building requires the development of a 'strategic architecture' or *strategic intent* (Hamel and Prahalad, 1989) to define the long-term direction of the firm, to establish the objectives of the process of accumulating capabilities, and to identify which core competencies and their *constituent technologies* to build (Prahalad and Hamel, 1990). Competence building can, therefore, be viewed as a 'guided' process of resource accumulation.

A new competitive model emerges. Competition is a matter of 'stretch' rather than 'fit'; it is not a question of understanding the relationship between the company and its competitive environment but of stretching objectives, leveraging resources and conceiving a consistent stream of efforts (Hamel and Prahalad, 1993).

In this chapter we will analyse how competence-based competition affects the strategic management of technology. We will focus on technology-intensive industries where competencies are essentially based on technological capabilities and enhanced through R&D investment and technology development. We first analyse each building block of a competence-based approach in order to identify the major implications for the strategic management of technology, especially the content and the process of technology strategy. We will then propose a model for formulating a technology-acquisition strategy and identify the characteristics of successful processes of technology strategy.

COMPETENCE-BASED COMPETITION AND TECHNOLOGICAL INNOVATION

From the above discussion, it can be argued that the building blocks of a competence-based competition are:

- Committing the organization to long-term objectives
- Accumulating resources
- A continuous process of learning.

In this section we analyse the major implications of each building block in terms of the strategic management of technology. At the end of each subsection the relevant concepts are summarized.

COMMITTING THE ORGANIZATION TO LONG-TERM OBJECTIVES

Competence building requires a clear definition of where the firm wants to be in the long term. It can be a fuzzy and weakly focused statement (Moenaert, 1992) but it addresses the firm's efforts. Sony's founders intended from the beginning to apply 'a mix of electronics and engineering to the consumer field'. Hamel and Prahalad (1989) call this *strategic intent*. This approach allows each action to be referred to the satisfaction of customer needs, in other words, to the delivery of *value*. It has been argued that strategic intent should consist of the 'functions' a product should perform (Abell, 1980). Product functions are more stable than technologies. Therefore, functions are the base for an organization to develop a long-term strategy, and the strategic intent guides the company towards specific actions enabling it to accumulate resources in a defined direction.

A strategic focal point ensures that resources are concentrated and efforts converge; this has been recognized as central to a strategy aimed at leveraging resources. Concentration involves convergence (preventing the diversion of resources over time) and focus (preventing the dilution of resources at any given time) (Hamel and Prahalad, 1993).

Other authors have suggested that technological choices and R&D investments should also be guided by the notion of strategic intent (Moenaert, 1992).

Competence-based competition requires that investments are focused on a limited number of competencies, knowledge assets and technologies which contribute to the perceived customer value and benefits.

ACCUMULATING RESOURCES

Hamel and Prahalad (1993) identify two ways of accumulating resources: *extracting* them from the company reservoir of experience and *borrowing* from other companies.

Extracting

It has been recognized that a company's assets are often invisible and refer to experience, intellectual competencies and insights of people (Imai, Nonaka and Takeuchi, 1985; Itami, 1987). Nonaka (1991) argues that successful companies are those that view the firm as a *knowledge-creating* 'machine'. Two different types of knowledge have been identified, *explicit* and *tacit* (obtained through experience), each of which requires an organizational 'machine' to exploit and embed it (Polanyi, 1966) so that it can contribute to the build-up of firm-specific competencies.

Creating knowledge is a matter of the whole organization: 'In the knowledge creating company, inventing new knowledge is not a specialized activity—the province of the R&D department or marketing or strategic planning. It is a way of behaving, indeed a way of being, in which everyone is a knowledge worker—that is to say, an entrepreneur' (Nonaka, 1991). The *learning organization* (Senge, 1990) is the only one able to extract efficiently knowledge from the experiences of every employee, i.e. maximize the insights that can be gained from them. Therefore, knowledge creation is a process involving different specialists and functions. It has been argued that knowledge inputs for any innovation draw on a wide variety of professional skills in science, engineering and management (Pavitt, 1991).

Innovation is the result of the interaction among functionally specialized groups and a variety of technological and managerial skills that are organizationally dispersed.

Borrowing

The other way to accumulate and leverage resources is by borrowing. Collaboration with other firms has been recognized as an integral part of a resource-based technological strategy (Hamel, 1991). It involves both gaining access to the partner's skills and internalizing them (Hamel and Prahalad, 1993; Anderson, 1982). Competencies lie in the embedded knowledge and skills of the organization and are accumulated through processes of continuous learning. Competitiveness is based on the ability of the organization to establish proprietary access to those resources that lead to a stream of sustainable competitive advantages. It does not mean that each piece of knowledge and technology required for innovation should be developed in-house. The increasing specialization of knowledge, skills and technological capabilities on a world-wide basis has increased the need for an organization to acquire outside knowhow and information and to tap into the global market for technology.

Sources of technical knowledge include scientific parks, but also regional or district concentrations which have become the main sources of technical and/or market knowledge in specific fields, such as Silicon Valley for semiconductors, the Sassuolo (Italy) area for ceramic manufacturers, the Zürich area for hard sciences, and the network of Japanese automotive suppliers.

Internalization of skills and knowledge gained from outside sources and their integration with internal resources become central to a resource-based technological strategy. Networking is a widely adopted practice (Chiesa and Barbeschi, 1992). De Meyer (1992) has indicated that the effectiveness of an international network of R&D activities depends on its ability to accelerate or improve some form of learning by the organization, such as different ways of doing research and approaching markets, learning customer needs, monitoring the most recent developments, or access to resources that can process the relevant information.

Innovation is the result of the interaction among functionally specialized groups and a variety of technological and managerial skills that are geographically dispersed.

LEARNING

The third leg of competence building is learning, which constitutes a sort of *fil-rouge* pervading all the activities of the firm. Indeed, given the nature of the cumulative development of competencies, their improvement requires continuous and collective learning. Learning can be defined as 'the ways firms build and supplement their knowledge bases in technologies, products and processes, and develop and improve the use of the broad skills of their workforce' (Dodgson, 1991). Sources of learning are very diverse and their relative importance varies according to the nature of the core competence of the firm: learning is concerned with both internal activities (learning by doing, using, failing, studying) and the outer context (learning from competitors, customers, suppliers, technological sources). Learning is the process that allows a continuous adaptation of firm-specific competencies in the light of experience and further information. In other words, '. . ., *process of learning allows a continuous feedback between the content of a resource-based technological strategy and knowledge of the context outside together with the inner context within the firm and its competences'* (Pavitt, 1991).

TECHNOLOGY STRATEGY IN COMPETENCE-BASED COMPETITION

This renewed context poses great challenges to the strategic management of technology and has major implications for the way to approach a technology strategy (Hax and Majluf, 1991; Hax and No, 1992). Traditional approaches to technology strategy have been related to a conventional generic framework, as in Porter (1985), and to a problem of market positioning. At the core of a technology strategy there is the type of competitive advantage a firm is trying to achieve and the question whether a firm should be the 'leader' or a 'follower' in these technologies. This view suggests that R&D and technology development programs should be consonant with the generic strategy that is being pursued (Booz-Allen and Hamilton, 1981; Little, 1981; Roussel, Saad and Erickson, 1991). The problem with generic strategy is that it addresses the problem of where the firm would like to be but not of how to get there (Grindley, 1991).

On the other hand, competence-based competition emphasizes that a firm's source of sustainable competitive advantage is the result of capability development along a given trajectory which is stable in the long term, that the innovative opportunities open to a firm are strongly dependent on its accumulated competencies and that competitive performance is the result of how a firm is able to leverage its resources, invest in a small number of distinctive competencies and shape the competition. It can be argued that a resource- or competence-based technology strategy should address the following areas:

What are the company's core competencies in technology?
What are the core and complementary core technologies?
Where does the company need to be strong and where can it rely on alternative sources?

and therefore

- Understand how technological choices affect the inner context (firm-specific competencies)
- Define a trajectory for technological resource acquisition and internalization.

Given that, as we have seen, the content of a technology strategy is heavily affected by the process of learning about the context, it is also relevant to adopt a process-based view of technology strategy in order to understand the relationships between a firm's technology management system and decision-making process and its technological innovation performance (Chakravarthy and Doz, 1992; Pavitt, 1990). More simply, the processes whereby technological strategies are generated and chosen are relevant to the definition of the content of the technology strategy itself. Therefore, it is relevant to our discussion to identify good practice and the characteristics of successful processes adopted for the formulation of a technology strategy.

In the next subsection we first propose a framework to formulate a technology acquisition strategy and subsequently study the characteristics of successful technology strategy processes in a competence-based approach.

TECHNOLOGY STRATEGY—THE CONTENT

The process of knowledge creation is central to competence building. Producing knowledge can be viewed as a manufacturing industry, in which the object of transformation is knowledge rather than physical goods. As in any manufacturing or service industry, a 'value chain' can also be identified in the knowledge-production industry. A technology to be used in a product or a process is the result of a process of knowledge transformation/production. This process comprises various stages, traditionally classified as basic research, applied research and development. Each stage represents a set of segments of knowledge needed to apply science and engineering to products, services or processes. A firm should identify the segments of knowledge which generate value in each of the constituent technologies of its competence.

The value of each segment of knowledge is related to four main dimensions:

- How it contributes to give value to customers
- The degree of appropriability
- The coherency: this refers to how each segment of knowledge contributes to the accumulation of resources in the direction undertaken
- How it contributes to the characteristic of uniqueness of the competence.

A segment of knowledge is defined as:

1. *Core* when it contributes to the perceived customer value, to the build-up of competence and is highly appropriable in itself, or to the creation of a unique pattern of knowledge accumulation and co-ordination;
2. *Competence-refreshing* when it contributes to the perceived customer value, is not highly appropriable but if combined with the available competence can lead to a stream of innovations;
3. *Non-core* when it refers to available basic knowledge.

This view suggests that:

- Each technology should be viewed as composed of a series of segments of knowledge each contributing differently to the constitution of the competence. This depends on two dimensions that are inherent in the segment itself: the contribution to the perceived value for the customer and the degree of appropriability.
- The two other dimensions which identify the value of a segment of knowledge refer to how it relates to competence and how it integrates with the latter. Therefore, the contribution of a piece of knowledge to the building of competence is also dependent on the type of competence (technology-integration-based versus single-technology based).

We argue that a technology acquisition strategy should be defined according to these two factors. The analysis of a number of cases supports our hypothesis and provides evidence of how key decisions related to a technology-acquisition strategy are dependent on these factors. The analysis relies both on our own empirical study on the technology acquisition process in multinational companies and on cases taken from the literature.

Cases of Competence-based Technology Strategies

The core competencies of Canon are linked to a unique form of integration of different technologies, microelectronics, optics and electronic imaging. NEC identified a stream of technologies, such as semiconductors, computing and communication, to integrate. Northern Telecom has focused its competence building on telecommunication technology; Honda and Cummins Engine found their competitive advantage in the unique mix of applications of one base technology, engine technology.

NEC and Canon are good examples of a creative conjugation of different technologies: Kodama's concept of *technology fusion* points out that innovations are often the result of horizontal integration (among different disciplines) rather than of vertical research, as was the case in the recent past: '. . . either a company can invest in R&D that replaces an older generation of technology—the "breakthrough" approach—or it can focus on combining existing technologies into hybrid technologies—the *technology fusion* approach' (Kodama, 1992). NEC provides a good example of a combination of technologies and of how to build up a competence (that mixes computing and communication) through a series of alliances (Prahalad and Hamel, 1990): each piece of knowledge required to create these competencies has been acquired through interpartner relationships. Its competence lies in the ability to integrate different technologies. Internal research activities are aimed at ensuring that there are internal resources and technical skills to absorb knowledge from the alliances and co-operative ventures. In-house R&D is aimed at increasing the *absorptive capacity* (Cohen and Levinthal, 1990). This concept emphasizes that the ability to evaluate and utilize outside knowledge is largely a function of the level of prior related knowledge, i.e. of the basic skills available within the firm. Moreover, R&D activity addresses some complementary areas, such as fibre optics, bioelectronics, artificial intelligence, new techniques for software development and neural computing in order to create a base of absorptive capacity in areas which be combined with the present knowledge to produce potential future competencies. NEC's approach has been very different from that of other multinationals operating in the electronics and computing industries, which have attempted to enter telecommunications through one or more large acquisitions, paying less attention to the integration of the skills from different disciplines and fields of study.

Canon is another case of competence based on a combination of technologies. The competence has been built by mixing different segments of knowledge available internally. It is helpful to our framework to analyse the strategy followed to build up the next-generation competence, to produce the aligners for laying out DRAM (Dynamic Random Access Memory) chips. Chip manufacturers are searching for technologies to design circuits with increasingly larger data storage capacity. The increase in capacity is linked to laying out the lines that compose the circuit in smaller and smaller dimensions. In 1986, Canon decided to develop the competencies to manufacture these aligners. The first aim was to acquire the knowledge to develop the skills needed. The company started research X-ray lithography, where it needed to create an absorptive capacity. At the same time, the vacuum microelectronics (a new technology based on the use of electron beams) emerged as a promising technology in this field. Canon therefore decided to promote actions to acquire knowledge of this technology. One of the most important experts in the technology was recruited and a co-operation agreement was made with Lepton, a company founded by several scientists who had worked at Bell Labs on the development of electron beam machines for the laying out of microchips. Through the acquisition of a capital share of Lepton, Canon was able to access the electron beam technology and knowledge developed at Bell Labs. This is being combined with its competencies in manufacturing and laser beam technology (that represent the platform of the present competencies) to build up a unique form of competence and a prospective key source of long-term competitive advantage. In this case, electron beam technology is a constituent technology that has been acquired from external sources in order to be combined with the existing competence and build up future competence. The existing competence also provides the basis for assimilating external knowledge.

The examples of NEC and Canon show that when a competence is based on the integration of various technologies internal R&D resources are allocated to increase the absorptive capacity and to integrate the knowledge absorbed from outside sources with internal capabilities. R&D resources are also allocated to create a base of absorptive capacity in complementary areas that could lead to technologies, refreshing the existing competence and providing the basis for the next-generation competence. The knowledge acquisition strategy concerning each constituent technology is essentially based on a number of alliances, joint ventures and acquisitions.

Northern Telecom recognized the need for a window on some basic research areas identified as potential sources of competence refreshing knowledge to be integrated into its current competence in telecommunication. It participated in the foundation of a university and started through this a series of research programs in these areas.

Honda and Cummins Engine represent a significant case of competence based on a single technology. Their R&D efforts are focused on basic research activities, such as the ceramic engine, looking to the prospective competence of the future. Major technical efforts are devoted to the application of engine technology, gaining advantages from the unique knowledge and cross-fertilization from a wide number of applications of the same technology. Their knowledge-acquisition strategy is essentially based on internal

R&D efforts and on a process of internal exchange of application experience.

The analysis of these cases provides evidence that the technology acquisition strategy is essentially dependent on the two factors identified above:

1. The value of the segment of knowledge (*core, competence-refreshing, non-core*)
2. The type of competence (based on the integration of different technologies or on one constituent technology).

Decisions on a technology acquisition strategy should be related to these factors. Key decisions are concerned with:

- Whether to use external sources or in-house R&D
- The aim of in-house R&D effort: producing new knowledge or enhancing the *absorptive capacity*.

From our analysis it can be argued that internal R&D efforts should be devoted to the core or to the competence-refreshing segment of knowledge. The amount and the direction of internal R&D efforts are defined according to the need to have proprietary access to a certain set of knowledge that represents an element in building a unique competence. The aim of the effort, i.e. developing new knowledge or creating an absorptive capacity, depends on how the technology relates to the competence.

In Table 12.1 we summarize the knowledge acquisition strategies according to the two dimensions indicated: (1) the value of the segment of knowledge (*core, competence-refreshing, non-core*) and (2) the type of competence ('technology-integration-based' or 'single-technology-based').

A technology strategy should be viewed as a 'trajectory' that determines how to acquire and internalize technical knowledge in the light of the characteristics of the current and future competence. The mode of acquisition of a piece of knowledge and technology, i.e. the extent to which the firm relies on its own internal efforts to develop internal capabilities rather than resorting to external sources, should not be decided by the technology, but be dependent on how the technology relates to the competence. Moreover, it is not simply a matter of developing in-house critical resources to compete and outsource non-critical resources: a central point is the level of absorptive capacity in a given technical area. It is imperative

TABLE 12.1   Technology-acquisition strategies

		Segment of knowledge		
		Core	Competence-refreshing	Non-core
Type of competence	Single-technology-based	In-house R&D efforts aimed at developing new knowledge	In-house R&D to enhance absorptive capacity	Buy
	Technology-integration-based	In-house R&D efforts aimed at enhancing absorptive capacity	Resort to external sources	

that resources and knowledge gained from outside sources are internalized and integrated with skills and knowledge available and/or developed internally.

TECHNOLOGY STRATEGY—THE PROCESS

We have argued that a process-based view of technology strategy is central to our discussion. The complex process by which organizations decide to change their strategic technological capabilities are strongly challenged by competence-based competition.

First, the above discussion has indicated that innovation is often the result of the interaction of resources, skills and capabilities that are organizationally and geographically dispersed. The organizational and geographical dispersion of sources of knowledge requires that planning processes and organizational mechanisms are defined to integrate the knowledge and information gained and to synthesize innovative capabilities.

Second, as competence (rather than the single product or the single business) is the unit of analysis of the technology strategy process, technological developments should be carried out in an integrated way on the basis of a cross-business view. This suggests putting more of the power to allocate R&D funding in the hands of corporate. Nevertheless, the need for reducing time-to-market, improving responsiveness to customer requirements and increasing quality and manufacturability have given business units more power to define the R&D projects to be undertaken. Therefore, a balance between the need for linking technology development to the marketplace and a competence-based view of technology planning is required. As a result, a further relevant question related to the technology strategy process is at what level of the firm should responsibility for planning technology development and allocating resources be placed.

Third, we have pointed out that learning processes affect the content of a technology strategy; it can be argued that the results of the learning processes should be taken into account in formulating a technology strategy. Moreover, forms of learning develop with the innovative projects themselves. It is therefore relevant to audit and self-assess the innovative capability and to measure the resource transformation occurring along with the innovative activities. In other words, a firm should measure the process of learning to give valuable inputs to the technological resource allocation, i.e. the technology strategy content.

The analysis of a powerful empirical case can give a series of insights into the characteristics of a successful technology strategy process and of good practices adopted to face these managerial challenges. In our own field research, we analysed the organization of a number of multinational Japanese companies operating in consumer electronics.

The activities of planning and control of the technical activities tend to be concentrated in one function that operates at corporate level, the *Technology Planning Unit* (TPU). Planning activities take into account technical inputs from the corporate R&D units (in charge of developing constituent technologies of the competence), market requirements from the headquarter business units and from the foreign market-sensing units, and technical inputs from business unit R&D labs and foreign technology-scouting units. The international technical network is composed of many small units that monitor the technological developments and sense the market evolution world-wide. The strategy underlying the process of dispersion of technical units lies in the need for screening, recognizing and absorbing knowledge from outside sources. The TPU is in charge of collecting from all these units information and knowledge which will be taken into account in the planning phase. The technological activity planning occurs in an annual general meeting, involving top management, marketing people, corporate R&D, business unit R&D and the TPU. The technological development activities of both corporate R&D labs and business unit R&D labs are planned on the basis of the inputs received and try to mediate the business units' requirements with the corporate (competence-oriented) view of technology development. The TPU is responsible for the progress of the projects at both corporate and business unit level. The progress of the work in the business unit R&D labs is cross-controlled by the business unit itself and the TPU. A member of the TPU usually follows the projects from the beginning (when they are carried out by corporate R&D) to the end (commercialization phase). The TPU is then responsible for changing project plans and activities while they are in progress. A top manager supervises all the planning activities and is responsible for the progress of the works. Moreover, TPU is outside the control of R&D. This ensures that choices are made on the basis of both technical inputs and market requirements. Indeed, a key factor of this unit is the concentration of marketing and technological skills. Technological developments are planned to satisfy functional performance requirements and also consumer taste, for example product appearance.

From these cases we can argue that:

- Synthesizing innovative capability and integrating knowledge from dispersed sources require that the processes of technology planning, acquisition and exploitation are centrally co-ordinated. This ensures that the firm can exploit the information and knowledge gained and plan internal efforts in an integrated way. Technical functions play a key role because they are central in all the dimensions of learning, representing a form of institutional continuity (Pavitt, 1991) in the process of competence building;
- The technology development planning process should not be viewed as the traditional negotiation between corporate and R&D on the resources to be allocated to R&D projects, nor as the usual conflict between business unit and corporate interests. It is central to competence building that the efforts from the various technical functions of the firm at all levels are centrally planned and co-ordinated. Technology planning is a corporate activity that should combine an end-product-oriented view of R&D from the business units with a competence-oriented view of technical activities from corporate. Each project should be seen in terms of its contribution to the innovation of the end products or to the development of a technology and to competence building. A matrix-type control is suitable to this end. This requires that there are units at

corporate level specifically devoted to looking after the development of competencies;

- A competence-based approach to technology strategy requires the creation of organizational units involving both marketing and technical skills which are devoted to the collection of knowledge and information from all the units of the organization in a specific technical field, so making it possible to exploit the learning process in the dispersed units and control the development trajectory in a given technical area.

Two further considerations emerge from our analysis. For this process to be effectively implemented, it is essential that:

1. Technological activities are evaluated and chosen on the basis of a series of projects rather than a single project.
2. Mechanisms, processes and tools should be defined for measuring the learning process and monitoring capabilities accumulated in different functions and in different countries.

1. A competence is built through a series of innovation projects that contemporarily represent the way the firm exploits its competencies and help to enhance the competencies themselves. This indicates a new view of innovation. Moenaert (1992) suggests that innovation should be viewed in a new way:

> By focusing on immediate commercial project success, we have ignored a large part of the transformation process taking place within an innovation process. The resources . . . do not remain unmodified in the course of the project life-cycle. 'Possibly the greater value of an aggregate project plan over the long-term is its ability to shape and build development capabilities, both individual and organizational' (Wheelwright and Clark, 1992). Past innovation research has looked at innovation projects as a set of resources which, through their allocation to project operations, effectuate a—hopefully positive—change in the firm's financial resources. However, all the resources are changed through project operations! People acquire new skills, there will be investments or disinvestments in technological infrastructure, and when changes in procedures are introduced or the company culture undergoes changes, the organizational resources are altered. External resources are acted as well. . . . Hence, innovation processes can be viewed as *resource transformation processes*.

In this sense, he argues that a more appropriate unit of analysis is the *innovation program*, defined as 'a related set of consecutive or overlapping innovation projects' rather than the project.

2. As stated earlier, the process of accumulation of capabilities is a long-term process fed by a series of short-term learning cycles: each set of innovation projects should be valued in terms of how it contributes to enhancing the firm's resources needed for competence building. Learning and innovative activities enhance both the breadth and the depth of technical skills (technical learning) and resources/techniques for managing technical projects (organizational learning). A continuous technological audit enables the enhancements in technical skills gained through a project and the technical skills available at the end of a series of innovative projects to be monitored. This provides valuable inputs to the technology planning process and to resource allocation. The embodiment of technical knowledge mainly involves people and technical systems. Technological audit frameworks should mainly address these two dimensions of knowledge in a firm (Chiesa and Barbeschi, 1993).

Learning also concerns techniques and procedures adopted to manage the process of technological innovation. Their adaptation and change in the light of experience is organizational learning. Therefore the process of organizational learning leads to a definition of the disciplines to be adopted in the organization. Disciplines become the tangible output of the learning process with regard to managerial systems; they are routines and procedures that can be easily transferred within the organization. Useful examples are the product development process in Honda and process engineering in Toshiba and Nissan. Disciplines also represent a tool for homogenizing activities world-wide. They have often been the key factor used by the Japanese to restructure acquired Western concerns. Innovation practice benchmarking can help understand and exploit the learning process and a firm's knowledge set in its managerial systems, culture and norms (Voss, Chiesa and Coughlan, 1993; Adler, McDonald and MacDonald, 1992).

CONCLUSIONS

In this chapter we have looked at the implications of a competence-based approach for the content and the process of strategic management of technology in technology intensive firms. We have identified three main points:

1. A new framework is required to define a technology acquisition strategy. A technology strategy should be seen as the definition of a trajectory to internalize technological resources and integrate them with those internally available with a view to competence building. Technology should be understood as a set of knowledge segments. Each segment of knowledge should be evaluated in terms of its contribution to building the competence. The value of a segment of knowledge can be interpreted in a number of dimensions as the contribution to the perceived customer value, the degree of appropriability, the coherency with the competence to be built or the contribution to its uniqueness. The other relevant factor affecting a technology acquisition strategy is the type of competence ('single-technology-based' or 'technology-integration-based'). These two variables, i.e. the value of the segment of knowledge and the type of competence, provide a framework in which to make decisions in terms of technology acquisition strategy, particularly with regard to the extent to which internal efforts are preferable to resorting to external sources, and the direction the internal efforts should take (developing new knowledge versus creating an absorptive capacity).

2. Competence building requires: (a) gathering knowledge inputs from organizationally (different functional competencies are required to innovate) and geographically (sources of knowledge are internationally distributed, because of a progressive international specialization of the activities of the knowledge production industry) dispersed units; (b) the conception and implementation of innovation projects leading to both end-product innovation and competence enhancement; (c) exploitation of the learning process of the whole organization. It is argued that a central element of the formulation of a technology strategy is the definition of the process whereby a technology strategy is generated. This analysis shows that a centrally co-ordinated plan of technical activities, a corporate-led technology development planning process, the creation of units responsible for looking after the development of competencies and co-ordinating the firm's technical efforts at all levels are among the required organizational solutions. The technology strategy process should be viewed as an element of the learning process: a technology development plan that is the result of a process shared by technical and marketing units at all levels of the organization ensures that there is a stronger link through

improved learning between technology strategy and corporate strategy.

3. Crucial support to the process of technology strategy is provided by tools to audit and self-assess the technological and innovative capabilities of the firm. These help to exploit the learning that occurs along with the innovative activities which relates both to the managerial capabilities needed to manage technological innovation projects and to the technical skills. The first process leads to the definition of the disciplines and practices to be adopted in managing innovation projects in order to underline the contribution of a project to learning, while the second provides valuable inputs to the process of resource allocation with a view to the building of firm-specific competence.

REFERENCES

Abell, D. F. (1980). *Defining the Business: the Starting Point of Strategic Planning*. Englewood Cliffs, NJ: Prentice-Hall.

Adler, P. S., McDonald, W. D. and MacDonald, F. (1992). Strategic management of technical functions. *Sloan Management Review*. Winter, 19–37.

Anderson, J. R. (1982). Acquisition of cognitive skill. *Psychological Review*, **89**, 369–406.

Bertelè, U. (1991). Strategie competitive e Tecnologie di decisione: la dinamica evolutiva. In U. Bertelè and S. Mariotti (Eds) *Impresa e Competizione Dinamica* (pp. 3–46). Milan: Etas Libri.

Booz-Allen and Hamilton (1981). The strategic management of technology. *Outlook*, Fall-Winter.

Chakravarthy, B. S. and Doz, Y. (1992). Strategy process research: focusing on corporate self-renewal. *Strategic Management Journal*, **13**, 5–24.

Chiesa, V. and Barbeschi, M. (1992). Globalization models and R&D management. *Proceedings of the International Engineering Management Conference '92*. Eatontown, New Jersey, October.

Chiesa, V. and Barbeschi, M. (1993). Technology assessment in competence-based competition. R&D Management Conference 'Technology Assessment and Forecasting', Zürich, Switzerland, July.

Cohen, W. M. and Levinthal, D. A. (1990). Absorptive capacity: a new perspective on learning and innovation. *Administrative Science Quarterly*, **35**, 128–152.

Collis, D. (1991). A resource-based analysis of global competition: the case of the bearings industry. *Strategic Management Journal*, **12**, 49–68.

De Meyer, A. (1992). Management of an international network of industrial R&D laboratories. R&D Management Conference 'Managing R&D Internationally', Manchester, July.

Dodgson, M. (1991). Technological learning, technology strategy and competitive pressures. *British Journal of Management*, **2**, 3.

Grindley, P. (1991). Turning technology into competitive advantage. *Business Strategy Review*, Spring.

Hamel, G. (1991). Competition for competence and interpartner learning within international strategic alliance. *Strategic Management Journal*, **12**, 83–103.

Hamel, G. and Prahalad, C. K. (1989). Strategic intent. *Harvard Business Review*, **67**, 3, 63–76.

Hamel, G. and Prahalad, C. K. (1993). Strategy as stretch and leverage. *Harvard Business Review*, **71**, 2, 75–84.

Hax, A. C. and Majluf, N. S. (1991). *The Strategic Concept and Process: A Pragmatic Approach*. Englewood Cliffs, NJ: Prentice-Hall.

Hax, A. C. and No, M. (1992). Linking technology and business strategies: a methodological approach and an illustration. Working Paper No. 3383-92BPS, February.

Hedlund, G. and Rolander, D. (1990). Action in heterarchies: new approaches to managing the MNC. In C. A. Bartlett and Y. Doz (Eds) *Managing the Global Firm* (pp. 15–47). London: Routledge.

Kaplan, R. B. and Murdock, L. (1991). Core process redesign. *The McKinsey Quarterly*, **2**, 27–43.

Kodama, F. (1992). Technology fusion and the new R&D. *Harvard Business Review*, **70**, 4, 70–78.

Imai, K., Nonaka, I. and Takeuchi, H. (1985). Managing the new product development process: how Japanese companies learn and unlearn. In K. B. Clark, R. H. Hayes and C. Lorenz (Eds) *The Uneasy Alliance: Managing the Productivity-Technology Dilemma*. Cambridge, MA: Harvard Business School Press.

Itami, H. (1987). *Mobilizing Invisible Assets*. Cambridge, MA: Harvard University Press.

Leonard-Barton, D. (1992). Core capabilities and core rigidities: a paradox in managing new product development. *Strategic Management Journal*, **13**, 111–125.

Little, A. D. (1981). The strategic management of technology. European Management Forum, Davos, Switzerland.

Moenaert, R. K. (1992). Firm resources and the meaning of innovation success. International Workshop on Core Competence, Genk, Belgium, November.

Nonaka, I. (1991). The knowledge-creating company. *Harvard Business Review*, **69**, 6, 96–104.

Pavitt, K. (1990). What we know about the strategic management of technology. *California Management Review*, **32**, 3, 17–26.

Pavitt, K. (1991). Key characteristics of the large innovating firm. *British Journal of Management*, **2**, 41–50.

Polanyi, M. (1966). *Tacit Dimension*. New York: Doubleday.

Prahalad, C. K. and Hamel, G. (1990). The core competence of the corporation. *Harvard Business Review*, **68**, 3, 79–91.

Roussel, P., Saad, K. and Erickson, T. (1991). *Third Generation R&D*. Cambridge, MA: Harvard Business School Press.

Senge, P. M. (1990). *The Fifth Discipline*. London: Century Business.

Stalk, G., Evans, P. and Shulman, L. E. (1992). Competing on capabilities: the new rules of corporate strategy. *Harvard Business Review*, **70**, 2, 57–69.

Voss, C. A., Chiesa, V. and Coughlan, P. (1993). Developing and testing benchmarking and self assessment framework in manufacturing. EIASM Conference, London, April.

Wernefelt, B. A. (1984). A resource-based view of the firm. *Strategic Management Journal*, **5**, 171–180.

Wheelwright, S. C. and Clark, K. B. (1992). Creating project plans to focus product development. *Harvard Business Review*, **70**, 2, 70–82.

Conclusions: Which Theory of Strategic Management Do We Need for Tomorrow?

A theory of management should describe, derive, explain and prescribe appropriate courses of decision making and action with respect to two basic problems facing the business community: the long-term survival of the company and the maximization of profits throughout the company's lifetime. As regards the first problem, remember that the average life expectancy of companies is much smaller than that of human beings (Senge, 1990), and regarding the second problem, many companies suffer from losses, 'roller-coaster' results or below-average profitability for most of their lifetimes.

Sustaining a profitable existence and thus creating welfare and reducing poverty in society is the basic mission of any company. Academics (as well as consultants) should develop concepts, techniques, approaches and frameworks to assist business people in fulfilling this basic mission. Based on this general mission, a theory of strategic management should primarily focus on the dynamics of 'sustainable competitive advantage' as one of the most prominent driving forces for long-term profitability and survival.

Though considerable work has been done in the past decades on developing a workable theory of strategic management, many

Competence-Based Competition.
Edited by G. Hamel and A. Heene.
Copyright © 1994 The Strategic Management Society. Published 1994 by John Wiley & Sons Ltd.

questions and problems remain unresolved and require further research and development. In the editors' opinion the core competence concept offers suggestions for the development of the theory of strategy management along four axes: interpreting the concept of 'sustainability' from a dynamic point of view, resolving the dilemmas inherent in the process of pursuing apparently 'conflicting' competitive advantages, integrating the metaphor of 'the learning organization' into the theory of strategic management and developing the theory of corporate strategy.

INTERPRETING THE CONCEPT OF 'SUSTAINABILITY' FROM A DYNAMIC POINT OF VIEW

The first axis concerns the interpretation of the concept of 'sustainability' of competitive advantage. As Porter (1985) pointed out, the concept of 'sustainability' can be interpreted in both a static and dynamic way. Approaching 'sustainability' from a static point of view means determining a necessary (portfolio of) competitive advantage(s) (given the objectives, the environment and the available resources of the company) and then deploying a course of decisions and actions to defend that competitive advantage against the competitor's moves (imitation, alienation and substitution being the most important categories). One of the major problems with this approach is that not a single competitive advantage can be 'sustained' in this way in the long run. Sooner or later, all competitive advantages will be eroded through competition and reduced to 'competitive prerequisites' or 'competitive conditions', which, in turn, will lead to a reduction in the company's profitability to the level of the 'average' profitability within its industry. Some competitive advantages may be more 'sustainable' than others, meaning that it will take the competition more time and effort to destroy the competitive advantage. As argued in a number of chapters in this book, establishing a competitive advantage around the core competence of the corporation may be more defensible over time before it falls victim to substitution, imitation or alienation.

Thinking about the competitive advantage as never being 'defensible' in the long run compels one to look at 'sustainability' from a different, more dynamic point of view. In a static approach, (strategic) decisions and deployment of resources are primarily aimed at defending an existing competitive advantage. Whereas with the dynamic approach sustainability is accomplished through the continuous renewal of the competitive advantage itself and the sources of that advantage.

Under the dynamic approach, sustainability means substitution, a continuous process covering the replacement of previously defined competitive advantage(s) and its (their) sources by newly defined advantages and sources in order to keep ahead of the competition. 'Sustainability' means 'keeping ahead' of the competition through processes of 'challenging' and 'changing' the rules of competition and through deliberately creating misfit.

Strategic management from this point of view has less to do with the search for 'defensible' sources of competitive advantage than with the search for sources that allow for a continuous renewal of the competitive position. In the dynamic approach of sustainable competitive advantage 'knowledge', for instance, will not be considered a core competence and (thus) a defensible source of competitive advantage. Rather it is the processes of 'knowledge creation' and 'knowledge engineering' that are considered to be the ultimate sources of competitive advantage.

Interpreting 'sustainability' from a dynamic point of view requires that the theory of strategic management become a theory of processes through which corporate renewal can be maintained.

The editors believe that a detailed research of the processes through which competitive advantage is developed, declared 'obsolete' long before the advantage is destroyed or eroded by competitor's actions and renewed and substituted by new competitive advantages, is one of the principal axes to be followed in developing today's theory of strategic management.

RESOLVING THE DILEMMAS INHERENT IN THE PROCESS OF PURSUING 'CONFLICTING' COMPETITIVE ADVANTAGES

The company that manages to sustain its competitive advantage in a dynamic way has to face the problem of resolving apparent dilemmas, such as the Porter dilemma of 'cost leadership versus differentiation'. Imagine a company that, in order to remain competitive, focuses on cost leadership after a period of strictly and successfully pursuing an innovation-based strategy. The company may have to face the problem of resolving conflicts that potentially exist between these concurrent strategies—for instance, in terms of the organizational make-up of the company or in the nature of the resources required to be competitive under each strategy. It goes without saying that the problem of reconciling conflicting competitive advantages becomes more prominent if the company pursues simultaneously several 'conflicting' competitive advantages (e.g. cost leadership and flexibility) rather than sequentially over time.

Interpreting 'sustainability' in a dynamic way forces the company to address which set of tools, techniques and approaches it needs in order to gain the 'strategic flexibility' and thereby either avoid (organizational, motivational) conflicts or resolve those conflicts in cases where they seem to be unavoidable. Proposing theoretically sound and 'workable' solutions to avoid and resolve the potential dilemmas incorporated into the processes of renewing sources of competitive advantage represents a second axis for shaping the forthcoming theory of strategic management.

INTEGRATING THE METAPHOR OF 'THE LEARNING ORGANIZATION' INTO THE THEORY OF STRATEGIC MANAGEMENT

The continuous renewal and 'resourcing' of competitive advantages can most probably be fulfilled by a 'learning organization' that maintains a degree of strategic and operational flexibility and bears the following characteristics:

- Systemic thinking and action by all members of the organization, taking account of the interrelationships between the different functional management domains
- A permanent striving for renewal, and not just improvement of past and present practices, enabling the company to rethink continuously the fundamentals of its competitive advantage
- A free flow of information between the members of the organization and between the company and its environment, made possible by an appropriate information infrastructure and suitable information technology
- A flat, non-hierarchical organization, consisting of large, self-regulating teams, creating room for all members of the organization to deploy creativity and initiative in the competitive battle

- A predominant emphasis on the maximal use of already-existing knowledge, skills and attitudes, which implies a constant search for alternatives to current habits and routines
- A concise, explicit and shared vision of the future to act as a touchstone for co-ordinated action and decision making and as a driving force behind all attempts to reorient decisions and actions within the company
- Acceptance and use of transrational processes such as intuition, symbolism and metaphors as a basis for creativity, renewal and reframing of resources.

As 'continual corporate renewal' is considered one of the most central themes to be explored in strategic management today, integrating the metaphor of 'the learning organization' (with the above-mentioned characteristics) is—in the opinion of the editors—the third axis along which a future-oriented theory of strategic management should be developed.

DEVELOPING THE THEORY OF CORPORATE STRATEGY

A theory of strategic management can never be regarded as 'grown-up' unless it can be fully described in terms of 'corporate strategy' problems and unless theoretically sound and pragmatic answers to important 'corporate strategy' problems are clearly presented and empirically tested. Core competence as a paradigm for long-term profitability and survival forces one to concentrate on corporate strategy issues, particularly the problem of building a 'strategic architecture' for the company. 'Strategic architecture' refers to combining and recombining resources that are traditionally scattered over the company's 'business units' in order to build, develop and acquire (existing or new) core competencies. In this respect the core competence concept provides a new and insightful lens through which to view the 'synergy' issue and stimulates one to rethink the traditional product-market-based 'portfolio' and diversification models in the theory of strategic management.

It is the opinion of the editors that (despite respectable efforts by many scholars in the past) much theoretical and empirical research still needs to be undertaken in order to develop theories of corporate strategy to a level where they can really support and sustain the ideas and paradigms incorporated in the 'core competence' approach. Therefore the editors believe that developing concepts, tools, techniques and models on the level of corporate strategy is the fourth axis on which the theory of strategic management can be advanced.

The editors hope that this book will provide a source of inspiration to readers to challenge existing concepts, constructs, assumptions and beliefs about (the theory of) strategic management and that, in turn, they might contribute to the development of the theory and practice of strategic management in the years to come, be they academics, consultants or those 'who make strategy happen': business people.

REFERENCES

Porter, M. (1985). *Competitive Advantage*. New York: Free Press.
Senge, P. (1990). *The Fifth Discipline* (p. 17). New York: Random Century.

Index

Thomson, 29
time compression diseconomies, 41–2, 64, 86, 99, 156, 208
time orientation metaskill, 189
Toshiba, 20, 23, 310
Toyota, 12, 13, 20, 29, 44, 45, 230
tradability, 46, 85, 95
transaction cost economics, 224
transaction costs, 85, 235

umbrella, 67, 69
uncertainty, 71

understanding, 117, 282
Upjohn, 133, 175, 179

value chain, 5, 24, 42, 153, 215, 295, 301
values, 270, 283
vision, 70, 117, 256, 319

Wal-Mart, 12, 87, 118–19, 186
Warner-Lambert, 175, 179–80
Weyerhauser, 228
what-if-simulations, 201–4
worldview, 271